Transactions of the Royal Historical Society

SIXTH SERIES

XVI

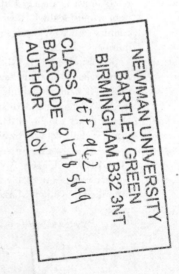
CAMBRIDGE
UNIVERSITY PRESS

Published by the Press Syndicate of the University of Cambridge
The Edinburgh Building, Cambridge CB2 8RU, United Kingdom
32 Avenue of the Americas, New York, NY 10013–2473, USA
477 Williamstown Road, Port Melbourne, VIC 3207 Australia
Ruiz de Alarcón 13, 28014 Madrid, Spain

A catalogue record for this book is available from the British Library

First published 2006

ISBN 0 521 862574 hardback

SUBSCRIPTIONS. The serial publications of the Royal Historical Society,
Royal Historical Society Transactions (ISSN 0080–4401) and Camden Fifth Series
(ISSN 0960–1163) volumes may be purchased together on annual subscription.
The 2006 subscription price (which includes print and electronic access) is £84
(US$136 in the USA, Canada and Mexico) and includes Camden Fifth Series,
volumes 28 and 29 (published in July and December) and Transactions Sixth
Series, volume 16 (published in December). Japanese prices are available from
Kinokuniya Company Ltd, PO Box 55, Chitose, Tokyo 156, Japan. EU subs-
cribers (outside the UK) who are not registered for VAT should add VAT at their
country's rate. VAT registered subscribers should provide their VAT registration
number.

Subscription orders, which must be accompanied by payment, may be sent to
a bookseller, subscription agent or direct to the publisher: Cambridge University
Press, The Edinburgh Building, Shaftesbury Road, Cambridge CB2 8RU, UK; or in
the USA, Canada and Mexico; Cambridge University Press, Journals Fulfillment
Department, 100 Brook Hill Drive, West Nyack, New York 10994–2133, USA.
Prices include delivery by air.

SINGLE VOLUMES AND BACK VOLUMES. A list of Royal Historical
Society volumes available from Cambridge University Press may be obtained
from the Humanities Marketing Department at the address above.

Printed and bound in the United Kingdom at the University Press, Cambridge

CONTENTS

Transactions of the RHS 16 (2006), pp. 1–38 © 2006 Royal Historical Society
doi:10.1017/S0080440106000405   Printed in the United Kingdom

TRANSACTIONS OF THE

ROYAL HISTORICAL SOCIETY

PRESIDENTIAL ADDRESS

By Martin Daunton

BRITAIN AND GLOBALISATION SINCE 1850: I.
CREATING A GLOBAL ORDER, 1850–1914

READ 25 NOVEMBER 2005

ABSTRACT. The world economy has experienced a cycle of globalisation, de-globalisation and re-globalisation since 1850. In each period, there has been a trade-off between various policies: fixed exchange rates, capital mobility, labour movement and free trade, and their international and domestic consequences. This essay establishes an analytical framework for understanding these trade-offs in the case of Britain, and proceeds to consider the choices made between 1850 and 1914. A case is made that the gold standard and fixed exchange rates secured widespread domestic support, and that they were not imposed by financial interests at the expense of domestic considerations.

In the last quarter century, Britain has experienced the second great age of globalisation. The first major episode of globalisation was located in the half century prior to the First World War, with unprecedented levels of labour migration, trade flows and capital mobility – as well as imperialism and dispossession of indigenous peoples. During this period, currency levels were 'pegged' by the widespread adoption of the gold standard. The interlude between the outbreak of the First World War and the end of the Second World War was marked by de-globalisation, with restrictions on labour movement, high levels of tariffs and the creation of trade blocs and limits on capital mobility. The gold standard collapsed and exchange rates 'floated'. Re-globaliation started at the end of the Second World War with the Bretton Woods agreement of 1944 and the General Agreement on Tariffs and Trade in 1947. Currency stability reappeared through a formal agreement to 'peg' currencies to the dollar which was in turn pegged to gold. The American administration hoped that currency stability would allow a reduction of tariffs and the

emergence of multilateral trade, but it was only with the collapse of the
Bretton Woods system in the early 1970s that capital mobility started to
return to the level found prior to the First World War. By the 1980s and
1990s, globalisation had returned to its earlier peak and the so-called
'Washington consensus' of trade liberalisation, market de-regulation and
privatisation was in the ascendant.[1] Of course, globalisation and the
'Washington consensus' have been contested by demonstrators at Seattle
and Genoa, by farmers and industrial workers facing competition, by the
advocates of debt redemption and the end to world poverty and by critics
of currency speculation and capital mobility. Time will tell whether such
discontents will lead to a reverse of the seemingly inexorable process of
globalisation.

In the course of four presidential addresses I cannot aim to cover
the entire process of globalisation, de-globalisation and re-globalisation
between 1850 and the present.[2] Rather, my aim is to focus on British
involvement in these long-term trends as the country moved from the
leading economic and political actor in the global economy before the
First World War to a more subsidiary role in the early twenty-first century.
Each of the four addresses will cover a particular period. In the present
address, I deal with the emergence of a highly global economic order
between 1850 and 1914. The second address turns to the collapse of
globalisation between 1914 and the Second World War. In the third
address, attention focuses on partial re-globalisation under the Bretton
Woods system from the Second World War to the early 1970s, and the
fourth address concludes with the emergence of a highly global economic
order since the 1970s. Above all, I will reflect upon debates over British
economic policy: was the crucial consideration to be domestic prosperity
or internationalism? Were these two concerns in tension or were they
complementary? If they were in tension, how was the choice between
the different priorities made? The question is central to British history
since 1850, and not only for economic historians: it relates to the cultural
identity of Britain as insular or cosmopolitan, and it was at the heart of
political debates from the repeal of the corn laws to the vexed matter of
entry into the Euro.

Globalisation and nationalism have been in tension throughout the
entire period covered by these lectures. In *The End of Globalisation:
Lessons from the Great Depression*, Harold James remarked that 'reactionary

[1] For a definition of the 'Washington consensus', see J. Williamson, 'What Washington
Means by Policy Reform', in *Latin American Adjustment: How Much Has Happpened?*, ed.
J. Williamson (Washington, DC, 1990), ch. 2, and his subsequent reflections in 'What Should
the World Bank Think about the Washington Consensus?', *World Bank Research Observer*, 15
(2000), 251–64. I return to the issue in the fourth address.
[2] Since delivering this lecture, an overview has appeared: J. A. Frieden, *Global Capitalism:
Its Fall and Rise in the Twentieth Century* (New York and London, 2006).

resentment [against globalisation] remains astonishingly similar over long periods'.[3] He posed the question: why was resentment against globalisation contained more successfully in some periods than in others? He points to three possible answers to his query. The first possibility is that the global economy suffered auto-destruction through the forces of financial volatility: collapse provided an opportunity for nationalistic controls on capital movement and financial speculation. In his analysis of the demise of the global economy in the 1930s, John Maynard Keynes concluded that capital mobility was a destructive, speculative force which might strangle trade rather than playing its 'proper auxiliary role of facilitating trade'. It should therefore be constrained by controls introduced by the Bretton Woods system which 'accords to every member government the explicit right to control all capital movements. What used to be heresy is now endorsed as orthodox.' More recently, James Tobin argued for a tax on currency transactions to limit speculation and volatility.[4] The implication of Keynes's and Tobin's analysis is that the collapse of globalisation in a spasm of speculation, with a destructive impact on domestic economies, could be prevented by carefully devised policies to limit the disruption caused by speculators.

The failure to put such policies in place leads to a second possible explanation of the demise of globalisation: a nationalistic response to resentment at the perceived injustices of competition from abroad which led to a loss of jobs or to pressure on wages and social spending in order to drive down costs. In the opinion of Kevin O'Rourke and Jeffrey

---

[3] H. James, *The End of Globalization: Lessons from the Great Depression* (Cambridge, MA, 2001), 1.

[4] James, *End of Globalization*, 2–3; J. M. Keynes, quoted in A. van Dormael, *Bretton Woods: Birth of a Monetary System* (1978), 33, 10; J. M. Keynes to R. F. Harrod, 'Your Memorandum on Forthcoming U.S. Conversations', 19 Apr. 1942, in *The Collected Writings of John Maynard Keynes*, XXV: *Activities, 1940–1944. Shaping the Post-War World: The Clearing Union*, ed. D. Moggridge (1980), 149; *Collected Writings of John Maynard Keynes*, XXVI: *Activities, 1943–1946. Shaping the Post-war World: Bretton Woods and Reparations*, ed. D. Moggridge (1980), 17. Tobin's proposal to tax international financial transactions to reduce speculative currency trading was proposed in the Janeway lectures in 1972 and published in *The New Economics One Decade Older: The Eliot Janeway Lectures in Historical Economics in Honor of Joseph Schumpeter, 1972* (Princeton, 1974), and 'Prologue', in *The Tobin Tax: Coping with Financial Volatility*, ed. M. ul Haq, I. Kaul and I. Grunberg (New York and Oxford, 1996), ix–xviii. His aim was to increase stability after the collapse of the fixed exchange rate regime of Bretton Woods; the idea has been appropriated by opponents of globalisation, and in particular the French organisation ATTAC (Association pour la Taxation des Transactions pour l'Aide aux Citoyens) founded in 1998: see I. Ramonet, 'Disarming the Market', *Le Monde Diplomatique*, Dec. 1997, and www.france.attac.org. Tobin distanced himself from this appropriation of his tax, which led to the change from Tobin to Transactions in the name of the organisation: see 'They Are Misusing My Name', *Der Spiegel*, 2 Sept. 2001, English translation at http://cowles.econ.yale.edu/news/tobin/jt_01-09-02_ds_misusing-name.htm.

Williamson, the seeds of nationalistic reactions to globalisation were planted in the 1870s in response to its real or perceived impact on the distribution of welfare as a result of cheap grain imports in Europe, mass migration to the New World and competition between manufactures. The result might be tariffs on imports of food or manufactures, and restrictions on migration; or, as in the case of Britain, it could be continued adherence to the ideology of free trade. These seeds germinated and grew as globalisation developed up to the First World War; and bore fruit between the wars.[5]

A third approach, and the one favoured by James, points to the ability or inability of institutions to mediate the tensions and resentments created by globalisation. In his view, late nineteenth-century globalisation rested on nation-states which 'evolved as a defensive mechanism against threats to stability coming from outside'. The result was protection of domestic industries in Germany and the USA, protests against mass immigration in the USA and Australia, the pursuit of nationalistic monetary policies and the emergence of costly welfare systems to provide benefits to citizens. The nation-state intruded nationalism into economic policy and made globalisation difficult to sustain unless international organisations could prevent politicians from succumbing to domestic political pressures. Before the First World War, globalisation rested on the willingness of each state to accept free trade and capital mobility without any formal commitment. Currency stability rested on the gold standard which depended on mutual self-interest, and there were no treaties or institutions to underwrite commitment. The gold standard was a 'contingent rule': it might be abandoned in an emergency such as a war, but there was a strong expectation that it would soon be reintroduced; and the market assessed the credibility of the commitment in deciding the terms on which finance might be provided.[6] Although international organisations were created after the First World War, the institutions of the League of Nations located at Geneva were too weak to deal with the strains in the world economy and the nationalistic backlash against globalisation. As Anne Orde has remarked, a leading theme after the war was 'the limited capacity, conceptually and intellectually, of the liberal capitalist order for the task of reconstruction'. New international institutions emerged in a world of 'fiercely independent nation states' with serious tension between the two. Although President Wilson espoused 'liberal internationalism', the treaty of Versailles also reflected the desire for national sovereignty

5 James, *End of Globalization*, 4–5; K. O'Rourke and J. Williamson, *Globalization and History: The Evolution of a Nineteenth-Century Atlantic Economy* (Cambridge, MA), 93–4, 286–7.

6 M. D. Bordo and A. J. Schwartz, 'The Operation of the Specie Standard: Evidence from Core and Peripheral Countries, 1880–1910', in *Currency Convertibility: The Gold Standard and Beyond*, ed. J. B. de Macedo, B. Eichengreen and J. Reis (1996), 12.

and did nothing to resolve the contradiction. The Bank of International Settlements was created in 1929 to deal with the divisive issues of debts and reparations rather than to stabilise the international financial system, and the World Economic Conference of 1927 was too weak to check the spread of protection. The 'Geneva consensus' of the interwar period was implicated by the retributions of Versailles: institutions could not cope with the strains in the international economy and globalisation collapsed in acrimony and mutual hostility.[7]

By concentrating on the difficulties between the wars and the triumph of the forces of nationalism over internationalism, James shows that globalisation can come to an end – a salutary warning at a time when the process seems inexorable. He asks if the same pattern could be repeated in the twenty-first century. Will liberalisation continue or will there be a backlash? He sees some grounds for the continuation of internationalism on the grounds that the 'Washington consensus' is more securely based on 'sustained reflection about appropriate policy' which is 'internally generated as a consequence of calculations about advantage'. Furthermore, international organisations are stronger and more secure – and the opponents of globalisation are too disparate and incoherent to create an alternative policy. He is therefore optimistic that the reaction against globalisation is less marked than in the interwar period.[8]

At the heart of James's account is the relationship between nationalism and cosmopolitanism in response to the forces of economic integration. But is he right in assuming that nation-states were necessarily nationalistic or insular in their economic policies? Britain remained remarkably loyal to a liberal, international policy before 1914, and we might wonder why the seeds of economic nationalism were so slow to develop. The answer is only in part that other nations were reacting against the economic power of Britain; after all, British agriculture and some industries were threatened by globalisation before 1914.

We might also wonder how far the 1930s really do hold lessons for the present. James used the depression of the 1930s and the collapse of globalisation to reflect on the present phase of globalisation; he did not directly compare the inner dynamics of the two processes of globalisation in the late nineteenth and late twentieth centuries. Alan Milward correctly

---

[7] A. Orde, *British Policy and European Reconstruction after the First World War* (Cambridge, 1990), 4; Z. Steiner, *The Light that Failed: European International History, 1919–1933* (Oxford, 2005), 603–4, 626; James, *End of Globalization*, 6–7, 13–21, 25–30, 208.

[8] James, *End of Globalization*, ch. 6. See also Frieden, *Global Capitalism*, for another reflection on the question. He warns (476) that economies work best when open to the world and – a crucial rider – 'when their governments address the sources of dissatisfaction with global capitalism'. The challenge, he concludes, is 'to combine international integration with politically responsive, socially responsible government'. The task, as he sees it, is to show that globalisation and social advance are compatible.

6 TRANSACTIONS OF THE ROYAL HISTORICAL SOCIETY

pointed out in his review of *The End of Globalization* that 'If we want to know whether the present epoch of globalization will last, should we not inspect it in at least comparative detail with its predecessor?'[9] Globalisation is not a single, undifferentiated phenomenon: reactionary resentment may be less constant than James assumed, for the nature of globalisation itself changed over time and accordingly stimulated different responses. Hence free trade held the moral high ground in late nineteenth-century Britain as a guarantor of peace and prosperity in a way that has now been lost in the present age of globalisation, when the moral high ground has passed to opponents of globalisation and advocates of the cancellation of debt and the end of poverty.[10] Above all, globalisation in both the late nineteenth and the late twentieth centuries consisted of a number of elements that could be combined in different ways.

Exchange rates were fixed in the late nineteenth century; they floated in the late twentieth century. Labour was free to migrate in the late nineteenth century, but more constrained by immigration laws in the late twentieth century. Capital mobility could be rejected as destructive of economic stability and hence a threat to free trade, as it was at Bretton Woods; or it could be encouraged as an engine of economic development as in the late nineteenth century or the present. Monetary policy might reflect international concerns in the late nineteenth century, but more domestic considerations in the late twentieth century. The trade-off between these different constituent parts of globalisation and domestic economic policy varied between the two ages of high globalisation, and influenced the extent and nature of nationalistic reactions to internationalism.

These trade-offs have been termed the 'trilemma' by Maurice Obstfeld and Alan Taylor. They point out that it is possible to have two but not three of the following: a fixed exchange rate; capital mobility; and an active domestic monetary policy.[11] Why can all three elements in the 'trilemma' not be combined? The explanation is found in the so-called Mundell-Fleming model developed in the 1960s, at a time when exchange rates were fixed under the Bretton Woods system of 1944 and capital mobility was reasonably free, though not yet at the same level as before 1914 or in the late twentieth and early twenty-first centuries. Under these conditions, what would happen if a country wished to raise interest

[9] A. S. Milward, 'Revolt of the Losers', *Times Literary Supplement*, 26 Oct. 2001, 4.
[10] This is the argument of the forthcoming study of Frank Trentmann, to whom I am very grateful for continuing discussion on the themes of these addresses.
[11] M. Obstfeld and A. M. Taylor, *Global Capital Markets: Integration, Crisis and Growth* (Cambridge, 2004), 29–33, and also their 'The Great Depression as a Watershed: International Capital Mobility in the Long Run', in *The Defining Moment: The Great Depression and the American Economy in the Twentieth Century*, ed. M. D. Bordo, C. D. Goldin and E. N. White (Chicago, 1998), 353–402.

rates and tighten monetary policy for domestic reasons in order to stop inflationary pressures or over-heating of the economy? Given free movement of capital, funds will move into the country in order to take advantage of high interest rates. The inflow of capital creates a balance of payments surplus and the exchange rate appreciates. Since the country is committed to fixed exchange rates, the central bank must intervene to hold down the value of its own currency. Hence monetary contraction is reversed, the domestic money stock rises and interest rates return to their initial, lower level. The argument runs the opposite way if a country wishes to reduce interest rates in order to stimulate the economy and boost employment. In this case, monetary supply increases and interest rates drop; capital now flows out of the country to seek a higher return elsewhere and the balance of payments weakens. Any benefit to the domestic economy from lower interest rates is countermanded by the outflow of capital. Instead of stimulating the domestic economy, lower interest rates encourage capital exports; and low interest rates are not sustained because of the priority given to maintaining the fixed exchange rate. The outflow of capital results in depreciation of the exchange rate and the central bank has to intervene in order to maintain the fixed parity. Monetary expansion is reversed and interest rates return to the initial level. The outcome, in the words of Rudiger Dornbusch, is that

> Under fixed exchange rates and perfect capital mobility, a country cannot pursue an independent monetary policy. Interest rates cannot move out of line with those prevailing in the world market. Any attempt at independent monetary policy leads to capital flows and a need to intervene until interest rates are back in line with those in the world market.[12]

An active domestic monetary policy would be possible if exchange rates were flexible and capital were mobile. Let us assume that interest rates are reduced for domestic reasons, to stimulate the economy and increase employment. Capital flows out of the country and the exchange rate depreciates. The exchange rate can be allowed to float downwards which leads to increased competitiveness in world markets, always provided that any outflow of capital does not become so serious that it might harm the domestic economy. The trade-off would also be different where exchange rates are fixed and capital movements are controlled. In these circumstances, fixed exchange rates and domestic monetary policy may be combined: interest rates are reduced to stimulate the domestic economy, and capital cannot leave the country; there is no pressure on the exchange rate which remains fixed. These differing policy trade-offs are shown in Table 1.

---

[12] I follow the outline in R. Dornbusch and S. Fischer, *Macroeconomics*, 6th edn (New York and London, 1994), 168.

Table 1 *Policy trade-offs between domestic economic polities, capital mobility and fixed exchanges, c. 1870–1990*

	Fixed exchanges	Capital mobility	Active economic policies
Gold standard to 1913	yes	yes	no
1925–31	yes	less	tentatively
Off gold, 1931–9	no	no	yes
Bretton Woods to 1973	yes	no	yes
Float from 1974	no	yes	yes

Source: Adapted from Obstfeld and Taylor, *Global Capital Markets*, 40.

The trilemma may be extended to an 'inconsistent quartet' by adding free trade versus protection, and to an 'incompatible quintet' by inserting labour mobility versus restrictions. In the 'inconsistent quartet', free trade, capital mobility, fixed exchange rates and autonomy in domestic monetary policies cannot all be combined. Tommaso Padoa-Schioppa indicates the problems in the European Monetary System in the 1980s: the removal of capital controls and barriers on the movement of goods and services with the creation of a single market, and the pursuit of fixed exchanges between European currencies, led to a surrender of domestic monetary policy. In Britain, the strains of pegging the pound against other currencies in the Exchange Rate Mechanism proved too much in 1992, and the attempt was abandoned on 'Black Wednesday' with the restoration of floating exchanges and domestic monetary policy. In this case, Britain opted for free movement of goods and capital, and preferred domestic monetary policy over fixed exchange rates.[13]

Before 1914, the choice of the British government within the 'inconsistent quartet' was free trade, capital mobility, fixed exchanges and a loss of autonomy in domestic monetary policy. In other countries, free trade was less readily accepted, and the trade-offs were different. The figures in Table 2 indicate that the level of tariffs and engagement in international trade varied widely between four countries committed to fixed exchange rates in 1913. Britain and the United States were at two

[13] For the 'inconsistent quartet', see Obstfeld and Taylor, *Global Capital Markets*, 29 n. 35; T. Padoa-Schioppa, 'The European Monetary System: A Long-Term View', in *The European Monetary System*, ed. F. Giavazzi, S. Micossi and M. Miller (Cambridge, 1988), 372–3. Papers on Black Wednesday are on the Treasury web-site at www.hm-treasury.gov.uk/about/information/foi.disclosures/foi_erm4_090205.cfm. I will deal with this episode in my fourth address.

Table 2 *Import duties as a percentage of total imports and total trade as a percentage of GNP, 1913*

	Import duties as % of total imports	Total trade as % of GNP
France	8.7	39
Germany	7.9	40
UK	5.6	48
USA	21.4	11

Source: A. Estevadeordal, 'Measuring Protection in the Early Twentieth Century', *European Review of Economic History*, 1 (1997), 91.

extremes. The high level of protection in the United States was reflected in greater autonomy in monetary policy, for the creation of the Federal Reserve System in 1913 gave much more power to domestic interests and concerns than did the Bank of England whose directors were drawn almost entirely from international bankers. The aim, in the words of the Federal Reserve Act, was 'to furnish an elastic currency'. Although the Act assumed that the gold standard would operate automatically, it also provided that the amount of notes should reflect 'actual commercial transactions'. The Act also gave considerable discretion to the directors of the regional Reserve Banks and the Federal Reserve Board who were dominated by domestic rather than international interests. In the United States, tariffs and a low level of engagement in the international economy gave more autonomy in monetary policy – with serious consequences between the wars. In Britain, free trade and a high level of engagement in the international economy did not permit autonomy in monetary policy.[14]

The 'incompatible quintet' inserts the labour market and migration into the equation. The successful maintenance of fixed exchange rates is often taken to mean flexible wages in order to adjust the balance of payments: the 'sticky' wages of the interwar period were blamed for the difficulties encountered by the gold standard. Pressure on the exchanges created by a deterioration or deficit in the balance of payments could not be corrected by allowing the exchange rate to fall and so making exports more competitive. Rather, costs needed to be reduced by cutting wages (or increasing productivity to reduce unit labour costs). If wages were rigid or 'sticky' in a downward direction, and productivity did not

[14] On the Federal Reserve System, see M. Friedman and A. J. Schwartz, *A Monetary History of the United States, 1867–1960* (Princeton, 1963), 187–93.

increase, fixed exchange rates came under pressure. The maintenance of high wages might also lead to protection to stop the importation of cheaper foreign goods. Equally, if capital were mobile and trade barriers were removed, as in the later twentieth century, labour market flexibility would be needed even with floating exchanges in order to retain markets against competitors from low-wage countries.

International migration and adjustment of the exchange rate were, to some extent, alternatives. Scandinavia provides a good example. The level of emigration was both high and volatile, operating as 'a vulnerable margin that responded to labor market conditions with a powerful multiplier'. The countries of Scandinavia remained on gold before 1914 and traded almost entirely with other gold countries, so that they could not adjust their balance of payments by modifying the exchange rate either through domestic monetary management or through variations in exchanges with non-gold currencies. Hence fluctuations in migration provided an alternative adjustment process: when costs were reduced or jobs lost, more people emigrated. In other countries, such as Japan and Russia, emigration was low and was not available as an adjustment mechanism. Britain was somewhere between these two poles, for trade to non-gold countries allowed a degree of exchange rate movement, and there was a reasonably high level of emigration before 1914. Lower emigration after 1914 reduced the availability of an alternative adjustment mechanism.[15]

The volatility of migration helped adjustment to the balance of payments. More significantly, the overall high level of migration raised the labour force in the New World by about a third and reduced it in Europe by about an eighth between 1870 and 1914. In this period, labour migration was probably the single largest factor in wage convergence in the Atlantic economy, surpassing the influence of capital mobility with which it was associated. Movement of labour into receiving countries – the USA, Canada and Argentina – moderated pressure for increased wages as a result of labour shortages; in the countries exporting labour, wages rose and labour surpluses were reduced. During this first age of globalisation, movements of labour and capital were connected: most capital exports followed migration to settler economies with scarce labour. In the later twentieth and early twenty-first century capital movements and labour migration are distinct. Not only has labour migration been at a lower rate in the second age of globalisation, but it has a different relationship

[15] L. A. V. Catao and S. N. Solomou, 'Effective Exchange Rates and the Classical Gold Standard Adjustment', *American Economic Review*, 95 (2004), 1273; see T. J. Hatton and J. G. Williamson, *The Age of Mass Migration: Causes and Economic Impact* (Oxford, 1998), 19, 67–74.

with capital mobility and does not act as a complementary force leading to convergence.[16]

These different trade-offs provide the framework for a consideration of the four periods to be covered in each presidential address. My aim is to move beyond the somewhat schematic approach of economists such as Mundell and Fleming or Obstfeld and Taylor in order to probe the reasons for the particular choices, and for their change over time. This brings me to the period of my first lecture, the half century before 1914 which was characterised as an age of high globalisation with fixed exchanges, capital mobility, free trade, migration and an inactive domestic monetary policy.

Why was this particular trade-off made before 1914 and why was it more powerfully held in Britain than in other countries where the double gold and silver standard had a more recent history and pressure for bimetallism revived in the later nineteenth century? Barry Eichengreen, in his major study *Golden Fetters*,[17] argues that the gold standard before 1914 rested on 'the credibility of the official commitment to gold and international co-operation'. The credibility depended on the ability of the government to commit to the policy, which was possible because those who stood to lose from fixed exchanges and to gain from active monetary policies lacked political voice which was only secured after the First World War. In his view, workers suffered as a result of the priority given to international monetary stability and the failure to vary interest rates to create domestic economic stability. He implies that organised workers were hostile to the gold standard and internationalism, but could not make their voice heard; survival of the gold standard and the credibility of the commitment before 1914 depended on the ability of the state to ignore those who suffered from its domestic economic impact. Despite the rise of trade unions and the extension of the franchise, and a growing realisation that high interest rates harmed trade and investment, bankers had no difficulty in giving priority to external over domestic targets. Hence the British government's unquestioning commitment to gold at the international conferences of 1867, 1878, 1881 and 1892, and its claim that gold was widely supported, did not reflect the views of critics who were silent or unheard.

---

[16] O'Rourke and Williamson, *Globalization and History*, 14–15, 119–20, 145, 165–6; Hatton and Williamson, *Age of Mass Migration*, 3; on early appreciations of the different links between capital and labour movements before the First World War and after the Second World War, see R. Nurkse, 'International Investment Today in the Light of Nineteenth-Century Experience', *Economic Journal*, 64 (1954), 744–58, and H. W. Singer, 'The Distribution of Gains between Investing and Borrowing Countries', *American Economic Review*, 40 (1950), 473–85.

[17] B. Eichengreen, *Golden Fetters: The Gold Standard and the Great Depression, 1919–1939* (New York and Oxford, 1992). For his argument as summarised here, see xi, 5–12.

Eichengreen's argument is compatible with the notion of 'gentlemanly capitalism', the belief that the international financial interests of the City and south of England controlled economic policy and favoured the gold standard and capital exports. According to this interpretation, the 'gentleman capitalists' were able to define their own economic interests as being the same as the nation's, while defining the northern industrialists' interests as sectional and selfish. In this view, the gold standard was rightly criticised by bimetallists in the 1880s and early 1890s for creating falling prices, depression and loss of employment – arguments that came to nothing as a result of the dominance of the City and its allies in the Treasury. According to such an interpretation, the City was dominant, industry subservient and workers lacked voice.[18]

Furthermore, Eichengreen argues that opposition to the trade-off between domestic and international concerns was ineffective before 1914 because economists had only a limited theoretical understanding of the link between international monetary policy, high interest rates and domestic stability. According to Eichengreen, workers and industrialists could not make a coherent link between policies designed to protect the gold standard and unemployment or depression. If he is right, then it follows that resistance to the gold standard between the wars arose both from the extension of the franchise which gave workers political voice; and the development of economic theories which allowed them to make the link between the pursuit of international economic policies and their own welfare.

The third reason for the particular trade-off, and the one stressed by Eichengreen, is that the commitment to gold was international and not just national: central bank cooperation was possible before 1914 but not after. In his opinion, the gold standard survived up to the First World War because central bankers were able to cooperate, whereas between the wars they could not. Eichengreen argues that the ability of bankers to work together after the war was limited by a loss of discretion and independence, for governments were scarred by the experience of

---

[18] In addition to Eichengreen, see P. J. Cain and A. G. Hopkins, *British Imperialism: Innovation and Expansion, 1688–1914* (Harlow, 1993); L. Davis and R. Huttenback, *Mammon and the Pursuit of Empire: The Political Economy of British Imperialism, 1860–1912* (Cambridge, 1986); and on the intermarriage and social fusion of financial elites and the aristocracy, Y. Cassis, *City Bankers, 1890–1914* (Cambridge, 1994). For the view that many industrialists and workers supported bimetallism, see E. H. H. Green, 'Rentiers versus Producers? The Political Economy of the Bimetallic Controversy c. 1880–1898', *English Historical Review*, 103 (1988), 588–612: in his account, landowners were hostile to the City as a result of the gold standard and its impact of falling prices in the agrarian economy. For critiques of gentlemanly capitalism as an interpretative device, see M. J. Daunton, 'Gentlemanly Capitalism and British Industry, 1820–1914', *Past and Present*, 122 (1989), 119–58; and A. Porter, "Gentlemanly Capitalism" and Empire: The British Experience since 1750?', *Journal of Imperial and Commonwealth History*, 18 (1990), 265–95.

inflation or hyperinflation in the early 1920s. In order to prevent a repeat of the devastating consequences of inflation on social relations, political legitimacy and economic stability, central bankers in many countries were obliged to abide by various rules imposed by their national governments, so removing their ability to work together and making the collapse of the gold standard more likely.

These explanations are open to various objections, and I will suggest a different approach to the acceptance of fixed exchanges and gold prior to 1914, with different implications for our understanding of economic policy and the British state. In the first place, did acceptance of the gold standard arise from a lack of voice prior to 1914 which prevented the expression of opposition and so allowed the British government to continue with its support of gold? Might it be that many workers supported or at least tolerated the gold standard as a natural and even desirable element in the institutional structure of Britain's political economy? Many workers had voice or representation under the second and third reform acts, and the crucial consideration was not their silence but the fact that they were at least indifferent to the monetary regime and at best active supporters of gold. The gold standard was firmly embedded in the political culture of Britain between 1850 and 1914.

The gold standard attracted widespread support far beyond the City for at least four reasons. First, the gold standard was automatic and therefore offered freedom from manipulation by financiers and speculators which was possible in a system with more discretion. Secondly, the gold standard offered access to the world's largest trade bloc, and in particular Britain which adopted a *de jure* gold standard in 1816 and fully restored convertibility in 1821; it was the leading world economy in the mid-nineteenth century, and other countries adopted gold to facilitate trade. Consequently, the gold bloc brought together most of the world's major economies. Thirdly, gold was linked with peace and civilisation. Fourthly, the gold standard made economic sense to organised workers who associated it with higher real wages in the later nineteenth century. The balance between these assumptions changed between 1850 and 1914, and the centrality of monetary issues also waxed and waned as other concerns dominated political debate – and not least the controversy over free trade and tariff reform in Edwardian Britain.

The basis for the belief that the gold standard was 'knave proof' (to use the phrase of the 1920s)[19] was laid in the debates over the resumption of the

---

[19] The phrase was used by John Bradbury and P. J. Grigg at the Treasury, and by Stanley Baldwin: see P. J. Grigg, *Prejudice and Judgement* (1948), 183, quoting Bradbury; P. J. Grigg to P. Snowden, 11 Oct. 1929, National Archives, T160/426/F11548, cited in P. Williamson, *National Crisis and National Government: British Politics, the Economy and Empire, 1926–1932* (Cambridge, 1992), 74; Baldwin in *(Conservative Party) Gleanings and Memoranda*,

gold standard in 1819 and the Bank Charter Act of 1844 which marked the triumph of the 'currency school' or bullionists against the 'banking school' or anti-bullionists. Rather than allowing banks discretion to increase the supply of money, the issue of bank notes was limited by the reserves held by the banks. 'Hard money' or the currency school offered a way of purging the financial system of 'fictitious bills' which allowed speculation; monetary bills should be 'real' or securely based on trade. After all, most economic disturbances could be blamed on the over-expansion of credit as a result of lack of control of the money supply rather than on a fall in commodity prices caused by shortages of money. Resumption and the Bank Charter Act were therefore designed to remove the corrupting power of money over business and over the state, much as the repeal of the corn laws and other protective duties removed the corrupting power of special interests.[20]

The problem with the currency school's approach was that it might impose constraints on the supply of money and so limit trade. The knaves might be expelled from finance, but at what cost? Crucially, the constraints of the Bank Charter Act were overcome by the discovery of gold in California and Australia in the late 1840s which led to an increase both in the amount of bullion and in the issue of notes, and so helped to embed the system in Britain's political economy. The gold discoveries, expansion of trade and a breakthrough to higher levels of per capita GNP in the 1850s helped to establish the legitimacy of the Bank Charter Act and the gold standard for the next half century or more.[21] The impact of the gold discoveries was a matter of intense debate and controversy in the 1850s and 1860s, provoking many books and pamphlets. W. S. Jevons remarked with some justice that the literature was 'very extensive and, to most readers, dreary in the extreme'.[22] Nevertheless, it does merit attention

---

December 1925, cited in R. Boyce, 'Government-City of London Relations under the Gold Standard, 1925–1931', in *The British Government and the City of London in the Twentieth Century,* ed. R. Michie and P. Williamson (Cambridge, 2004), 216.

[20] See in general B. Hilton, *Corn, Cash and Commerce: The Economic Policies of the Tory Governments, 1815–30* (Oxford, 1977); idem, *The Age of Atonement: The Influence of Evangelicalism on Social and Economic Thought, 1785–1865* (Oxford, 1988); S. G. Checkland, 'The Birmingham Economists, 1815–50', *Economic History Review,* second series, 1 (1948–9), 1–19; F. W. Fetter, *The Development of British Monetary Orthodoxy, 1797–1875* (Cambridge, MA, 1965); T. L. Alborn, 'Economic Man, Economic Machine: Images of Circulation in the Victorian Money Market', in *Natural Images in Economic Thought: 'Markets Read in Tooth and Claw',* ed. P. Mirowski (Cambridge, 1994), especially 186–93.

[21] For the 1850s as the crucial breakthrough in pre capita GNP, see C. H. Feinstein, 'Pessimism Perpetuated: Real Wages and the Standard of Living in Britain during and after the Industrial Revolution', *Journal of Economic History,* 58 (1998), 650–2; on the political resolution, see G. Stedman Jones, *Languages of Class: Studies in English Working-Class History, 1832–1982* (Cambridge, 1983), 107.

[22] W. S. Jevons, *Money and the Mechanism of Exchange* (1875), 137.

for the issues were of vital importance for economic thought and policy, inspiring studies of trends in prices and trade, and leading to serious concern over the structure of the European monetary system.

In their two-volume account of prices and circulation between 1848 and 1856, William Newmarch and Thomas Tooke estimated that the gold production of California and Australia meant that 'the Metallic Circulation of the leading portions of the Commercial World has been increased to the extent of *One Third*, or say about 30 *Per cent*'.[23] Tooke and Newmarch were proponents of the 'banking school'; in their eyes, Divine providence (or Nature) had intervened to solve the limitations of the Bank Charter Act and the rigidities of the 'currency school'. Here, in the words of the *Quarterly Review*,

> we can recognise Divine design more plainly than in other facts of history. The singular manner in which gold is spread over certain tracts of the earth, the ease with which it can be collected by individual effort, and the universal opinion entertained of its value, seem to point it out in an especial manner as one of the agencies by which intercourse between nations is to be promoted, and the social condition of man raised.[24]

Newmarch did not succumb so explicitly to providentialism, but T. E. Gregory noted that 'an almost theological ardour inspires the rather uneasy eloquence' of his analysis of the gold discoveries. The discoveries had a redemptive power, calling forth 'influences of which it seems to be the special mission to contribute by the aid of these great Discoveries, and by the aid of concurrent advances of Knowledge, to the removal or mitigation of many chronic evils against which successive generations have striven almost in vain'.[25] Gold was diffused across the world, and the result was a

> great Emigration – the transfer of large masses of population from their old seats to new ones, – the vast and sudden spread of civilised mankind over the earth, making deserts and waste places to bloom, cities to rise amid the solitude, and seas, whose virgin waters had hardly been stirred by a single prow, to grow white with the sails of golden argosies.

California had 'seemed the last in the world that would be peopled by civilised man'; and gold might equally provide the impulse to the European 'invasion' of Africa, 'that greatest waste place of the earth'.[26]

---

[23] T. Tooke and W. Newmarch, *A History of Prices and the State of the Circulation during the Nine Years 1848–1856 in Two Volumes Forming the 5th and 6th Volumes of the History of Prices from 1792 to the Present Time* (1857), VI, 158. See also an earlier estimate in W. Newmarch, *The New Supplies of Gold. Facts, and Statements Relative to their Actual Amount; and their Present and Probable Effects* (revised edn, 1853), 87.

[24] 'Gold Discoveries', *Quarterly Review*, 91 (1852), 540 quoted in T. E. Gregory, *An Introduction to Tooke and Newmarch's A History of Prices and of the State of the Circulation from 1792 to 1856* (London, 1928), 115 n. 1.

[25] Gregory, *Introduction*, 115; Tooke and Newmarch, *History of Prices*, VI, 236.

[26] R. H. Patterson, *The Economy of Capital, or Gold and Trade* (Edinburgh and London, 1865), 29–34. For a more prosaic account, see H. Fawcett, *Manual of Political Economy* (1863), 505–8.

The interpretation of the gold discoveries as beneficial was not self-evident, for the result might be inflation, upsetting relations between debtors and creditors, and hitting recipients of fixed incomes. Richard Cobden, for one, was alarmed. The Bank Charter Act was introduced to 'prevent those fluctuations in the amount of the currency which were alleged to have arisen from the arbitrary action of the Bank of England, and which rarely exceeded two or three millions in the course of a long series of years'. In his view, the gold discoveries were not a providential solution to the constraints of the Act but an alarming temptation to commercial immorality. How much more serious, he argued, was the large and sudden increase in gold output than the dangers formerly posed by the Bank's discretion over money:

> The tendency to a general rise of prices would lead to an expansion of credit, and an increase of speculation, which would be followed by panics and convulsions of greater violence and more frequent recurrence than have been hitherto experienced. Instead of a crisis visiting the commercial world once in each decade, its return would be expected every five years.[27]

Cobden's concern was a minority position in Britain, but it was much more potent in France with its double gold and silver standard where changes in the relative value of the two metals could lead to problems.

The existence and degree of variations in the relative values of gold and silver were contested by economists in Britain and France. Had gold discoveries resulted in a depreciation of gold and hence caused a rise in prices? Had they created currency instability by upsetting the ratio between gold and silver? The French liberal economist Michel Chevalier is well known for signing the eponymous treaty with Richard Cobden in 1860. A year earlier, in a book translated by Cobden, he predicted a large fall in the value of gold and a rise in prices which would produce 'a deeply-felt derangement of interests, and a modification more or less radical in the different sectors of society'. Creditors, affected by the rise in prices, 'will be flung headlong, without rule of measure, down to a lower station'. Even those members of society who could hope to adjust their wages, rents and fees would experience a period of painful transition with 'innumerable shocks and sufferings'. The gold discoveries seemed a curse rather than a blessing, and the evils had so far been avoided because France acted as a 'parachute'. The value of gold and silver was fixed in a ratio of 15.5 to 1 by the law of 7th Germinal, an XI (27 March 1803) so that depreciating gold could be exchanged for silver in France on favourable terms, and the drop in price was slowed down. But Chevalier believed

---

[27] Preface to M. Chevalier, *On the Probable Fall in the Value of Gold*, trans., with a preface, by Richard Cobden (Manchester and Edinburgh, 1859), vi, x.

that it was only a matter of time before serious problems would emerge, with a depreciation of gold and a rise in prices.[28]

By no means all French economists agreed with Chevalier's gloomy prognosis. The French free trade liberal economist Louis Wolowski argued that gold and silver were compensating or equilibrating, acting as a force for stability which should on every account be preserved. If silver were more valuable than the ratio of 15.5 to 1, it would be imported, coined and exchanged for gold which would then be exported. The result, according to Wolowski, was that each currency would vary less than it would otherwise have done. The analogy was not a parachute merely slowing descent before the inevitable crash. Rather, France's double standard acted, in the words of Jevons, as 'a great compensatory currency pendulum'. The 'equilibratory action' was explained for an English audience by Jevons:

> Imagine two reservoirs of water, each subject to independent variations of supply and demand. In the absence of any connecting pipe the level of the water in each reservoir will be subject to its own fluctuations only. But if we open a connection the water in both will assume a certain mean level, and the effects of any excessive supply or demand will be distributed over the whole area of both reservoirs. The mass of the metals, gold and silver, circulating in Western Europe in late years, is exactly represented by the water in these reservoirs, and the connecting pipe is the law of the 7th Germinal, an XI, which enables one metal to take the place of the other as an unlimited legal tender.[29]

Such considerations led Wolowski to warn against demonetising silver in Europe, which would end the compensating or equilibrating action, leading to a rise in the value of gold with a consequent fall in prices and increased burdens for debtors. He rejected a single gold standard as a source of social disorder; the case for maintaining a dual standard rested on its supposed ability to maintain equilibrium and to prevent creditors from gaining at the expense of debtors.[30]

Most British economists were more relaxed about the impact of the gold discoveries than their French counterparts, and were less concerned about the compensating role of the double standard. Fawcett remarked that additional supplies of gold coincided with 'the commencement of a new era in the commerce of this country ... Our commerce and trade, released from the trammels of protective duties, at once showed

---

[28] *Ibid.*, 6, 14, 60. The material first appeared in the *Revues des Deux Mondes* in 1857. See also an assessment of Chevalier by J. E. Cairnes, *Essays in Political Economy: Theoretical and Applied* (1873), which first appeared in the *Edinburgh Review* in 1860. He argued that the fall in gold values was less than assumed by Chevalier, and that when it did occur it would be beneficial rather than harmful for the working classes in England. Although fixed incomes from bonds or loans would suffer, taxpayers would benefit from reduction in the burden of the national debt, and mortgagors would gain. Society would experience major changes with the balance being favourable (146–58).

[29] Jevons, *Money and the Mechanism of Exchange*, ch. XII , 139–40.

[30] L. Wolowski, *L'or et l'argent* (Paris, 1870).

a more extraordinary developement [*sic*].' Gold discoveries therefore complemented free trade and prevented a sudden rise in its value:

The gold discoveries were made at a most opportune time, and ... they averted a most serious evil; for, if we had been left to the old sources of supply for obtaining gold England's commerce could not have expanded as it has during the last few years without a large and sudden fall in general prices.[31]

Newmarch took the same line. Although he accepted that prices might start to rise, he remained optimistic that the result would be 'almost wholly beneficial', with higher wages, extended trade and new enterprise. Far from the destructive impact predicted by Chevalier,

the great revolution pursues its course so gradually; it is moderated and checked in modes so infinite and subtle; and moulded by influences too delicate to be laid bare by any appliance of statistics: – that so far as we can judge of the Future by that which now occurs around us, we may contemplate without fear, a change in the economical condition of the world; – new, and startling doubtless; – but already adjusting itself, without shocks or convulsions, to the expanding intelligence and resources of mankind.[32]

Far from being destructive, Jevons believed that any increase in prices would be so 'slow and imperceptible' that most people would not notice the change. Indeed, the rise in prices was more likely to have

a most powerfully beneficial effect. It loosens the country, as nothing else could, from its old bonds of debt and habit. It throws increased rewards before all who are making and acquiring wealth, somewhat at the expense of those who are enjoying acquired wealth. It excites the active and skilful classes of the community to new exertions, and is, to some extent, like a discharge from his debts is to the bankrupt long struggling against his burdens. All this is effected without a breach of national good faith, which nothing could compensate.[33]

The supplies of gold encouraged desirable social and economic change. As T. E. Cliffe Leslie pointed out

the emancipation of the Russian serfs affords, in the payment of wages it involves, an example of the useful employment which the progress of civilization may provide for an increase of silver and gold in the world. The history of the last fifteen years bids us believe that, if the sword can be kept in its sheath, the precious metals will become less precious, chiefly in places where they are too precious at present; that prices will rise fastest where they are now lower than they should be, or could be, if commerce had convenient pathways; and that commodities will finally be multiplied as much as pieces of money on the market.

[31] Fawcett, *Manual*, 498–9.
[32] Newmarch, *New Supplies*, 88–9; Tooke and Newmarch, *History of Prices*, VI, 230–6. See also W. Newmarch 'Results of the Trade of the United Kingdom during the Year 1859; with Statements and Observations Relative to the Course of Prices since the Year 1844', *Journal of the Royal Statistical Society*, 23 (1860), 76–110, and 'Results of the Trade of the United Kingdom during the Year 1860; with Statements and Observations Relative to the Course of Prices since the Year 1844', *Journal of the Royal Statistical Society*, 24 (1861), 74–124.
[33] W. S. Jevons, *Investigations in Currency and Finance*, ed. H. S. Foxwell (1884), ch. II, 'A Serious Fall in the Value of Gold Ascertained, and its Social Effects Set Forth' (1863), 97.

The abundance of gold would mean that prices would fall in economies which were already monetised and commercialised; prices would rise in other areas as they were incorporated into a more advanced market economy. This process of convergence was 'a sign of advancing civilization and prosperity', showing that

> distance as well as war had ceased to separate mankind . . . [T]he history of prices proves that, while many obstacles to human fellowship remain, more has been done since the new gold mines were discovered to make the world one neighbourhood than was done in the 300 years before.[34]

The dominant view amongst British economists was that the double standard was destabilising, leading to more extreme fluctuations in both metals.[35] Fawcett felt that both gold and silver were liable to some variation in value as mines were exhausted or new deposits were found – and that the shifts in the relative values of the two metals allowed everyone to chose in which metal to make a payment in order to reduce their debt. 'It is evident', he pointed out, 'that this unfortunate and most mischievous disturbance would be avoided if gold was the only standard of value.'[36] Even Jevons, who accepted that the double standard acted as a compensatory or stabilising influence, nevertheless believed that it could be abandoned without difficulty, and without the serious consequences predicted by Wolowski. The compensating function of the double standard was fulfilled by the East which acted as a 'great reservoir' to absorb bullion, whether from gold discoveries or demonetised silver, so maintaining price levels and allowing Europe to adopt a gold standard. Jevons rejected Wolowski's fears that the action of European countries in demonetising silver would lead to instability by appreciating gold and depreciating silver. After all, Europe was only part of the world:

> The hundreds of millions who inhabit India and China, and other parts of the eastern and tropical regions, employ a silver currency, and there is not the least fear that they will make any sudden change in their habits . . . Although the pouring out of forty or fifty millions sterling of silver from Germany may for some years depress the price of the metal, it can be gradually absorbed without difficulty by the eastern nations, which have for two or three thousand years received a continual stream of the precious metals from Europe. If other nations should one after the other demonetise silver, yet the East may be found quite able to absorb all that is thrust upon it, provided that this be not done too rapidly.[37]

---

34 T. E. Cliffe Leslie, *Essays in Political Economy* (Dublin, 1888 edn), ch. XIX, 'The Distribution and Value of the Precious Metals in the Sixteenth and Nineteenth Centuries' (first published in *Macmillan's Magazine*, 1864), 300.

35 According to Jevons, *Investigations*, ch. XI, 'Gold and Silver' (1868), 303; also *Money and the Mechanism of Exchange*, 137.

36 Fawcett, *Manual*, 351–2.

37 Jevons, *Money and the Mechanism of Exchange*, 142. This book appeared in 1875 after the gold standard had been adopted in Germany and France, and gold did indeed appreciate as Wolowski warned; Jevons's argument dated from 1868 in response to enquiries from

As R. H. Patterson remarked in 1865, the movement of bullion from Europe to Asia made the impact of the gold discoveries global rather than 'local and evanescent'. He predicted that 'If this drain continues, the Golden Age may last for a hundred years; and as a result of the ever-widening commerce, all nations both of East and West will be drawn together in bonds of mutual interest and sympathy.'[38]

The gold discoveries were, on these arguments, continuing the work of free trade in creating peace and prosperity. The result was not to undermine the stability of gold as a means of value (as claimed by Chevalier) but to make it the 'pre-eminent and natural standard of value' in 'advanced nations'. In Jevons's words,

> The greatly increased mass of gold in use, the extended area of production, and the greater variety of nations which share in its production, will finally render it far more steady in value even than it has been. In becoming more abundant gold will become more than ever the natural international currency, by the flow of which the balances of the exchanges of nations are adjusted. It will become more generally the money of the world. So far from our changing from gold to silver as a standard, many years will probably not pass before several countries, which still cling to silver, will be constrained to change to gold ... Gold has not lost its character of a standard by the late gold discoveries ... The character of gold is no more changed by these discoveries than is the game of whist by the occurrence of an extraordinary hand of cards.[39]

By 1867, even the French government was coming to share the belief that the future was golden.

Despite French adherence to the double standard and its adoption by the Latin Monetary Union in 1865, sentiment turned towards gold at the International Monetary Conference in Paris in 1867 which was held under the auspices of Napoleon.[40] The French delegation rejected Wolowski's concerns, arguing that the double standard was not compensatory, that gold was more stable, that the attempt to maintain a fixed ratio between the value of gold and silver was 'against nature' and that countries with a double standard were more susceptible to financial crises. Henri Baudrillart, professor of economic history at the Collège de France, remarked that

> the system of double standard legalised an injustice, by making it optional to use either of the two metals; it put the creditor in the arbitrary power of the debtor, and sacrificed entirely the small fundholder, the professional man, and the workman. The alleged compensation between the two metals was an illusion, because one cannot calculate at pleasure whether the variations of the one counter-balanced those of the other, and if

Wolowski, and his letter was partly printed in *L'or et l'argent*, 62 (see Jevons, *Money and the* · *Mechanism of Exchange*, 141).
[38] Patterson, *The Economy of Capital*, 41–2.
[39] Jevons, *Investigations*, ch. II, 101–3.
[40] For accounts of the international conferences and debates between the United States, France and Britain, see F. A. Walker, *International Bimetallism* (1896), and S. P. Reti, *Silver and Gold: The Political Economy of International Monetary Conferences, 1867–1892* (Westport, CT, 1998).

the immense influx of gold of the last years had not produced a greater crisis, it was not to the double standard that we owed it, but it was to the enormous movement of business which had taken place, and which supplied an unusual outlet to coinage. Lastly, the adoption of a double standard would have the immense inconvenience of rendering impossible any arrangement with England and America.[41]

The example of Britain was highly pertinent: its prosperity and economic dominance were associated with its adherence to the gold standard, and the French were eager to secure British participation in the conference in 1867.[42] Despite the fact that only two of the twenty states represented at the conference were on gold, much to the delight of the British delegation the conference adopted a resolution in favour of gold 'with a unanimity as remarkable as it was unexpected'.[43] Britain and France now had a common interest in disseminating the gold standard, extending their earlier collaboration on free trade.

The gold standard seemed to offer prosperity and economic progress. Its widespread adoption started with Germany in 1872; the Netherlands followed in 1875, Belgium in 1878, France in 1878, the United States in 1879, Italy in 1884, Japan and Russia in 1897. Chris Meissner's recent statistical test of the various interpretations of the adoption of gold allows us to measure which economic variables had most impact. He finds that the crucial point was the level of trade with other gold standard countries. The important consideration was not that the gold standard reduced the risks of exchange rate volatility between two different monetary regimes, but that a single standard reduced the transaction costs of trade. Gold was adopted in those countries with the largest trade with the gold bloc relative to their GNP, and the potential savings rose as the size of the bloc increased. Lopez-Cordova and Meissner find that countries on the gold standard traded almost 30 per cent more amongst themselves than with non-gold countries; and that global trade would have been 20 per cent lower between 1880 and 1910 without the widespread adoption

---

[41] Parliamentary Papers [hereafter PP] 1867–8 XXVII, *Report of the International Conference on Weights, Measures and Coins Held in Paris, June, 1867 Communicated to Lord Stanley by Prof Leone Levi and Report of the Master of the Mint and Mr Rivers Wilson on the International Monetary Conference Held in Paris, June 1867*, 858–9 and 872–8. See also H. B. Russell, *International Monetary Conferences* (New York, 1898).

[42] See the comments of PP 1867–8 XXVII, *Report from the Royal Commission on International Coinage*, 14.

[43] PP 1882 LIII, *International Monetary Conference, 1881. Copy of the Report of the Hon. L. W. Fremantle, the Delegate Appointed to Represent Her Majesty's Government at the International Monetary Conference Held in Paris, 1881*. On the background to French debates on the double standard and the shift to gold, see L. Einaudi, *Money and Politics: European Monetary Unification and the International Gold Standard, 1865–1873* (Oxford, 2001), and M. Flandreau, *The Glitter of Gold: France, Bimetallism, and the Emergence of the International Gold Standard, 1848–1873* (Oxford, 2004), which argues that the French operation of the double standard and a fixed ratio was indeed stable, and its collapse not preordained.

of the gold standard. Hence the decision to adopt the gold standard was encouraged by Britain's early adherence to gold, and its financial and trading significance in the mid-nineteenth century. The French government realised this point in 1867, when it saw the virtues of adopting the same monetary system as Britain. The rationale for the choice is apparent in a survey of French opinion in 1868: merchants trading with Britain supported a gold standard, whereas eastern and southern France trading with silver regions in Germany, Austro-Hungary and Russia favoured silver. Of course, the more countries joined the system to benefit from membership of the world's major trading bloc, the more reason Britain had to remain loyal to gold.[44]

The gold standard also allowed preferential access to international capital by reducing exchange rate risks for lenders. It offered what Michael Bordo and Hugh Rockoff call the 'good housekeeping seal of approval': exchange rate risks for lenders were reduced, so that the government was able to borrow on international capital markets on more favourable terms. The Japanese adoption of the gold standard, for example, was encouraged by this consideration.[45] Adoption was delayed where banks were unregulated and fiscal policies were weak, for in these circumstances gold might flee in search of safety elsewhere, and maintenance of a fixed exchange rate would be difficult. A successful switch from paper money or silver to gold depended on political reform to control government debt and ensure stable banking. Late-comers to the gold standard needed time to introduce these fiscal and banking reforms.[46] By contrast, Britain had a reputation for fiscal prudence and stable banking as a result of the reforms of Sir Robert Peel with the reintroduction of the income tax in 1842 and the Bank Charter Act of 1844. British state finances were secure and stable, its national debt was falling and government bonds had a

---

[44] C. Meissner, 'A New World Order: Explaining the Emergence of the Classical Gold Standard', *National Bureau of Economic Research Working Paper 9233* (http://www.nber.org/papers/w9233); a version is forthcoming in *Journal of International Economics*. On the survey of 1868, see M. Flandreau, 'The French Crime of 1873: An Essay in the Emergence of the International Gold Standard, 1870–1880', *Journal of European Economic History*, 56 (1996), 880–2. J. E. Lopez-Cordova and C. M. Meissner, 'Exchange Rate Regimes and International Trade: Evidence from the Classical Gold Standard Era', *American Economic Review*, 93 (2003), 344–53; a longer version is available at Center for International and Development Economics Research (University of California–Berkeley), Working Paper COO-118, Nov. 2000.

[45] M. Bordo and H. Rockoff, 'The Gold Standard as a "Good Housekeeping Seal of Approval"', *Journal of Economic History*, 56 (1996), 389–428; on Japan, N. Sussman and Y. Yafeh, 'Institutions, Reforms and Country Risk: Lessons from Japanese Government Debt in the Meiji Era', *Journal of Economic History*, 60 (2000), 442–3, which argues that the adoption of the gold standard led to an immediate improvement in the rating of Japanese bonds on the London money market.

[46] Meissner, 'New World Order'.

high reputation which allowed the government to borrow on generous terms.[47] Membership of the gold standard was part and parcel of the wider fiscal constitution of nineteenth-century Britain.

Generally, gold came to be viewed as a symbol of economic modernity and sophistication – above all, in Britain. Gold was linked with peace, prosperity and civilisation as part of the wider political culture of free trade, and was placed on an evolutionary scale. As Henry Fawcett remarked, any general measure of value should vary as little as possible. Gold and silver fulfilled this criterion, for their production did not change to a great extent, and their other uses did not vary very much; they had intrinsic value which was high in relation to their bulk. Above all, gold was superior to silver as the general standard of value, for 'gold is the more costly metal of the two, and it therefore contains greater value in small bulk'. Furthermore, the cost of obtaining gold (and hence its value) varied less than silver, a vital consideration given 'the importance of possessing, as a standard of value, that substance whose value is most uniform'.[48] Gold was the most appropriate standard for advanced economies. 'Is not gold becoming', asked Jevons,

> by the progress of industry, the most suitable medium of exchange? Could we in this country ever replace our gold currency by a silver currency fifteen times as heavy? . . . It seems to me that as nations become more and more wealthy, they naturally pass from a silver to a gold currency. Such is now the progress of wealth in many parts of the world that this change is becoming natural and inevitable to them . . . The conveniences of a single gold standard are of a tangible and certain nature. The weight of the money is decreased to the least possible amount, without the use of paper representative money. There is a simplicity and convenience about the system which has recommended it to the English during the half century which has passed since our new sovereigns were issued. The operation of our law of 1816 has, in fact, been so successful in most respects that I should despair altogether of the English people or Government ever being brought to adopt the double standard in place of it.[49]

Jevons used an evolutionary language of progress in order to criticise American advocates of a double standard who 'would be stepping back from the gold age into the silver age. This seems to me about as wise as if the men of the bronze age had solemnly decided to reject bronze, and to go back into the stone age.' If the United States rejected gold, it would set itself 'against irresistible natural tendencies'; silver should be left 'to those Eastern nations who are too poor and ignorant to employ gold'. There was, he remarked,

---

[47] For the creation of fiscal legitimacy, see M. Daunton, *Trusting Leviathan: The Politics of Taxation in Britain, 1799–1914* (Cambridge, 2001); on the lower costs of British government debt, see N. Ferguson, *The Pity of War* (1998), 127, 131.

[48] Fawcett, *Manual*, Book III, ch. V , especially 351.

[49] Jevons, *Investigations*, ch. XIII, 'Bimetallism', first published in *Contemporary Review* (1881), 305–6.

a broad, deep distinction. The highly civilised and advancing nations of Australasia, and some of the better second-rate states, such as Egypt, Brazil, and Japan, will all have the gold standard. The silver standard, on the other hand, will probably long be maintained throughout the Russian empire, and most parts of the vast continent of Asia; also in some parts of Africa, and possibly in Mexico . . . In such a result there seems to be nothing to regret.[50]

Gold complemented free trade in a vision of peace and prosperity. It was at the heart of the political culture of free trade liberalism. The convertibility of bank notes into gold imposed morality and discipline, both on businessmen and on the government, so containing the threats to order posed by a liberated and competitive economic system. The discipline of gold prevented militaristic ministers from printing notes to wage war; and it limited speculation by preventing an over-expansion of credit. A highly commercialised capitalist economy created difficulties in measuring value – in knowing whether a piece of paper was really worth what it claimed. Gold was a measure of intrinsic value in a complex world. It was easily assumed that only prosperous countries with a highly developed cash economy could afford to use such an expensive form of currency; and equally that less advanced and civilised countries were condemned to the lesser metal of silver.

Indeed, a gold coin was 'Sovereign' – a point not lost on the banker Lord Overstone who remarked in 1869 that 'I have stuck up stoutly for the unimpeachable integrity of the Sovereign in affairs of the Mint as much as in those of Church and State.'[51] To question gold was tantamount to an attack on the queen whose head appeared on the newly designed gold sovereigns and half-sovereigns of 1893 as DF and Ind Imp – Defender of the Faith and Empress of India. The gold sovereign was celebrating nationalism as well as a world without economic frontiers; it was both a symbol of national identity and readily exchanged into the gold coins of other countries. The gold standard and gold sovereign were not technical issues for bankers and economists but were embedded in political culture.

Of course, proponents of the 'gentlemanly capitalist' interpretation of Victorian Britain could still counter that this political culture was propagated by financiers and their allies in the Treasury and political elite, so obscuring the 'real' interests of workers and industrialists who suffered as a result of the dominance of the gold standard. Such an interpretation does seem strained: the case for the gold standard was much wider than the self-interest of the City, and plausible arguments could be made for the gold standard as central to economic progress

[50] Jevons, *Investigations*, 309, 316; Jevons, *Money and the Mechanism of Exchange*, 149.
[51] Overstone to G. W. Norman, 18 Sept. 1969, quoted in T. Alborn, 'Coin and Country: Visions of Civilisation in the British Recoinage Debate, 1867–91', *Journal of Victorian Culture*, 3 (1998), 252.

and prosperity. Indeed, we can go still further and argue that the gold standard made sound economic sense to organised workers who gained from rising real wages. In the words of Anthony Howe, the gold standard – with free trade – was 'an essential part of the "social contract" between the working class and the State', resulting in lower prices and rising real wages rather than a loss of jobs.[52]

By the 1880s, the debate over the economic consequences of the gold standard had moved from the dangers of depreciation after the gold discoveries in California and Australia to concern that gold was in short supply and was appreciating against abundant silver, partly created by its demonetisation in Europe. Two problems arose which were considered at international monetary conferences in 1878 and 1881 called by the United States government with the aim of creating a double standard with fixed relative values. In both cases, the British government only agreed to attend on condition that the terms were modified to allow free discussion rather than merely consideration of the American proposals. The first issue was that a shortage of gold meant that prices fell in countries on a single gold standard, so increasing the burden on debtors, and fuelling demands to re-monetise silver. The issue was particularly important in the United States, where it became a central plank of the populist programme. The second issue was the exchange rate with silver-based currencies, above all in India. The decline in the value of the rupee affected both Britain and India: it meant that British exports to India, a major market for Lancashire cotton and other manufactures, became more expensive; and it meant that India's costs of paying the 'home charges' and debt payments mounted.[53] Would the British government shape its policy to assist India which was so crucial to the 'gentlemanly capitalists'; or would it be more concerned to guard the domestic interests of Lancashire cotton manufacturers and workers? How did these issues resolve themselves in the last quarter of the nineteenth century?

In the United States, popular opposition to the gold standard formed the basis of mass political movements in favour of bimetallism. Ewan Green has argued that bimetallism attracted support from many industrialists and workers in Britain who were concerned at the impact of the depreciation of the rupee, and eager to create modest prices rises in order to stimulate trade and employment. In his view, their case was

---

[52] A. C. Howe, 'Bimetallism, c1880–1898: A Controversy Reopened?', *English Historical Review*, 105 (1990), 389–90.

[53] For the concerns of India, see *inter alia*, PP 1876 VIII, *Report of the Select Committee on the Causes of the Depreciation of the Price of Silver and the Effects of Such Depreciation upon the Exchange between India and England*; PP 1882 LIII, *Report to the Secretary of State for India on the International Monetary Conference, 1881*; PP 1888 XLV, *Final Report of the Royal Commission Appointed to Inquire into the Recent Changes in the Relative Values of the Precious Metals*.

successfully contained by the gold lobby of the City.[54] Is he correct, or was bimetallism marginal with most workers and industrialists accepting gold as economically beneficial? By contrast to the United States, or even the continued interest in France, support for bimetallism was slight and the Bank Charter Act and the gold standard took monetary issues out of politics for a generation. The fall in prices in the later nineteenth century resulted in an unprecedented increase in real wages and, like free trade, seemed to offer prosperity to consumers. Few organised workers supported bimetallism which was, according to Howe, confined to one element of the Lancashire cotton industry (whose signifance was in any case declining) and a 'rump of protectionist squires'. The City and workers' adherence to gold was, he suggests, a better guide to policy.[55] Bimetallism was a sign of eccentricity or obsession, and a source of amusement. In Oscar Wilde's *An Ideal Husband*, Mabel Chiltern recounts the frequent proposals of marriage from Tommy Trafford.

> At luncheon I saw by the glare in his eye that he was going to propose again, and I just managed to check him in time by assuring him that I was a bimetallist. Fortunately I don't know what bimetallism means. And I don't believe anyone else does either. But the observation crushed Tommy for ten minutes. He looked quite shocked.[56]

A general belief in the superiority of gold did not necessarily require that it should benefit workers; policies are not always adopted after a careful (and certainly not accurate) assessment of self-interest. The relationship was contingent. But it was certainly possible to make a connection between gold and gains in welfare in the later nineteenth century. The gold standard benefited British workers because money wages did not drop in line with prices. Between the wars, many economists felt that the failure of the gold standard arose from the fact that wages were now 'sticky' in a downward direction, unlike before 1914. In reality, wages were also sticky before 1914: money wages were stable and hence real wages rose. The phenomenon explains the interest in price trends and wage rates of Robert Giffen, George Wood and Arthur Bowley who continued the analysis of Tooke and Newmarch. In 1889, Giffen reported 'a revolution in the quality of labour and the general conditions of life of the working classes' which would continue, despite growing competition from abroad, so long as socialism were avoided. Wealth was growing and

---

[54] Green, 'Rentiers versus Producers?', and his response to Howe, 'The Bimetallic Controversy: Empiricism Belimed or the Case for the Issues', *English Historical Review*, 105 (1990), 673–83. See the slight account in T. Wilson, *Battles for the Standard: Bimetallism and the Spread of the Gold Standard in the Nineteenth Century* (Aldershot, 2000). For bimetallist arguments, see H. C. Gibbs, *A Bimetallic Primer*, 2nd edn (1896), and H. H. Gibbs and H. R. Grenfell, *The Bimetallic Controversy: A Collection of Pamphlets, Papers, Speeches and Letters* (1886).
[55] Howe, 'Bimetallism', 390–1.
[56] O. Wilde, *An Ideal Husband: A Woman of No Importance* (1899), Act II .

was more equitably distributed.[57] A similar conclusion was reached by the Royal Commission on the Depression of Trade and Industry. Although the commission did admit that unemployment was higher, its overall assessment was highly positive:

> There is no feature in the situation which we have been called upon to examine so satisfactory as the immense improvement which has taken place in the condition of the working classes during the last twenty years... there can be no question that the workman in this country is, when fully employed, in almost every respect in a better position than his competitors in foreign countries, and we think that no diminution in our productive capacity has resulted from this improvement in his position.

The major change was in the distribution of the increased wealth of the country, 'to give a larger share than formerly to the consumer and the labourer, and so to promote a more equal distribution'. The Royal Commission was optimistic about the future, and did not lay the blame for any immediate depression on monetary factors so much as excessive productive capacity, investment of capital and competition from other countries. As we shall see, when attention turned to 'distress owing to the want of regular work', the causes and solutions were found in non-monetary factors.[58]

The question of 'sticky' wages was a matter of considerable debate in the 1920s and 1930s, and it is often seen as a major constraint on the successful operation of the gold standard compared with the period before 1914. A. C. Pigou, for example, argued that

> before the Great War there can be little doubt that wage-rates in Great Britain were adjusted in a broad way to the conditions of supply and demand... In the post-war period, however, there is strong reason to belief that an important change has taken place in this respect.[59]

Various reasons were suggested for the change, and will be considered in the second presidential address. However, there is little evidence that

---

[57] R. Giffen, 'Gross and Net Gain of Rising Wages', *Contemporary Review* (Nov. 1889), 839; *idem*, 'The Progress of the Working Classes in the Last Half Century', *Journal of the Royal Statistical Society*, 46 (1883), 593–622; *idem*, 'Further Notes on the Progress of the Working Classes in the Last Half Century', *Journal of the Royal Statistical Society*, 49 (1886), 28–100; *idem*, 'The Recent Rate of Material Progress in England', *Journal of the Royal Statistical Society*, 50 (1887), 615–47. See also M. Mulhall, *Fifty Years of Material Progress, 1837–1887* (1887); G. J. Goschen, 'The Increase of Moderate Incomes', *Journal of the Royal Statistical Society*, 50 (1887), 589–612; G. H. Wood, 'Some Statistics relating to the Working-Class Progress since 1860', *Journal of the Royal Statistical Society*, 62 (1899), 639–75; A. L. Bowley, 'Changes in Average Wages (Nominal and Real) in the United Kingdom between 1860 and 1891', *Journal of the Royal Statistical Society*, 58 (1895), 223–85; L. Levi, *Wages and Earnings of the Working Classes* (1885). For a discussion of the emergence of statistical time series, see J. L. Klein, *Statistical Visions in Time: A History of Time Series Analysis, 1662–1938* (Cambridge, 1997).

[58] PP 1886 XXIII, *Final Report of the Royal Commission Appointed to Enquire into the Depression of Trade and Industry*, 521–3, 527, 529.

[59] A. C. Pigou, 'Wage Policy and Unemployment', *Economic Journal*, 147 (1927), 355.

wages were in reality flexible before the First World War, and later economists might have been looking back in nostalgia to a world which did not exist. The stability or increase in money wages at a time of falling prices reflected a change in work practices. Many employers realised that an increase in the standard of living meant gains in efficiency, and that a more sensible strategy than cutting money wage rates was to increase productivity by tighter control over the work effort. Money wages did not fall; unit labour costs did.[60] Keynes suggested another reason in his *General Theory*: workers are concerned about protecting their relative wages; a reduction in their money wage at a time of falling prices might well lead to an increase in their own real wage, but to a decline relative to other occupations. They would therefore resist a cut in their money wage. The same argument meant that an erosion of real wages caused by inflation would be more difficult to resist, for it affected all occupations and so did not upset relative incomes.[61] If Keynes was right, money wages would be sticky in the period of falling prices between 1873 and 1896 as well as in the 1920s and 1930s. Of course, 'stickiness' might be more marked between the wars as a result of other changes in the labour market and improved welfare benefits. It might also be that the capacity of employers to reduce unit labour costs was constrained by the nature of the 'effort bargain' negotiated in the late nineteenth century. Rather than tight, hierarchical control by managers, it gave considerable power to skilled, often unionised, workers on the shop-floor to determine the pace of work and to control subordinates.[62] Consequently, British wage costs might be less easily reduced between the wars – a point considered in the next address.

Workers had little reason to oppose the gold standard and support bimetallism from concern about their standard of living. The problems created by a deteriorating value of silver for relationships between Britain and India were more serious, both for British export industries (above all Lancashire cotton) and for the government of India which faced higher 'home charges'. But was the solution to reject the gold standard? At the international monetary conferences of 1878, 1881 and 1892, the British delegates were 'perfectly determined' to retain gold as the basis

[60] R. Price, *Master, Unions and Men: Work Control in Building and the Rise of Labour, 1830–1914* (Cambridge, 1980); E. J. Hobsbawm, 'Custom, Wages and Work-Load in Nineteenth-Century Industry', in *Essays in Labour History*, ed. A. Briggs and J. Saville, revised edn (1967), 113–39; E. H. Phelps Brown with M. H. Browne, *A Century of Pay: The Course of Pay and Production in France, Germany, Sweden, the United Kingdom and the United States of America, 1860–1960* (1968).
[61] J. M. Keynes, *The General Theory of Employment, Interest and Money* (1936), 14.
[62] W. Lazonick, *Competitive Advantage on the Shop Floor* (Cambridge, MA, 1990); W. Lewchuck, *American Technology and the British Vehicle Industry* (Cambridge, 1987).

of prosperity, with the general support of all parties. Nevertheless, the British delegates believed that silver had a continuing, important, role in the world economy as the 'partner or natural ally of gold in all parts of the world, where it might be possible to do so'. Extension of the gold standard would mean the disposal of existing stocks of silver, and it was much better for the world's currency to rest on two metals in order to provide an outlet. 'We considered that, while a universal double standard was a utopian impossibility, a single gold standard throughout the world would be a false utopia, and that further steps in that direction might tend to produce incalculable disasters to the commerce of the world.' A fixed ratio was also rejected as an unjustified interference in free markets:

> It has been the policy of this country to emancipate commercial transactions as far as possible from legal control and to impose no unnecessary restrictions upon the interchange of commodities. To fix the relative value of gold and silver by law would be to enter upon a course directly at variance with this principle, and would be regarded as an arbitrary interference with a natural law, not justified by any pressing necessity.

Britain's argument against the further demonetising of silver was given additional force by its policy in India. 'What would have been the position of silver, we were able to ask, if the metal had been demonetised in India as it had been demonetized elsewhere?'[63]

The Indian government was separately represented in 1881, and was less sanguine, complaining that the relationship between silver and gold was causing 'deep interest and anxiety'. In 1881, Louis Mallett complained that India was losing income because two-thirds of its trade was with gold-based countries. Furthermore, the burden of the 'home charges' – payments to Britain for administration and defence – was rising, with a consequent need to cut expenditure or increase taxes. The Indian budget became, in the words of one finance minister, a 'gamble in exchange'. Although Mallett emphasised the drawbacks of depreciation of the rupee for India, it had some benefits: Indian exports were highly competitive in gold-based economies. India's trade with the rest of the world was central to multilateral clearances in the late nineteenth century through its trade deficit with Britain and surplus with the rest of the world. The appreciation of gold also hit British exports to India, not least Lancashire cotton goods. The potential problems for British exporters were increased by the Indian government's response to the growing burden of the 'home charges'. It needed more revenue, and there were obvious political dangers in imposing taxes on land or salt. A duty on imports of cotton goods was more attractive. Not surprisingly, the

[63] PP 1882 LIII, *International Monetary Conference 1881. Copy of the Report of the Hon C. W. Fremantle, the Delegate Appointed to Represent Her Majesty's Government at the International Monetary Conference Held in Paris, 1881*, 797–803; PP 1878–9 XXI, *Report of the Commissioners Appointed to Represent Her Majesty's Government at the Monetary Conference Held in Paris in August 1878*, 105–15.

Lancashire cotton industry was unsympathetic to the plight of India – and the secretary of state for India, as a member of the British cabinet, was as concerned about the electoral consequences in Lancashire as he was for the difficulties of the viceroy.[64]

Not surprisingly, Mrs Prism instructed her pupil Cecily that in reading her manual in political economy, 'The chapter on the Fall of the Rupee you may omit. It is somewhat too sensational. Even these metallic problems have their melodramatic side.'[65] Her warning was salutary, though more as a result of the complexity and technicality of the issues than their drama. In any event, the Lancashire cotton industry was less concerned to press for bimetallism that to maintain free trade in India – a demand in which it succeeded.[66] The concerns of India were given little credence by the Royal Commission on the relative values of gold and silver. Were the falls in the price of Indian commodities the result of changes in their production rather than in the standard of value? Could the difficulties experienced by the government of India which were known and measurable be removed without creating others which were unknown and unmeasurable? Would a double standard really produce the benefits claimed for it? What would be gained by attempting to reduce the burden on India, only to threaten the financial position of Britain by abandoning the gold standard? A 'leap in the dark' was too risky to contemplate, and 'the wiser course is to abstain from recommending any fundamental change in a system of currency under which the commerce of Great Britain has attained its present development'.[67] Certainly, there is little sign of any sustained pressure against gold from organised workers compared with their support for free trade with the sub-continent.

The international campaign for the restoration of the double standard petered out with a final monetary conference in 1892 which adjourned without a vote. The government of India was in a dilemma at the conference: should it back a fixed bimetallic rate to resolve its difficulties; or should it admit defeat and instead ensure stability by closing the mints to silver and adopting gold? The lack of any positive result from the conference settled the issue: in 1893, the Indian mints were closed to

[64] Sir David Barbour, cited in A. P. Kaminsky, '"Lombard Street" and India: Currency Problems in the Late Nineteenth Century', *Indian Economic and Social History Review*, 17 (1980), 309; PP 1882 LIII, *Report to the Secretary of State for India on the International Monetary Conference, 1881*, 779–95; PP 1886 XLIX, *Correspondence between the British and Indian Governments Respecting the Silver Question*; S. B. Saul, *Studies in British Overseas Trade, 1870–1914* (Liverpool, 1960), chs. III, VIII; I. Klein, 'English Free Traders and Indian Tariffs, 1874–96', *Modern Asian Studies*, 5 (1971), 251–71.
[65] O. Wilde, *The Importance of Being Earnest* (1895), Act II.
[66] Klein, 'English Free Traders'.
[67] PP 1888 XLV, *Final Report of the Royal Commission Appointed to Inquire into the Recent Changes in the Relative Value of the Precious Metals*, 295, 336, 375, 383, 384, 386, 388, 400.

silver. The silver rupee became a token with its value distinct from its silver content. The decision led to contention and controversy in India, but the government of India pressed ahead and in 1898 proposed the adoption of a gold standard. The suggestion was not universally welcomed. After all, the British government's position was that silver was a vital element in the world's currency, and City bankers feared a loss of gold to India and consequently higher interest rates. Indeed, Giffen argued that India should return to silver. The committee appointed to consider the government of India's proposal recommended the adoption of gold, with silver rupees as legal tender at a fixed value: the reform was introduced in 1899. In fact, the outcome was a 'gold exchange standard' or more accurately a 'sterling exchange standard', that is a gold standard with a local non-gold currency fixed at an exchange rate of 1s 4d per rupee.[68] The defeat of William Jennings Bryan in the presidential election of 1896 closed the debate in the United States, and prices started to rise modestly up to the First World War. Monetary issues were not central to political debate in Britain before the war – the major concern was free trade and its challenge from tariff reform. Whatever their other disagreements, the gold standard was not central to controversies between the free traders and tariff reformers.

I have concentrated on Eichengreen's claim that acceptance of the gold standard rested on a lack of voice by workers. I have suggested that support extended beyond the City of London and its allies, and was firmly embedded in political culture, alongside support for free trade and fiscal probity. The implication of my argument is also that support of the gold standard cannot be understood in terms of ignorance or a lack of theoretical understanding. Economists from Tooke and Newmarch to Giffen debated the impact of the depreciation or appreciation of gold, and the consequences for prices, wages, interest rates and growth. They lacked the technical sophistication of later economists, but they were not unaware of the importance of monetary influences. It was easy to assume that the gold standard led to improvements in welfare, economic stability and growth rather than to conclude that the gold standard meant a lack of autonomy in setting interest rates, a sacrifice of domestic prosperity, high unemployment and depression.

Perhaps the most thorough study of the influence of the gold standard on interest rates was the report of R. H. Inglis Palgrave (the editor of the *Bankers' Magazine*) on Britain, France and India for the Royal Commission

[68] PP 1893–4 LXXXIX, *International Monetary Conference, Brussels, 1892: Instructions to the Delegates of Great Britain and their Report, Together with the Proceedings of the Conference*, 489–98; PP 1893–4, LXV, *Report of Committee Appointed to Enquire into Indian Currency*; PP 1898 LXI, *Correspondence Respecting the Currency Proposals of the Government of India*; PP 1899 XXXI, *Report of the Committee Appointed to Enquire into Indian Currency*; Kaminsky, '"Lombard Street" and India', 311–27; J. M. Keynes, *Indian Currency and Finance* (1913).

on the Depression of Trade and Industry. He pointed out that

The influence of the quantity of money on prices is very different when, as in civilized countries at the present time, credit and the various forms of 'book transfer' utilized by the system of banking in existence in those countries, come into play as a means of purchase and exchange than in countries which possess only a metallic circulation. The countries in which the credit system is most completely developed appear to be the most readily influenced.

Palgrave doubted that the French bimetallic system had the benefits claimed by its advocates of lower and more stable interest rates. He found that interest rates in Germany were higher than in Britain and France, both when it was on silver and on gold. Similarly, the interest rate in England was lower than in France both when it was on a double standard and on gold.

It does not appear as a matter of observation that the fact of the Standard of Value being mono-metallic or bi-metallic has a very distinct effect on either the number of variations in the rate of interest or on the rate charged. Other causes . . . appear to regulate these points.[69]

When unemployment emerged as a political concern from the 1880s, monetary issues were largely irrelevant to discussion of its causes. The explanation was located in other factors. The Royal Commission on the Depression of Trade and Industry noted the presence of unemployment alongside gains in welfare; the enquiries of Charles Booth still laid much of the blame on deficiencies of character and an overstocked metropolitan labour market. By the early twentieth century, attention turned to the structure of the labour market. William Beveridge urged reform of the labour market through unemployment insurance to tide workers over periods of unemployment, and decasualisation of the labour market with Labour Exchanges to provide better flows of information. In the Labour party's analysis, the solution was a legal right to work and redistribution of income and wealth. Unemployment implied a lack of demand for domestically produced commodities; by taking money from the rich and giving it to the poor, the market would stimulate high, stable levels of production and employment. Of course, Joseph Chamberlain campaigned for imperial preference in order to provide steady domestic work behind tariff walls. The striking point about these debates is that monetary issues were largely absent.[70]

---

[69] PP 1886 XXIII, *Third Report of the Royal Commission Appointed to Inquire into the Depression of Trade and Industry*, Appendix B, 'Currency and standard of value in England, France, and India, and the rates of exchange between these countries', memorandum laid before the Commission, prepared by R. H. Inglis Palgrave, 340–1.

[70] On Booth, see J. Brown, 'Charles Booth and Labour Colonies, 1889–1905', *Economic History Review*, 21 (1968), 349–60; E. P. Hennock, 'Concepts of Poverty in the British Social Surveys from Charles Booth to Arthur Bowley', in *The Social Survey in Historical*

Finally, what of Eichengreen's claim that survival of the gold standard rested on cooperation between central banks? Marc Flandreau reads the evidence in a very different way and argues that 'central bank co-operation was probably not decisive in the operation of the gold standard'. He argues that the benefits of stable exchanges could just as well have been achieved through France's double standard as the gold standard, and that the adoption of gold was not preordained. Rather, it was 'an accident of history', arising from a 'massive co-ordination failure'. The timing was determined by *force majeure* rather than negotiation. The problem for countries contemplating adopting gold was how to dispose of their silver. Prussian victory over France in 1870 provided the answer. Germany's indemnity of 5 billion francs from France secured gold; its silver was then sent to France to take advantage of its double standard which could no longer be so readily portrayed as a stabilising force. In order to restrict German silver sales, the French government limited silver coinage in 1873 in an attempt to prevent Germany's adoption of gold. The attempt failed, and reinforced the shift to gold. As Flandreau remarks, 'the emergence of the gold standard was a blatant failure of international cooperation'. His detailed analysis of the subsequent behaviour of central banks shows that cooperation was 'exceptional, never reciprocal, and always failed to institutionalize': their approach may better be understood as a mixture of 'hatred, neglect and indifference'. The banks only helped each other if it was in their own interest, and not out of concern for the system as a whole. The conflicts of the 1870s reappeared in the run-up to the First World War as central bankers became part of the armaments race, building up their war chests of gold. Inter-bank cooperation was less significant than the fact that politicians in each country pursued their own independent policies to maintain gold and to secure the advantage of belonging to the major trade bloc of the world. Contrary to Eichengreen's claims of cooperation prior to 1914, 'most of the evils at work during the interwar years (competition among nations to attract gold, inability to enforce a co-ordinated outcome, neglect of the international effects of national monetary policies, and the Franco-German rivalry) were already operating during the 1870s'. The implication of Flandreau's argument might even be that the 'trilemma' is mis-specified, and that the gold standard was a domestic or nationalistic economic policy.[71]

Perspective, 1880–1940, ed. M. Bulmer, K. Bales and K. K. Sklar (Cambridge, 1991), 189–216; E. P. Hennock, *British Social Reform and German Precedents: The Case of Social Insurance 1880–1914* (Oxford, 1987); idem, 'Poverty and Social Theory in England: The Experience of the Eighteen-Eighties', *Social History*, 1 (1976), 67–91; J. Harris, *Unemployment and Politics: A Study in English Social Policy, 1886–1914* (Oxford, 1972).

[71] M. Flandreau, 'Central Bank Co-operation in Historical Perspective: A Sceptical View', *Economic History Review*, 50 (1997), 735–63; idem, 'The French Crime of 1873'; idem, *The Glitter of Gold*.

A further implication follows: the successful operation of the gold standard depended less on cooperation between the 'core' countries and more on the ability of the core economies to use the periphery (such as India), if necessary by coercion or influence. Gold-based economies traded on a large scale with non-gold economies with more flexible monetary regimes, based on silver or inconvertible paper: about two-thirds of the merchandise trade of the European core economies was with such countries, and about 40 per cent of the United States' trade. Changes in the nominal exchange rate on the periphery led to considerable fluctuations in the real effective exchange rate. The explanation was not only the variation in the price of silver relative to gold which so obsessed contemporaries, but also monetary policy in the core and movements of capital. When high levels of exports of capital led to a fall in reserves, the central banks in the core increased interest rates, so checking capital exports to the periphery and forcing the periphery to adjust parities to resolve the ensuing balance of payments problems. These changes in parities had significant impact on trade balances, so allowing adjustments in international payments. A reduction in exchanges rates in the periphery in response to cuts in capital led to falling import prices in the core countries; when capital exports from the core were high, rising activity in the periphery reduced the impact of weaker investment in the core. In the words of Catao and Solomou, such adjustments

> obviated the need for the kind of massive monetary sterilization by central banks often observed in the post-World War II world. As such, exchange rate flexibility in the periphery seems to help explain a key puzzle of the classical gold standard . . ., namely, how significant relative price adjustments were accomplished without jeopardizing the gold peg in the absence of massive reserve accumulation by the core central banks.[72]

Hence the pegging of the rupee to the pound, and the grant of fiscal autonomy to India after the First World War, imposed strain on the operation of the gold standard by removing an element of flexibility. This is a point to which I shall return in the next address.

In this address, I have concentrated on the gold standard, seeking to place it in mainstream political debates rather than isolating it as a rebarbative technical issue. It should be placed in a broader context of international and domestic politics, interpreted not just as a highly complex matter of monetary economics but as an integral part of Britain's political culture. Frank Trentmann has done the same, in greater depth and with more subtlety, for free trade which so dominated debates in the decade before the First World War. As he indicates, support for free trade was more than a matter of a rational, utility-maximising choice

[72] Flandreau, 'Central Bank Co-operation', 760–1; Catao and Solomou, 'Effective Exchange Rates', 1272. See also Bordo and Schwartz, 'Operation of the Specie Standard', on the frequent suspension of the specie rule in peripheral countries.

determined by concrete social and political interests; it reflected cultural meanings, definitions of national identity and notions of the morality of consumption. I do not need to repeat his evidence of the centrality of free trade to British political culture, and the way that its advocates responded to tariff reform. But, as he points out, the demise of free trade came about as much through its redefinition by its proponents at the point of victory as from attacks by its opponents. The Labour party and organised workers supported free trade, but in a different way from old Liberals: they argued that free trade was only equitable provided that it was linked with a 'fair' distribution of income and wealth at home, so that exports did not rely on low wages at home, and imports did not fuel exploitation abroad.[73] Concern about the level of wages did not arise from the perceived impact of the gold standard so much as from changing notions of equity and social justice. These assumptions impacted on the taxation system and the need for redistribution to ensure that free trade was based on a 'fair' and not pathological social structure. The changing definitions of equity and social justice were crucial to the trade-offs between economic policies, and I will return to the issue in the next lecture.

In Britain, free trade and the gold standard survived as inseparable twins up to the First World War. The pattern differed in other countries where maintenance of the gold standard came at the cost of partial surrender to the forces of protectionism. We have seen that adherence to gold led to an increase in world trade, from which we can deduce that membership of the gold bloc was likely to be supported by interests and sectors committed to external trade. Yet at the same time as they joined or remained committed to gold, a number of countries adopted protectionist policies. This outcome might appear contradictory, but it reflects the complex trade-offs within different societies. The countries adopting gold in the 1870s seem to have made the decision without considering trade policy, and subsequently compensated losers by introducing tariffs. The process was not general, for outcomes differed according to circumstances.[74] In the next address, I will consider the implications of the weakening of the ideology of free trade in Britain for the gold standard: did the one impact on the other?

---

[73] See F. Trentmann, 'The Transformation of Fiscal Reform: Reciprocity, Modernization, and the Fiscal Debate within the Business Community in Early Twentieth-Century Britain', *Historical Journal*, 39 (1996), 1005–48; *idem*, 'The Strange Death of Free Trade: The Erosion of "Liberal Consensus" in Great Britain, c. 1903–1932', in *Citizenship and Community: Liberals, Radicals and Collective Identities in the British Isles, 1865–1931*, ed. E. F. Biagini (Cambridge, 1996), 219–50; *idem*, 'Wealth versus Welfare: The British Left between Free Trade and National Political Economy before the First World War', *Historical Research*, 70 (1997), 70–98; *idem*, 'Political Culture and Political Economy: Interest, Ideology and Free Trade', *Review of International Political Economy*, 5 (1998), 217–51.

[74] I discussed this issue with Chris Meissner. He did not find that the level of tariffs was significant in the decision to adopt gold.

There is not time to deal in any detail with another element of the 'trilemma': capital exports. Rather like the gold standard, the historical literature has been dominated by excellent accounts of the level, chronology and sectoral and geographical allocation of capital exports, and the impact on the domestic economy. By contrast, little has been written about the cultural meanings of capital movements. The scale of capital exports was considerable: in 1850 overseas assets were 6.8 per cent of net national wealth and in 1913 35.2 per cent. Overseas investment experienced a cycle, falling from 62 per cent of gross domestic fixed capital formation in the late 1880s to 37 per cent in the 1890s, before rising to an astonishing level of 76 per cent between 1905 and 1914.[75] Criticism was surprisingly muted at the time compared with the concerns expressed in the later historical literature that Britain's economic performance suffered from such a high level of investment overseas. The explanation of the scale of export of capital (and the lack of concern about its possible impact) favoured by some historians is that British economic policy was dominated by 'gentlemanly capitalists' who owned the foreign assets, securing a high rate of return as a result of the disproportionately heavy costs of imperial defence paid by the taxes of workers and northern industrialists.[76]

There are two interconnected debates. One debate relates to the question of the costs and benefits of imperialism: did it lead to excessive costs of defence, and would the benefits have been obtained even in the absence of empire? The issue has divided recent historians as it divided economists in the past. Adam Smith commented in 1776 that the empire was costly, distorted investment and led to political corruption. His line of reasoning was continued into the nineteenth and early twentieth centuries, amongst others, by J. E. Cairnes, Henry Fawcett and John Hobson. Against them were ranged other economists who believed that the empire paid, allowing an outlet for surplus labour and capital, providing a market for British exports and returning a flow of income and raw materials.[77] A second, narrower, debate relates to the desirability

---

[75] *Studies in Capital Formation in the United Kingdom, 1750–1920*, ed. C. H. Feinstein and S. Pollard (Oxford, 1988), 469; S. Pollard, *Britain's Prime and Britain's Decline: The British Economy 1870–1914* (1989), 61; L. Stone, *The Global Export of Capital from Great Britain, 1865–1914: A Statistical Survey* (Basingstoke, 1999), 7. For detailed accounts of the level, direction and domestic impact of capital exports, see also amongst others A. K. Cairncross, *Home and Foreign Investment, 1870–1913: Studies in Capital Accumulation* (Cambridge, 1953); M. Simon, 'The Pattern of New British Portfolio Investment, 1865–1914', in *The Export of Capital from Britain, 1870–1914*, ed. A. R. Hall (1968); S. Pollard, 'Capital Exports, 1870–1914: Harmful or Beneficial?', *Economic History Review*, 38 (1985), 489–514; L. E. Davis and R. E. Gallman, *Evolving Financial Markets and International Capital Flows: Britain, the Americas, and Australia, 1865–1914* (Cambridge, 2001).

[76] The argument above all of Davis and Huttenback, *Mammon and the Pursuit of Empire*.

[77] For the debate over the costs of the empire between recent historians, largely in response to Davis and Huttenback, *Mammon and the Pursuit of Empire*, see P. K. O'Brien,

of capital exports regardless of their direction. Indeed, a large part of British overseas investment went outside the empire which accounted for about 40 per cent of the total.[78]

The debates over the burdens (or benefits) of empire and the costs (or profits) of overseas investment were linked, and the precise nature of the connection needs to be traced over time. As with the debate over free trade, capital exports raised issues of equity and social justice. Robert Giffen, for example, defended capital exports in 1905, arguing that 'a rich class at home living on its foreign income is, on the whole, a desirable class for a country to possess'. His argument rested on the assumption that large fortunes and incomes led to savings, and hence to investment and employment – and that investment overseas was just as beneficial as investment at home in leading to the import of cheap goods and stimulating export markets. Indeed, 'the existence of a field for investment abroad is to be welcomed as a relief from a plethora that would be dangerous' – if funds were retained at home, the result would be to drive down yields on government bonds.[79] Giffen was arguing against Hobson who feared that overseas investment (and militarism) arose from a maldistribution of income and wealth which meant that domestic markets and investment opportunities were limited. In the words of Leo Chiozza Money,

> While capital has gone oversea [sic] in a never-ending stream, the people whose united activities produced the commodities embodied in that capital have remained poor for lack of the proper investment of capital at home...If a housing scheme at home promises to yield but three per cent, while the employment of coolies in South Africa promises ten per cent, South Africa and the coolies are 'developed' and the housing scheme collapses.

The solution was not necessarily to limit capital exports: it was to redistribute wealth at home to create a fair and just domestic market, so that capital exports did not arise from a pathological social structure, and

---

'The Costs and Benefits of British Imperialism, 1846–1914', *Past and Present*, 120 (1988), 163–200, who argues that 'massive public expenditure upon the apparatus of imperial rule and defence was neither sufficient nor necessary for the growth of the economy' (200); for sceptical views see P. Kennedy, 'The Costs and Benefits of British Imperialism, 1847–1914', *Past and Present*, 125 (1989), 186–92, who suggests that 'both in absolute and relative terms, . . . the British taxpayer was probably not bearing a disproportionate burden – although the small island-state of Britain itself *was* enjoying a disproportionate share of global lands, raw materials, power and influence' (191–2); A. Offer, 'The British Empire, 1870–1914: A Waste of Money?', *Economic History Review*, 46 (1993), 215–38, similarly concludes that 'The empire was an adjunct of British wealth' (236). They are following in the footsteps of many earlier economists, whose views are summarised in J. C. Wood, *British Economists and the Empire* (1983).

[78] Stone, *Global Export of Capital*, 26–7.

[79] R. Giffen, 'Notes on Imports versus Home Production, and Home versus Foreign Investment', *Economic Journal*, 15 (1905), 493.

their connection with militarism was ended. On this condition, capital exports could still lead to a Cobdenite vision of peace and prosperity.[80]

The chancellor of the Exchequer in the years prior to the war, David Lloyd George, continued to hope that the massive outflow of capital exports would lead to economic growth and higher real wages, by stimulating demand for British goods in foreign markets and producing cheap goods for British consumers. Only shortly before the war did he start to doubt that capital exports would lead to renewed improvements in the standard of living, and wonder whether lack of funds at home was driving up the costs of borrowing for social welfare.[81] These concerns mounted between the wars, with a growing realisation that investment overseas, and in imperial development, might collide with investment in industrial reconstruction and in public spending, not least given the huge costs of servicing the national debt. But should capital exports be controlled, given the concerns of the City to retain its role as an international financial centre, the desire of insurance companies to secure good returns for their policy holders and the wish of the Colonial Office to invest in imperial development? These concerns became increasingly pressing between the wars, and were linked with changing perceptions of the 'fair' or equitable distribution of income and wealth.

In this essay, I have tried to show that the particular choice of trade-offs in the half century or so before 1914 did not reflect vested interests and ignorance so much as a widely shared and understandable belief that the gold standard was beneficial. The question to which I turn in the next address is why the pattern changed after 1914 so that the trade-off came under increasing pressure.

---

[80] J. A. Hobson, *Imperialism: A Study* (1902), 134, 147–8; L. G. Chiozza Money, *Riches and Poverty* (1905), 43, 147–8. On Hobson's views on capital exports, see P. J. Cain, 'J. A. Hobson, Cobdenism, and the Radical Theory of Economic Imperialism, 1898–1914', *Economic History Review*, 31 (1978), 565–84, and *Hobson and Imperialism: Radicalism, New Liberalism, and Finance, 1887–1938* (Oxford, 2002); P. F. Clarke, 'Hobson, Free Trade, and Imperialism', *Economic History Review*, 34 (1981), 308–12.

[81] A. Offer, 'Empire and Social Reform: British Overseas Investment and Domestic Politics, 1908–14', *Historical Journal*, 26 (1983), 119–38.

Transactions of the RHS 16 (2006), pp. 39–74 © 2006 Royal Historical Society
doi:10.1017/S0080440106000430   Printed in the United Kingdom

LAND, FREEDOM AND THE MAKING OF THE MEDIEVAL WEST*

By Matthew Innes

READ 26 APRIL 2005 AT THE UNIVERSITY OF SOUTHAMPTON

ABSTRACT. In the course of the fifth and sixth centuries, barbarian warbands acquired property rights in the former provinces of the Roman west, in a process that established the broad structural characteristics of early medieval society in western Europe: that is the central contention of this essay. Focusing on the western Mediterranean heartlands of the Imperial government and senatorial aristocracy, it argues that these property transfers were fundamental to the emergence of ethnic identity as the crucial political marker in the post-Roman west. Latent conflict over the respective rights and obligations of barbarian 'guests' and their provincial 'hosts' structured the first attempts at post-Roman state-formation in the west, for the nature of the 'hospitality' offered to barbarian warbands accommodated within the Empire became a matter of contention as second and third generation 'guests' continued to enjoy the fruits of the property of their 'hosts'. Interpreting these new social relationships in the light of established legal forms, barbarian kings identified agreed mechanisms for the legitimate transfer of Roman property to their followers: this process allowed Roman landowners to seek remedies for illegitimate or violent seizure, but at the price of acknowledging a significant redistribution of land to a new class of barbarian soldiers whose liberty was rooted in their military service. The result was the emergence, by the seventh century, of regionalised and militarised elites who appropriated the language of ethnicity to legitimate their position.

I

Around the year 510, a funerary inscription was raised in the church of St Just in the city of Lyon. It commemorated a man named Sarwa Gastimodus, who had died at the age of forty. Sarwa Gastimodus's name, it told its readers, truly summed up the merits of his life. That this epitaph apparently required no further explanation to its contemporary audience is striking, for it turned on the literal meaning of Sarwa and Gastimodus, both words with Germanic roots. Sarwa denoted weaponry and here signified martial valour, whilst Gastimodus Latinised the Germanic noun

* I should thank John Arnold, Marios Costambeys, Caroline Humfress and Chris Wickham for their comments, my Birkbeck friends and colleagues for knocking a very early draft into a more promising shape and of course my audience at Southampton for their questions.

for 'guest'. So here we have an inhabitant of Lyon, named in Germanic with a hint of bastardised Latin 'Hard Man our Guest', commemorated in a resolutely Roman form in a Catholic church, but to an audience who were familiar enough with Germanic names to understand.[1]

Sarwa's epitaph is far from isolated: this aspect of Roman elite culture flourished in a Rhone valley now under Burgundian management. This material is but one of the many bodies of evidence now used to paint a picture of barbarian-Roman acculturation, with shifting social, cultural and political frontiers being negotiated through the framing of new identities.[2] Sarwa's epitaph belongs to a provincial society in flux, and his identity cannot be read as a biological given. The history of barbarian settlement behind Sarwa's presence in Lyon at the turn of the fifth century can hardly be understood in terms of arrows tracing the itineraries of homogeneous 'tribes' from German 'homelands' into Roman provinces.

The groups that were described by Roman observers as 'Burgundians' were highly discontinuous.[3] 'Burgundians' – the definite article that allows us to talk of 'the' Burgundians reflects our attempts to weld contemporary witnesses into a continuous narrative – are attested in a variety of locations beyond the Rhine frontier in the third and fourth centuries. In 407 'Burgundians' made an alliance with the provincials and generals supporting Jovinus's bid for the purple, settling along the frontier in the process. A generation later, after a calamitous defeat, the 'relics' of these Rhineland Burgundians were evacuated by the Roman general Aetius to Sapaudia, the frontier zone around Lake Geneva. Subsequent expansion into the Rhone basin took place in the decades after 450, in a series of uneasy alliances with provincial aristocrats.

The members of the Burgundian 'people' of the years around 500 were not a fixed group defined by descent from a core group of original settlers. The diverse warbands who settled in a number of distinct though obscure movements in the second half of the fifth century brought with them households, dependants and slaves. Traditions uniting these groups

---

[1] *Recueil des inscriptions chrétiennes de Gaul* 15, ed. F. Descombes (Paris, 1985), no. 263; my thanks to Wolfgang Haubrichs for explication.

[2] On the social meaning of inscriptions, Mark Handley, *Death, Society and Culture. Inscriptions and Epitaphs in Gaul and Spain, 350–700* (Oxford, 2003); on names and identity, Patrick Amory, 'Names, Ethnic Identity and Community in Fifth- and Sixth-Century Burgundy', *Viator*, 25 (1994), 1–30.

[3] The itinerary that follows has been rehearsed on many occasions; recent accounts are Justin Favrod, *Histoire politique du royaume burgonde 443–534* (Lausanne, 1997), and Reinhold Kaiser, *Die Burgunder* (Stuttgart, 2003). On Burgundian ethnogenesis and state-formation, see Ian Wood, 'Gentes, Kings and Kingdoms – the Formation of States. The Kingdom of the Gibichungs', in *Regna and Gens*, ed. Hans-Werner Goetz, Jörg Jarnut and Walter Pohl (Leiden, 2003), 243–69, and his 'Ethnicity and the Ethnogenesis of the Burgundians', in *Typen der Ethnogenese unter besonderer Berücksichtigung der Bayern*, ed. Herwig Wolfram and Walter Pohl (2 vols., Vienna, 1990), I, 53–69.

were shallow: when the Burgundian kings attempted to cultivate dynastic memory, they could not traverse the middle decades of the fifth century.[4] And the crystallisation of a territorial kingdom in the Rhone valley did not involve a corresponding stabilisation of populations: in laws and letters we again and again encounter endemic slave-taking fuelling the coming and going of captives whose allegiances and identities were undergoing renewed transformation.[5] By the first decades of the sixth century the various subjects of the Burgundian king could be referred to as 'our people', whatever their origin, and the label 'barbarian' reserved for those outside the kingdom.[6] Even if we focus on its political and ethnic dimensions, ignoring issues of status, gender, locality and religion which should loom large, Sarwa's identity must, then, be seen as a construct, not an index of descent or cultural affiliation, which in this context can hardly but have been mixed. His parents and peers, through his name, defined his membership of provincial society in terms of very specific gendered functions within that society, as a 'hard man' and a 'guest'.

So far, so familiar. Our mental world of the late antique west is now populated with scores of Sarwas. We are slowly being weaned off older models of clashes of civilisations, with the calamitous decline of Rome a tabula rasa on to which new groups could inscribe their ancestral cultures, and learning to read identities as processes, not givens.[7] But these great strides should not lead us to see an endless and continuous renegotiation, where barbarian ethnicities are only the logical outgrowths of ancient regional identities, and transformation is seamless and friction-free. After all, the notion of barbarians as 'guests', here used approvingly – is not the epitaph saying, Sarwa was not only a hard man, but he also behaved as a true guest? – could be more ambivalent. Several fifth-century Gallic authors counterpointed the official line on barbarians as 'guests' with the troubled experiences of provincial landowners. On a fairly light level, Sidonius Apollinaris's famous but playful comments on a band of Burgundian guests on his villa should remind us that not all guests are welcome, nor do they necessarily behave as their hosts would wish. In elegant Latin verse, Sidonius complained to a friend that the Burgundians had driven away his muse, with the noise of their

---

[4] Liber Constitutionum [hereafter LC], ed. L. von Salis, Monumenta Germaniae Historica [hereafter MGH] Leges Nationum Germanicarum 2.1 (Hannover, 1892); English trans. K. F. Drew, The Burgundian Code (Philadelphia, 1972), 3.

[5] See n. 34 below; the role of experiences of captivity in the reshaping of identities in this period serves proper study; its trauma may have played a part in encouraging dramatic change here. See also Recueil des inscriptions chrétiennes de la Gaule 15, ed. Descombes, no. 290.

[6] See Patrick Amory, 'The Meaning and Purpose of Ethnic Terminology in the Burgundian Laws', Early Medieval Europe, 2 (1993), 1–28.

[7] For why it matters, see Patrick Geary, The Myth of Nations: The Ethnic Origins of Europe (Princeton, 2001).

singing, eating and drinking, and their disgusting smell. For other authors, though, the joke was blacker: Paulinus of Pella, for example, lamenting the seizure of family property saw the rhetoric of 'hospitality' a sham that hid a reality of 'hostility' and expropriation.[8] That the ideology of barbarians as 'guests' enjoying 'hospitality' attracted grim humour points to something we really ought to know: that dramatic changes in social identity most likely relate to far-reaching social transformations fraught with tension.

It is such tensions, and their working out in the former heartlands of the western Empire in Italy, southern Gaul, Spain and Africa, that are the subject of this essay. In particular, in what follows I draw upon the strong and unambiguous evidence for friction over the distribution of land between barbarians and Romans from the 410s – when Paulinus's woes began – through Sidonius's public career in the second half of the fifth century, into the period of Justinian's 'reconquests' in the middle decades of the sixth century. By listening closely to the testimonies of those who took part in these events we will explore how a latent conflict over title to land shaped processes of acculturation and ethnogenesis. In the initial stages of settlement, particularly in the militarily denuded provinces of Gaul, violence and the threat of violence were central in allowing the systematic transfer of the fruits of landowning to barbarian incomers. In the second and third generations after the initial settlements, however, the legal and tenurial implications of these *de facto* transfers of rents and produce gave rise to litigation, as Roman landowners attempted to reclaim property, to assert their continuing title to lands which now housed barbarian settlers, even to claim rights over waste or woodland brought under the plough by newcomers. Practical problems over the definition of overlapping interests in the countryside gave rise to claim and counter-claim, which in turn generated legal rulings, preserved in the administrative instruments and law-codes issued by barbarian kings. Through their indispensable expertise in overseeing the machinery of late Roman government, Roman advisors at barbarian courts were thus able to order and reassert control over the devolution of property in the countryside, and the Gallic experience was used as a template for land transfer by administrative fiat in post-Roman Italy. But the price for this ordering of barbarian settlement was the acknowledgement of a large-scale transfer of resources that was a crucial mechanism in the

---

[8] Walter Goffart, *Barbarians and Romans: The Techniques of Accommodation, AD 418–568* (Princeton, 1980), 95–6, first pointed out Gallic hagiographers playing on the contrast between their experience of 'hostility' and the official line on 'hospitality'. Sidonius Apollinaris, *Poems and Letters*, ed. and trans. W. B. Anderson (2 vols., Cambridge, MA, 1938–65), *carmina* 12; Paulinus of Pella, *Eucharisticon*, lines 422–5, ed. and trans. H. G. Evelyn White, *Ausonius: Works* (Cambridge, MA, 1921), 295–351. Sidonius, *Letters*, 7.7, engages in similar word-play on 'hospitality' and 'hostility'.

restructuring of western society. As a result, now fragmented landowning elites were unable to sustain formal status boundaries and legal privileges of the kind that had marked off the Roman senatorial aristocracy; instead, they adopted ethnic identities that legitimated their bearers as representatives of a wider community of free landowners. This was a distinctively western development, which marked out a fundamental divergence in the historical trajectory of Europe.

Discussion of conflict over material resources is strangely lacking from much of the modern historiography on the transformation of the Roman west. Sophisticated treatments of identity politics have coincided with a relative dearth of research on the actual mechanics of social transition. This is no accident. The historiographical revolution which has encouraged narrative sources to be read as active texts designed to create identities has opened up exciting new vistas, but has left the sparse, difficult and highly technical source material on social structure unappealing to few but the hardcore. Indeed, the personal trajectory of one of the dominant figures of the 1970s and 1980s in barbarian studies, Walter Goffart, neatly articulates this turn to textuality. In his 1980 discussion of 'the techniques of accommodation' between barbarians and Romans, Goffart provided the last extended investigation of the effects wrought by barbarian settlement on the social structures of the Roman provinces, whilst his hugely influential 1988 study of 'the narrators of barbarian history' was a pivotal moment in the textual turn.[9]

Goffart has been far from the only figure teaching us to see barbarian identity not as a timeless given born out of a changeless 'Germanic antiquity', but rather as a product of interaction and negotiation between the Roman Empire and its neighbours: it is the work of Patrick Geary, and the development of German-language 'ethnogenesis' scholarship by Herwig Wolfram and Walter Pohl, that has exploded the old historiography.[10] But because the cornerstone of Goffart's earlier work

[9] *Barbarians and Romans*, published in 1980, still shapes the parameters of debate on settlement; in contrast *The Narrators of Barbarian History, 550–800* (Princeton, 1988) stands at the beginning of a debate which has altered out of all recognition in the past two decades (see e.g. Walter Pohl, 'History in Fragments: Montecassino's Politics of Memory', *Early Medieval Europe*, 10 (2001), 343–74). I should add that although my view of the earliest stage of barbarian settlement obviously differs from Goffart's, the interpretation advanced below is fundamentally shaped by his seminal demonstrations of the complex interrelationship between property law and fiscal liability in the late Roman world; the shame is that the 'Goffart thesis' as fossilised in much of the historiography ignores this by opposing 'tax' to 'land' in a way wholly alien to Goffart's own work.

[10] For the Anglophone, Patrick Geary's early work marked the real breakthrough, even though Wolfram had been publishing in English since the 1970s. For subsequent advances, spurred on by international collaboration, see e.g. *Strategies of Distinction: The Construction of Ethnic Communities, 300–800*, ed. Walter Pohl and Helmut Reimitz (Leiden, 1998), esp. Pohl's contributions; for different emphases within the 'ethnogenesis' paradigm, see Patrick

was that barbarians were 'accommodated' through relatively ordered processes that could be analysed in terms of late Roman administrative and fiscal practice, it has allowed social and economic organisation to go relatively neglected. Drawing on his earlier work which argued that the distinction between property rights and fiscal liability in the late Roman Empire was increasingly fuzzy, he claimed that the barbarian armies of the fifth- and sixth-century west were granted shares of tax revenue by provincial elites eager for protection, and that these originally fiscal transfers were slowly transformed into landownership. The dense exegesis on legal terminology on which these arguments were based continues to fuel debate among specialists.[11] But even those sceptical of the details have been profoundly influenced by Goffart's basic contention, that the apparent absence of any large-scale or concerted resistance to barbarian settlement by provincial landowners is incompatible with widespread expropriation. The administrative complexities of late Roman fiscal law are therefore consistently invoked as a mechanism for easing friction and tension out of the process even whilst qualifications to a wholesale fiscalist view of settlement are acknowledged. Barbarian settlement has become a self-contained issue in administrative history, and the evidence that the debate turns on – the richest material we have on relationships between barbarians and Romans on the ground – has thus been lost from the mainstream of the historiography.

The result has been a widespread perception of relatively ordered change, contested primarily by those wishing to reassert traditional views of barbarian violence.[12] Such a perception is the logical outcome of an

Amory, *People and Identity in Ostrogothic Italy 489–554* (Cambridge, 1997), and Peter Heather, 'The Making of the Visigoths', in *The Visigoths from the Migration Period to the Seventh Century*, ed. Peter Heather (Woodbridge, 1999), 47–73; for a stimulating overview of the state of play, see Walter Pohl, 'Ethnicity, Theory and Tradition: A Response', in *On Barbarian Identity: Critical Responses to Ethnicity in the Early Middle Ages*, ed. Andrew Gillett (Turnhout, 2002), 221–40.

[11] Goffart's major prominent supporter is Jean Durliat (e.g. 'Le salaire de la paix sociale dans les royaumes barbares', in *Anerkennung und Integration: zu den wirtschaftlichen Grundlagen der Völkerwanderungszeit 400–600*, ed. Herwig Wolfram and Andreas Schwarcz (Vienna, 1988), 17–70; 'Cité, impôt et integration des barbares', in *Strategies of Distinction*, ed. Pohl and Reimitz, 153–79; *Les finances publiques de Dioclétian aux Carolingiennes, 285–888* (Sigmaringen, 1989)), founder of a French school essaying hyper-continuity rooted in the survival of fiscal structures, and effectively demolished by Chris Wickham, 'The Fall of Rome Will Not Take Place', in *Debating the Middle Ages*, ed. Lester Little and Barbara Rosenwein (Oxford, 1998), 45–57. Sustained critiques, as opposed to passing criticism, are harder to find, but see Sam Barnish, 'Taxation, Land and Barbarian Settlement in the Western Empire', *Papers of the British School at Rome*, 54 (1986), 170–95, as well as Evangelos Chrysos, 'De Foederatis Iterum', and Wolfgang Liebeschuetz, 'Cities, Taxation and Barbarian Settlement: The Theories of Durliat and Goffart', in *Strategies of Distinction*, ed. Pohl and Reimitz, 185–206, 135–51.

[12] For example see B. Ward-Perkins, *The Fall of Rome and the End of Civilisation* (Oxford, 2004). Peter Heather's *The Fall of Rome: A New History* (London, 2005) appeared as this paper was in the final stages of preparation.

approach that seeks to distil from disparate legal sources a system, and so bypasses those very cases of conflict where we see divergent interests in sharp relief. Yet it is precisely these cases that reveal the immediate pressures that reshaped identities. Whilst we must never forget the late Roman foundations of early medieval society, we should not be so focused on the hunt for precedents that we forget the scale of change, or reduce the experience of change to a cosy cultural politics which presupposes free choice or an agency unrestrained by social and economic imperatives on the part of those adopting new allegiances. The sharp social hierarchy that underwrote the domination of the senatorial aristocracy in the west, after all, had vanished by the seventh century, as stratification shallowed and elite dominance came to be exercised in far less formal terms than it had been in Roman times. In place of the complex nexus of Roman fiscality and property law, in which the categorisation of rights over land had intersected with the registration of fiscal liabilities, we move into a world of free proprietors whose status was defined by their bearing of arms in the service of their king, and whose rights over property were manifest, rooted in physical fact. Ancient ideologies of freedom had presented citizenship as enabling access to the law that defined civilisation but also necessitating obligations to the state; by the seventh century, free status was articulated through honourable public activity on the wartrail and in assemblies, and was seen as incompatible with the humiliation of onerous service or the payment of tax.

The accommodation of barbarians in the west was, of course, not the only factor in these changes. But investigating the dynamics of barbarian settlement opens new perspectives on how they came about, for by insisting that a vague wave at 'social stress' is not an adequate explanation for change we demand precise connection between the economic, political and social. More than that, looking in detail at the reception of barbarian incomers can help restore an element of surprise to the historiography. After all, historians, professional explainers of why things turned out as they did, all too easily lose the sense of options urgently debated and a future at stake which animated their subjects. Given the energy that has been expended reconnecting Rome to the early middle ages, it is easy for us to forget that western Europe's post-Roman trajectory was unparalleled in the other ancient agrarian Empires of Eurasia.[13] Would an observer c. 400 have predicted that the absorption of barbarian warbands into western society would lead to the collapse of the structures of senatorial dominance? Historians of the late Roman world have traced the increasing importance of personal retinues and

[13] For discussion, with comparative and theoretical bibliography, from the perspective of the Carolingian endpoint of post-Roman transformation, see Matthew Innes, *State and Society in the Early Middle Ages: The Middle Rhine Valley, 400–1000* (Cambridge, 2000), 251–63; the current study is an attempt to trace the origins of the characteristics suggested there.

barbarian warbands in the late fourth- and fifth-century west, evoking a world where landlords were becoming warlords and warlords landlords.[14] Was not the logical outcome the fashioning of a hybrid elite combining extensive landownership and military leadership in the service of the Roman state? In the east, an Imperial edict issued from Constantinople in 409 insisted that Hunnic barbarians who wished to settle were to have the status of tied tenants (*coloni*) under the control of their landlords.[15] Yet barbarian settlement in the west was not to refashion, but to wrench loose and ultimately break the circuits of landlord power and Imperial authority that had powered late Roman society in the west. If we are to understand the making of the early medieval west, we must explain why this was the case.[16]

II

Students of the late antique experience of living with barbarians, and the transformations which cohabitation could render to the cultural and social norms of both hosts and guests, are lucky to enjoy a relative abundance of legal evidence. Pride of place must be given to the *Book of Constitutions*, a collection of royal edicts published at Easter 517 by the Burgundian king Sigismund, which contains over a dozen rulings relating to relationships between Burgundians and Romans and the mechanisms of barbarian settlement.[17] Sigismund's collection contains little predating the turn of the century; the rulings on settlement thus do not directly illuminate the initial settlements, but their consequences two or three generations later. This horizon is typical. From the Visigothic kingdom in southern Gaul and Spain, we have a handful of rulings preserved in the palimpsested fragments of the earliest surviving barbarian law-code,

---

[14] C. R. Whittaker, 'Landlords and Warlords in the Later Roman Empire', in *Warfare and Society in the Roman World*, ed. J. Rich and G. Shipley (London, 1993), 277–302.

[15] *Theodosian Code*, ed. T. Mommsen (Berlin, 1905), 5.6.3; my thanks to Caroline Humfress for drawing this edict to my attention.

[16] Chris Wickham, 'The Other Transition: From the Ancient World to Feudalism', *Past and Present*, 103 (1984), 3–36, to be read alongside his 'The Uniqueness of the East', *Journal of Peasant Studies*, 12 (1985), 166–96, is the classic theoretical discussion, subsequently nuanced by its author, but its basic modality accepted for the west even by those who have identified a 'tributary mode of production' in Imperial successor states elsewhere, e.g. John Haldon, *The State and the Tributary Mode of Production* (London, 1993).

[17] For a full discussion of this material, see Matthew Innes, 'On the Social Dynamics of Barbarian Settlement: Land, Law and Conflict in the Burgundian Kingdom', forthcoming in *The Burgundians from the Migration Period to the Seventh Century*, the proceedings of a symposium hosted by the Centre for International Research on Social Stress at San Marino in 2003; this paper draws on material developed and discussed there, and I would like to thank Giorgio Ausenda for his hospitality and Peter Heather and Ian Wood for sharing their insights. I accept Ian Wood's arguments on the date and context of LC, first advanced in his 'Disputes in Late Fifth- and Sixth-Century Gaul: Some Problems', in *The Settlement of Disputes in the Early Middle Ages*, ed. Wendy Davies and Paul Fouracre (Cambridge, 1986), 7–22 at 10.

that of Euric (466–84), half a century after the initial settlement.[18] Even from Italy, where we might expect the richest evidence, the mechanisms whereby the armies of Odoacer and Theodoric were settled between 476 and 493 remain elusive. Our insights come from a source of a different genre: the series of specific instructions issued by Theodoric and his successors, and preserved by their author, the Roman aristocrat and civil servant Cassiodorus, in the collection of official documentation he put together after leaving public life, as the Ostrogothic kingdom was coming to an end before Justinian's armies.[19]

The chronological horizon of the legal evidence is only a problem if we seek to read it in an outdatedly positivistic way, as an unproblematic window on to institutional arrangements. It is of value precisely because it allows us to investigate settlement not as a single event or the articulation of administrative principle, but rather in terms of the evolving relationships between barbarians and provincials as new generations of barbarians who were born and bred within provincial society came of age. It was precisely such questions and queries that inspired the royal rulings with which we must work.

If the chronological distribution of our evidence is no accident, neither is its geographical focus or its legal form. In the fourth century, the provincial elites of Italy, southern Gaul and Spain had been closely tied into the Imperial system, and these regions, along with the north African coastline, formed a distinct western Mediterranean economic, social and political system, moulded by senatorial wealth and Imperial patronage. The unpleasant necessity of settlement here rested on both unofficial and official negotiation between provincial elites and barbarian leaders that observed established administrative and legal forms, and was regulated through administrative and legislative instruments. Further north, where

[18] *Code of Euric* [hereafer CE], ed. K. Zeumer, MGH Leges Nationum Germanicarum 1 (Hannover, 1902), which includes internal references to laws issued by earlier kings; Visigothic kings continued to issue codifications of legislation through the seventh century, so the material assembled under Recceswinth (642–53) (*Liber Judicum* [hereafter LJ], ed. K. Zeumer, trans. S. P. Scott, *The Visigothic Code* (Boston, 1911)), is valuable in showing how later generations received the early material, not least as it marks some chapters as 'ancient', dating from the reign of Leovigild (569–85).

[19] Cassiodorus, *Variae*, ed. Theodor Mommsen, MGH Auctores Antiquissimi [hereafter AA], 12 (Berlin, 1894), a selection is available in English translation by Sam Barnish (Liverpool, 1990). The whole issue of Odoacer's army and the system for its reward needs urgent re-examination, but suffers from lack of sources. Procopius's account, which has Odoacer's troops demanding a third of the lands in Italy, is to be treated with extreme care serving as it does to underwrite Procopius's depiction of the settlement of Theodoric's Goths: see Goffart, *Barbarians and Romans*, 62–70. Whilst strictly contemporary sources are less than forthcoming, the mutiny that precipitated Odoacer's deposition of Romulus Augustolous must suggest that this was not a case of business as usual. *Variae* 1:18, discussed below pp. 55, 60–1 is crucial evidence here.

an increasingly distinct regional system focused on the Rhine frontier had been emerging since the third century, even a general lack of fifth-century evidence cannot hide huge differences: when we pick up the Salic law, we move into a society more or less unrecognisable from Sigismund's, Euric's or Theodoric's.

The coherence of the ties which had bound together the western Mediterranean coast and its hinterlands for the fourth and much of the fifth centuries explains the close similarities between the evidence from the Burgundian and Visigothic kingdoms, and the evident influence of these earlier settlements on arrangements in Theodoric's Italy. It is no accident that the one area of the western Mediterranean core that produced a different class of evidence, Africa, was settled in a radically different process. Here, military conquest and distinct economic and social structures allowed the Vandal kings to target the lands of the senatorial aristocracy and the Catholic church, manipulating Roman law to do so, and using administrative instruments of a familiar kind. No African counterpart to the Roman advisors responsible for Sigismund's and Euric's law-codes compiled a comparable artefact for the Vandal kingdom, and so our perspective is dependent on the pained voices of exiled senators and churchmen.[20]

Legal codifications of the kind on which we are reliant need careful handling. It was the late Patrick Wormald's brilliant achievement to demonstrate the ideological functions of barbarian law-codes: in law-giving, barbarian kings were legitimating their rule.[21] Wormald's insight holds good for our material. Sigismund's code was promulgated at a time of profound crisis within his kingdom, and presented his regime as resting on law and so guaranteeing the continuation of civilised social order; Cassiodorus's *Variae*, published in the middle of Justinian's 'reconquest', were clearly making a political statement about the nature of the Gothic regime and the aspirations of those who had served it; and Visigothic law-giving occasioned comment from Roman landowners.[22]

---

[20] These differences in the nature of the source material mean that the Vandal settlement of Africa is best treated separately from the Italian, Gallic and Spanish evidence used here. I hope to discuss the African situation in detail elsewhere.

[21] Above all is the still seminal 'Lex Scripta and Verbum Regis. Legislation and Germanic Kingship from Euric to Cnut', in *Early Medieval Kingship*, ed. Peter Sawyer and Ian Wood (Leeds, 1977), 105–38.

[22] Sigismund in 517: Ian Wood, 'Incest, Law and the Bible in Sixth-Century Gaul', *Early Medieval Europe*, 7 (1998), 291–303. Cassiodorus: most recently Andrew Gillett, 'The Purposes of Cassiodorus' *Variae*', in *After Rome's Fall: Narrators and Sources of Barbarian History*, ed. A. C. Murray (Toronto, 1998), 37–50. The context of Euric's legislation remains unknown, but for Visigothic state-formation in the fifth century see Ralph Mathisen and Hagith Sivan, 'Forging a New Identity: The Visigothic Kingdom of Toulouse', in *The Visigoths: Culture and Society*, ed. A. Ferreiro (Leiden, 1999), 1–62; note also, for the ideological meaning of law-giving, Sidonius's memorable character-assassination of the Roman official Seronatus

Attempts to interpret these codifications as compilations of barbarian custom, statements of the 'personal law' of Burgundians and Visigoths distinct from the Roman law of the provincial population, have failed because Sigismund's and Euric's codes deal with all sections of the population, Roman as well as barbarian.[23] They were demonstrations of the continued application of Roman legal practice in newly emerging barbarian kingdoms, and hence were soon supplemented by handbooks of the Roman law whose basic principles they adapted to a new situation.[24]

Legitimating statements they may have been, but these collections were not confections shaped solely by ideological concerns. The edicts codified under Euric and Sigismund and the administrative instruments collected by Cassiodorus arose in a context in which a lively intercourse of legal argument and appeal continued in full late Roman tradition. In dealing with the flood of business thus generated, barbarian kings relied on Roman advisors and their legal education: Sidonius Apollinaris even complemented one friend on becoming 'a new Solon among the Burgundians'.[25] We should not, then, dismiss this legal evidence as merely normative or of questionable practical application, nor should we treat it uncritically as merely descriptive, seeing tariffs of fines or labels for different groups as straightforward reflections of social structure. This material needs handling every bit as carefully as a literary source or an archaeological site. Like the Imperial rulings collected in the Theodosian Code, we should see it as arising from legal conflict and social change on the ground, requiring authoritative rulings from above. Like the Theodosian Code, our evidence should not be read as a static description of a monolithic system, but disaggregated and contextualised, ruling by ruling. In applying principles and expectations rooted in Roman administrative and legal practice to a series of new and concrete problems, this legislation thus attempted to order and regulate tensions.

---

who 'trampled the code of Theodosius beneath the laws of Theodoric [II, the Gothic king]': *Letters*, 2.1.

[23] See Wood, 'Ethnicity and Ethnogenesis', built upon by Amory, 'The Meaning and Purpose of Ethnic Terminology'.

[24] For the Visigoths, this took the form of the Breviary of Alaric, a condensation of the Theodosian Code issued around half a century after Euric's code, as Alaric II was attempting to rally support among the southern Gallic aristocracy and episcopate in the face of Frankish threats; for the Burgundians, an enigmatic tract known as the *Lex Romana Burgundionum*, which collects Roman legal precedents for issues dealt with in Sigismund's code, and is best therefore seen as a companion or commentary on the latter whose official status remains unclear. More work is urgently needed on this material.

[25] Sidonius, *Letters*, 5.5.

III

These tensions turned on the implications of the allocation of barbarian 'guests' to their Roman 'hosts'. The relatively late horizon of our legal evidence means that the precise workings of the process must remain obscure, although it clearly differed in both scale and implication from established mechanisms for the billeting of Roman armies.[26] The contemporary comments we do have on barbarian settlement – primarily asides in hagiography and poetry – are frustratingly sparse, but they are unanimous in pointing to allocations, whereby barbarian incomers were dispatched to specific estates in a process which was negotiated, yes, but in which the possibility of coercion and the experience of sporadic violence were never far away. Sidonius could thus criticise the Roman official Seronatus for having 'filled the woods with fugitives, and villas with "guests"'.[27] The language of hosts, guests and hospitality was rooted in social norms, not administrative procedures or legal rules.[28] Looking back from c. 460, Paulinus of Pella lamented his disastrous decision not to billet barbarian guests at his ancestral home near Bordeaux: as a result, it was pillaged, whereas Gothic 'guests' elsewhere 'strove most generously to serve their hosts by protecting them'.[29] To debate whether this primary stage of barbarian settlement rested on the transfers of tax liabilities or property rights is thus unhelpful, for contemporaries did not conceive of it in these terms. What mattered was the assignation of a place where barbarian soldiers and their dependants could reside whilst they were not generating plunder and tribute on the wartrail. As late as the 460s the Gallician chronicler Hydatius could describe Gothic settlement as the acquisition of 'seats' (*sedes*), whilst a decade later Sidonius could describe the Goths returning to their 'seats' after a campaign against his native Auvergne.[30]

The social relationships between 'hosts' and 'guests' that grew up in the aftermath of such arrangements remain elusive. Some 'hosts' at least were absent, among them senatorial landowners like Paulinus of Pella whose political careers ended in failure, exile and expropriation. The high personal costs of falling from political grace in the late Roman world must

[26] Following Goffart, *Barbarians and Romans*, ch. 2.
[27] Sidonius, *Letters*, 2.1.
[28] This terminology was adopted as early as 418: H. Sivan, 'An Unedited Letter of the Emperor Honorius to the Spanish Soldiers', *Zeitschrift für Papyrologie und Epigraphik*, 61 (1985), 273–87; H. Sivan, 'On Foederata, Hospitalitas and the Settlement of Gaul in AD 418', *American Journal of Philology*, 108 (1987), 759–72.
[29] Paulinus, *Eucharisticon*, lines 271–90: his *domus* was allowed to be pillaged because it was protected by no 'special right (ius)'.
[30] R. W. Burgess, *The Chronicle of Hydatius and the Consularia Constantinopolitana* (Oxford, 1993), s.a. 418, p. 82; Sidonius, *Letters*, 6.6.

have provided barbarian rulers with a ready-made and recurrent source of land for distribution, and because such expropriation did not target the senatorial class as a whole, but played on time-honoured rivalries within it as different factions sought to win royal favour, it did not arouse wholesale opposition: Paulinus could contrast the distribution of his family property to Goths according to the 'law of hostility' to the infamy of his Roman rivals who acted 'in defiance of all laws'.[31] But as time passed and guests became long-term residents, the need to regularise the stake enjoyed by barbarian guests in their hosts' estates became pressing. It is precisely such pressure that gives rise to the earliest layers of our legislation. They deal with the transformation of hospitality into property: Roman landowners were evidently under pressure from second and third generation guests aiming to turn their long-standing ties with the estates on which they lived into property rights.

Our fullest account of any barbarian settlement comes *c*. 500, in a complex decree issued by the Burgundian king Gundobad. Gundobad identifies successive stages of settlement: each of his 'people' had been assigned hospitality at a specified place (*locus*); some had subsequently been enriched by gifts of 'fields together with slaves' by Gundobad and his predecessors; earlier in his reign, Gundobad had issued a written instrument ordering that all those who had not benefited from royal gifts should receive 'a third of the slaves and two thirds of the land . . . from that place at which hospitality had been assigned to them'; now, Gundobad was legislating against those who had abused his earlier order.[32] Gundobad's reign had begun in 474, so this edict takes us back to the initial Burgundian settlement in the Rhone valley in the 450s and 460s: the allocation of a 'place of hospitality' and gifts of royal land to favoured followers had taken place under Gundobad's predecessors. Gundobad's granting to his people of a part of the 'land and slaves' of their Roman hosts can scarcely be construed as anything other than the transfer of real

---

[31] Paulinus, *Eucharisticon*, lines 422–5. Cf Sidonius, *Letters*, 5.7: Romans who make accusations against their countrymen are worse than barbarians.

[32] LC 54. The date of *c*. 500 has been suggested (by Goffart, *Barbarians and Romans*, 155–9) on the basis that the land-distributions discussed may well have taken place in the aftermath of the bloody civil war of 500, which according to Marius of Avenches resulted in the death, disgrace and expropriation of many major landowners; this is highly plausible, and would be strengthened if Gundobad's legislation on Burgundian settlement were to be equated with the 'milder laws' he was said to have issued after the civil war, as suggested in n. 44 below. LC 79, issued in 515 and decreeing a highly unusual fifteen-year term of possession for barbarians to establish permanent rights over land granted to them (the norm would be thirty) surely echoes a land distribution made in 500. In any case, the surviving output of Sidonius Apollinaris and Avitus of Vienne do not mention the grant of *sortes*: whilst argument from the absence of evidence is always shaky, it here might give us further encouragement to think of a land-distribution towards the very end of the fifth century.

property: the Latin terminology of *terra* and *mancipia* is unambiguous. We should not think of Gundobad rewarding individual settlers, but extended household units: another edict confirms the continued dependence of freedmen who had not received transfers of 'land and slaves'.[33] The imbalance implicit in the grant of two-thirds of the land, but only one third of the slaves, remains puzzling. On one level, it is of course a legal fiction, meaningless when abstracted from the reality of fields and soil. But the imbalance it makes explicit is most easily explained by the expectation that Burgundians had acquired not only plunder and tribute, but also human captives, on the wartrail: slave-taking is endemic in both the legislation and the written sources.[34] Gundobad's transfer of 'land and slaves' marked a fundamental shift, transforming his people from a warband economy of tribute and plunder to one rooted directly in the agrarian landscape.

The transfer of 'land and slaves' from Roman host to barbarian guest, as effected by Gundobad, in fact had very close precedents elsewhere in Gaul. In the Visigothic kingdom, there is good evidence for barbarian guests acquiring property from their Roman hosts in the first half of the fifth century, as rights of hospitality rooted in cohabitation were transformed into the possession of a carefully defined part of a Roman estate. Euric's code preserves a fragment concerning Goths entering their 'place of hospitality' to delimit a boundary; sixth-century legislators explained that 'a division of arable lands or forest between Goth and Roman' should not be disturbed, provided that it had been publicly made and each side had taken no more than the stated proportion, two-thirds for the Goths and one third for the Roman. The practice of *divisio* had plentiful precedents in Roman law, as a carefully controlled process for effecting an impartial separation of shared interests.[35] Although difficult, our legal evidence suggests a gradual process, with specific pieces of property transferred from Roman hosts to barbarian guests from the time of the very earliest settlements on, rather than a single and universal transfer by administrative fiat.[36] Euric's code, for example, also includes injunctions against Roman hosts who granted to their Gothic guests

[33] LC 57.
[34] LC Constitutiones Extravagantes 21 is vivid here. Redemption of captives was also a concern of bishops like Avitus of Vienne, Caesarius of Arles and Ennodius of Pavia.
[35] CE 276; LJ 10.1.7. Ernst Levy, *West Roman Vulgar Law: The Law of Property* (Philadelphia, 1951), 76–80 with – astoundingly – no historiographical follow up. On the Visigothic settlement see Mathisen and Sivan, 'Forging a New Identity', 13–18, 23–7, 34–7.
[36] The early date of these land-divisions is suggested by the fifty-year limitation on attempts to contest them, stated in CE 277 and transmitted to LJ 10.1.14, 10.2.1; the author of CE 277, whose absolute terminus *ante quem* is 484, must therefore have envisaged land-divisions which took place more than fifty years before his time. Paulinus's testimony confirms this chronological horizon.

estates to which they had no rightful title: the implication is that transfers from host to guest were commonplace, but that some hosts attempted to turn the process to their advantage by encouraging their Gothic guests to seize estates from other Romans.[37] Similar processes had in all probability been at work in the Burgundian kingdom before Gundobad's wholesale transfer of 'land and slaves': an edict of 515 confirmed and encouraged the 'long-standing' and 'well-known' practice whereby 'people belonging to a barbarian nation' might be 'voluntarily' granted land on which to live by the subjects of the Burgundian king.[38]

When discussing the recurrent agreements made between barbarian warlords and fifth-century elites, contemporary chroniclers regularly referred to them as resting on *divisiones*, drawing clear contrasts between such negotiated settlements and forced expropriation.[39] It would probably be mistaken to read the terminology too literally, and see recurrent divisions of individual estates. Division, the granting out 'allotments' or 'shares' (*sortes*), turned on the agreement of barbarian and provincial leaders on the principle of settlement, presumably followed by the assignment of hospitality to the barbarian rank-and-file in the specified areas. The term 'allotments' (*sortes*) is intriguingly ambivalent. Through the fifth century it had a territorial sense, denoting an area subject to agreed barbarian settlement, and by the time of the Visigothic and Burgundian legislation it was also the standard term for the specific stakes acquired by barbarian settlers in the Gallic countryside, that is for individual 'allotments'. The vocabulary evoked Roman legal usage, where *consortes* might share interests in a piece of property and indeed undertake agreed processes of division, but it also drew on extra-legal

[37] CE 312: these transfers could take the form either of outright donations from host to guest, or the grant of rights of 'occupation' without the transfer of legal title.

[38] LC 79: barbarians are invited to live amongst 'our people', which by this date had a territorial rather than a narrowly ethnic sense (see n. 6 above), and acquire permanent rights if they inhabit the land for fifteen years on certain conditions (the gift is not to be coerced, and the fifteen years' tenure must have taken place *sine testis/tertiis* – the MSS have variant readings which reflect Carolingian scribes trying to make sense of an obscure clause, which could mean either 'without disturbance', 'without rent' or 'without subsequently receiving thirds', i.e. the fruits of formal land-divisions).

[39] As late as 467, the Roman official Arvandus was found guilty of treason for allegedly suggesting that the Burgundians and Visigoths effect a *divisio* 'according to the law (*ius*) of *gentes*' of what remained of Roman Gaul: Sidonius, *Letters*, 1.7. For earlier settlements see e.g. the Gallic 'Chronicle of 452', ed. T. Mommsen, MGH AA 13, 660–6. Note the clear contrast between the smooth *divisio* undertaken by the Burgundians and the inhabitants of Sapaudia (s.a. 442) and local resistance to Aetius giving (the verb is *tradere*, transfer in property law) of rebellious 'further Gaul' to the Alans to 'divide' with the inhabitants, resistance which lead to expropriation as the Alans took possession of the land (s.a. 443); this surely counterpoints direct expropriation with negotiated *divisio*.

practices of drawing lots (*sortes*), and perhaps the sharing out of spoils on the wartrail.[40]

The ambivalence of the terminology of 'allotments' reminds us that we should not confuse continuity of legal form with continuity in social practice. For all their Roman precedents, the use of techniques of land-division to effect transfers to newcomers was unprecedented. The context and scale of the land-divisions in the fifth-century Visigothic kingdom must remain murky, but by the end of the century they fuelled the expectations of the barbarian rank-and-file elsewhere in the west, providing a template not only for Gundobad's wholesale transfer of 'land and slaves' to those Burgundians who had not been otherwise rewarded, but also for the accommodation of Theodoric's army in Italy.[41] The crucial witness for the latter is a letter of Theodoric's to the Senate in 509, nominating the young Roman nobleman Venantius for an honorary office. Written and preserved by Cassiodorus, it gives a lengthy panegyric on Venantius's father Liberius, who had served as Theodoric's Praetorian Prefect c. 493–500. Aside from his loyalty, and his care for the public purse, Liberius is particularly praiseworthy for ensuring the peaceful settlement of Goths in Italy:

> It is my delight to mention how, in the assignment of thirds, he united both the possessions and hearts of Goths and Romans. For though men usually quarrel when they are neighbours, here the sharing of rights in estates seems to have produced concord. For the result has been that both peoples (*nationes*), while living together, have achieved accord. Behold an unprecedented and wholly praiseworthy accomplishment: division of the soil has joined its title-holders in goodwill; the friendship of the people has grown through loss, for at the cost of a part of the land a defender has been purchased, and property preserved secure and intact. A single and just law embraces all. For sweet affection must develop among those who always preserve fixed boundaries. The Roman commonwealth owes its peace, then, not least to the aforementioned Liberius, he who has transmitted to such glorious peoples (*nationes* i.e. the Goths and Romans) the zeal for love.[42]

[40] For the territorial sense, often missed, see Hydatius, ed. and trans. Burgess, s.a. 411, p. 82, a crucial passage; Sidonius, *Letters*, 7.6, on the 'frontier (*limes*) of the Gothic *sortes*';Victor of Vita, *History of the Vandal Persecution*, ed. K. Halm, MGH AA 3.1 (Berlin, 1879), trans. John Moorhead (Liverpool, 1992), II:39, III:4, quoting Vandal royal edicts. In Paulinus of Pella, the language of *sortes* is pervasive. The links between this usage of *sortes* to refer to barbarian 'shares' of Roman provinces and Roman estates, the practices of taking *sortes Virgiliae* or *sortes Biblicae* by randomly selecting a passage, and the generic notion of drawing lots deserves sustained study.

[41] The example of the Vandals may also, of course, have played a role, but close and direct links between Visigothic, Burgundian and Ostrogothic practice are clear, and close contacts between the kingdoms must mean that they served as direct models; note in particular the chronological and geographical proximity of the transfers in Burgundy under Gundobad (who had spent his early career until 474 in Italy as master of the soldiers) and Italy under Theodoric (and probably already under Odoacer).

[42] *Variae* 2.16, trans. Barnish, 28–30.

Panegyric is a slippery source, but the vocabulary here is that of farms and soil, boundaries and land. Liberius is being praised for effecting an ordered land-division, here presented as a worthwhile price to pay for Gothic military protection; sharing out estates is thus a means for preserving the security of property.[43]

IV

The growing expectations of the barbarian warbands, which in the course of the fifth century had replaced the regular army as the military arm of Roman government in the west, culminated in systematic transfers of landed property. Unless we are prepared to swallow the huge pinch of salt necessary to make Cassiodorus's picture of two peoples united in loving neighbourliness palatable, we must ask how such transfers were received by provincial landowners. The wealth of evidence for forced and illegal expropriation by barbarians, too easily overlooked in our search for administrative structures underpinning settlement, should remind us that most had little room for manoeuvre here. In fact, barbarian rulers and their Roman advisors, in attempting to lay down rules governing land transfers, were in part attempting to control and structure processes which were already taking place on the ground; by doing so, they could label transfers taking place by approved mechanisms with their blessing legitimate, and so attempt to force the return of land taken by unapproved and so illegitimate means. Hence Gundobad, initiator of the systematic transfer of 'land and slaves' by administrative instrument, was remembered among the sixth-century descendants of those Roman landowners who would have lost out not as a despoiler but as the author of 'milder laws'.[44] Hence Theodoric, responding to the queries of two judges hearing cases that had arisen between Goths and Romans, ruled

---

[43] Cf. Goffart, *Barbarians and Romans*, 70–3 – why would Theodoric address the Senate in terms redolent of the division of land in the countryside to hide a reality of ordered transition through tax allocation? As Goffart notes, Ennodius of Pavia independently uses nearly identical language in his panegyric on Liberius (ed. Vogel, MGA AA 7 (Berlin, 1885), 9:23); this must encourage us to take the vocabulary of estate boundaries and farms seriously.

[44] Gregory of Tours, *Historiae*, ed. Bruno Krusch and Wilhelm Levison, MGH Scriptores Rerum Merowingicarum 1.1 (Hannover, 1951), 2:33: *leges mitiores* were issued in the aftermath of bloody civil war. This passage has traditionally been used to date the issue of the LC, long believed to be Gundobad's work, but this view has convincingly been challenged by Ian Wood, who has suggested that Gregory may be referring to a change in religious policy; others have attempted to identify specific laws within the LC e.g. the limitations of the 'ancient law of blame' which attempted to reduce the legitimate legal use of violence. I would suggest that in the aftermath of the disorder and expropriations, a firm ordering of the basis of Burgundian settlement is precisely what Gregory's family might have remembered as mitigatory laws.

that any estates which had been seized in his reign by barbarians without a warrant issued by the appropriate official were to be returned to their original Roman masters.[45]

Mention of official warrants effecting and limiting transfer reminds us that not every landowner in every province was subject to expropriation. Our understanding of the social impact of land transfer is hampered by a lack of documentary evidence, although the vulnerability of senators to expropriation for treason and 'political' crime is a recurrent feature, and both Lombards and Vandals systematically targeted senatorial wealth in the earliest stages of settlement. A single papyrus from Ravenna in 540 hints at agreements made between Roman landowners and provincial officials, through which the impact of land-division was mediated and negotiated: it transfers a portion of an estate to the church of Ravenna, guaranteeing that the property was immune from any public or private charge, and from transfer to barbarians as an 'allotment'.[46] We might well suppose that, for an individual landowner with sufficient influence, it would have been possible to volunteer a particular estate whilst safeguarding others, but we simply lack dense enough evidence to go further.

What is clear, nonetheless, is that barbarian settlement had important implications for tax liabilities. In a society where title to land was dependent on ability to meet fiscal demands, it could scarcely be otherwise. Here, thanks to Cassiodorus, our evidence is fullest for Italy; the intimate link between property and fiscality that it demonstrates persuaded some scholars to argue that barbarian settlement was

---

[45] *Variae* 1:18; special judges are here used to hear cases between soldiers and civilians, with the Goths having inherited the special status previously enjoyed by the Roman military. Goffart, *Barbarians and Romans*, 89–90, demonstrates that the vocabulary of *delegatio* by *pittachium* is generic, not specific to barbarian allotment; but the argument that *Variae* 1.18 cannot be relevant to the Gothic settlement as it concerns 'private law property' puts the cart before the horse, and cannot explain the implication of this letter that there had been systematic land transfer effected by such warrants.

[46] J.-O. Tjäder, *Die nichtliterarischen lateinischen Papyri Italiens aus der Zeit 445–700* (3 vols., Lund and Stockholm, 1954–82), no. 31. The fact that this is a portion of a larger estate encourages speculation that the immunity rests in the fact that this is a relic of a property previously subjected to division; whilst the guarantee of immunity from public or private charges, presumably implying that the donor had made arrangement for all personal and fiscal obligations from the remainder of his property, is a standard formula in sixth-century Ravennese donations (it presumably was a declaration by the former owner that he had met all liabilities so that the land, now owned by the church, was exempt from all charges); but the *sors* clause is unique; that this guarantee was given under a Roman regime after Justinian's 'reconquest' must strengthen the case that it rested on the estate's prior history i.e. it related to land that had already been subjected to the process of allocation and division so should not be so treated again.

essentially a reallocation of tax revenues.[47] In fact, Cassiodorus does show Gothic soldiers receiving donatives and payments funded out of tax, but also makes it clear that this form of reward complemented the grants of allotments (*sortes*). Theodoric's grandson and successor Athalaric could rally his army by reminding them that 'allotments of your own nourish you, and our gifts enrich you'. Enriching gifts of moveable wealth created personal bonds between ruler and warrior. But these were not the basis for settlement: allotments (*sortes*) nourished Gothic households.[48] Thanks to their official position as the military arm of the Roman state, Theodoric's Gothic army enjoyed the immunity from taxation that traditionally applied to Roman soldiers, and so estates granted out as *sortes* were likewise tax exempt.[49] Cassiodorus preserves an administrative instrument cancelling the tax due from an estate which Theodoric has just granted out as an allotment (*sors*) to the Gothic (i.e. Arian) priest Butila.[50] Given this direct evidence that the transfer of land as Gothic allotments led to an adjustment of tax liabilities, we might suspect that the loss of Roman property might have been made more palatable by a lightening of the tax burden. After all, fiscal exemptions of any kind were liable to imperceptible creep, particularly in the hands of the powerful or legally articulate. Another of Cassiodorus's letters, for example, deals with the case of 'ancient barbarians' settled on the Danube frontier, who had married provincial women and who were now claiming tax exemption for their wives' inheritances; although their claims were turned down, the potential elasticity of any concession is clear.[51] Beyond Theodoric's kingdom, the evidence is more sparse, but there are indications that land held by Burgundians or Visigoths was exempt from taxation, and we may assume similar processes to be at work.[52]

[47] Central to Goffart's argument is the evidence for the *illatio tertiarum* (*Barbarians and Romans*, 73–9); traditionally seen as an additional tax imposed on those landowners whose land was not divided and assigned as allotments, Goffart convincingly shows it is actually an earmarking of a portion of existing tax revenues (*Variae* 1.14 is crucial). *Variae* 2:17 clearly demonstrates that land granted as Gothic allotments no longer paid the *illatio*; it is difficult to read this as solely a matter of accountancy conventions with no effect on the ground.

[48] *Variae* 8:26. On grants of tax revenue to Goths, Goffart, *Barbarians and Romans*, 80–8.

[49] Goffart, *Barbarians and Romans*, 91–3, is conclusive.

[50] *Variae* 2.17. Goffart argued that this letter actually concerned the diversion of tax revenues from the local tax bureau to Butila, whose *sors* thus comprises the tax revenues from the stated estate; this seems forced, and there is no good reason to abandon the less complex reading that Theodoric was simply cancelling the liability on land granted out as a Gothic allotment.

[51] *Variae* 5.14.

[52] There is actually no direct evidence for the land tax under the Burgundians or the Visigothic kings of Toulouse, but in the later sixth century both the Merovingian and Visigothic kings taxed. That barbarian lands were exempt from tax is the implication of LJ 10.1.14 (Romans to reclaim lands of which they are unjustly deprived 'in order that the royal fisc may sustain no loss') and 10.1.16 for the Visigoths; for the Burgundians from a

If tax breaks may have helped Roman landowners accept the granting out of allotments, barbarian rulers were also keen to present this limited and ordered land-division as an acceptable price for the security of property, as in the panegyric on Liberius. For one thing, for all the established legal forms used to effect land-divisions, the precise legal status of estates transferred as *sortes* was debatable. Roman property law, rooted in the fundamental distinction between title (*dominium*) and possession, was able to separate distinct levels of right in a single piece of property; it also allowed various arguments for the reclamation of land wrongfully held. In provincial societies whose fabric was still shaped by litigatory complexities, ambiguity about the precise extent of the rights acquired by barbarians in their allotments inevitably gave rise to attempts by Roman landowners to use the law to re-establish control over estates now held by barbarians. Not that litigatory argument was not the sole preserve of Romans. Quite the opposite. Burgundian kings forbad their barbarian subjects from acting as advocates for Romans, and from representing their hosts in boundary disputes, precisely because such actions were possible stratagems of expropriation, whilst Boethius could look back on his career in Theodoric's service and lament 'how often have I protected such poor wretches as the unpublished covetousness of barbarians harassed with unending accusations?'[53] Legal complexities should not blind us to the raw fact of barbarian control of what had been Roman land in the countryside, but law here did not simply legitimate control rooted in coercion.

In fact, litigation over barbarian land reshaped notions of title. This is clearest in Sigismund's *Book of Constitutions*. Here, the rights of Burgundians over their allotments are consistently limited: they are to be subject to special inheritance rules to keep them in a restricted male line; they are only to be sold under certain strict conditions, and then only to the Roman host from which they had been received; litigation over the boundaries of 'fields which are possessed by barbarians through the law of hospitality' is to be conducted between Roman hosts, not barbarian guests. Allotments are thus a special kind of property, and the restrictions of Burgundian rights, and continuing interests of Roman hosts, in them are explicitly contrasted with the full ownership enjoyed by Burgundians over estates

---

comparison of LC 84 with *Lex Romana Burgundionum* [hereafter LRB], ed. L. von Salis, MGH Leges Nationum Germanicarum 2.1, 40 (the former limits the ability of Burgundians to sell land and dissipate allotments, whilst the latter, the equivalent clause in a compilation of Roman legal maxims, requires that (Roman) vendors meet the tax liability as a condition of sale). Tax exemption for barbarians is also witnessed for Vandal Africa and Merovingian Gaul.

[53] LC 22, 55; Boethius, *On the Consolations of Philosophy*, ed. and trans. E. K. Rand and H. Stewart (Cambridge, MA, 1918), 1.4.35.

they have received as 'public gifts', direct from the king. The substantive restrictions on rights over allotments are matched by a very careful use of legal terminology: whereas the standard terms for possession (*possidere* and its derivatives) are used in discussing the rights of Roman landowners and Burgundians in receipt of royal gifts, the vocabulary of unrestricted possession is never used of allotments.[54] The limitation of property rights enjoyed by Burgundians over their allotments is consistent and striking. It did not, however, rest on the wholesale application of any single distinction or tenurial template inherited from Roman property law; rather, in the material collected in the *Book of Constitutions*, it emerges piecemeal through a case by case application of established legal arguments and maxims to a new situation, as complaints over particular cases reach the king's ears, resulting in the issue of edicts clarifying the precise legal implications of Gundobad's transfer and of rulings delineating on the respective rights of 'host' and 'guest' over the land converted into Burgundian 'allotments'. We must suspect that the agency of the legally learned Roman advisors whose expertise shaped so much of this legislation played a crucial role here; the remarkable insistence on the limited nature of Burgundian rights in their allotments rests on their firm conviction that the granting of 'land and slaves' as allotments was not an absolute and outright transfer of rights in the relevant property from host to guest.

Learned distinctions over interlocking rights in property and closely drawn limitations on their disposition may seem technical in the extreme, but in at least one area we can see the legal arguments advanced by Roman landowners having a very real and tangible effect. In the recurrent legislation dealing with the legal status of land newly brought into cultivation, Burgundians undertaking clearances are repeatedly required to make real and sizeable concessions to their Roman hosts. The roots of this requirement lay in Roman legal rules dealing with common land, which was held to be shared in proportion to an individual's possessions. From this principle came the requirement that those making a clearance and bringing it into cultivation owed proportionate compensation to all those who had previously shared rights in the uncleared waste or wood. A series of case by case rulings preserved in the Burgundian *Book of Constitutions* show this logic being applied to common rights in woodland, and extrapolated to establish a new principle, that half of all clearances made by Burgundians are to be given to Roman landowners, further extrapolated to a series of rulings requiring that Burgundian guests compensate their Roman hosts for clearances and new build by offering

---

[54] See Innes, 'On the Social Dynamics of Barbarian Settlement', and note already Wood, 'Ethnicity and the Ethnogenesis', 68–9.

them half of all clearances, vineyards, orchards and farmhouses.[55] This logic is paralleled, in telescoped form, in the seventh-century Visigothic code. The compiler of this lawbook understood Euric's legislation on Gothic 'guests' delimiting boundaries within their hosts' estate as a description of a 'division of arable lands or forest': this involved a transfer of land to cultivate, or indeed to clear before bringing under the plough, and set up the barbarian guest with a small-holding carved out within the boundaries of a Roman estate. Another chapter concerns the respective rights of Goths and Romans over clearances made in 'undivided forests', and directly parallels the Burgundian laws.[56] These were meaningful acknowledgements of the priority of the Roman proprietorial grid, which involved barbarian settlers investing their Roman neighbours with a part of the fruits of their labour in order to establish outright possession unencumbered by the interlocking and overlapping rights rooted in Roman land registration and long-established estate boundaries.

Elsewhere, we lack the dense cluster of legislation that allows us to view the development of the 'law of allotments' in Burgundy. But we do have evidence for a similar dialectic of claim and counter-claim, appeal and ruling, as Roman landowners sought to preserve some form of title to land granted out to their barbarian guests. Crucial here were the various legal remedies for the reclamation of unjustly held property, and the defence of prescription allowed in Roman law, in which attempts to contest title were disallowed if the current possessor could demonstrate long and uninterrupted enjoyment of property (thirty years was the norm). The sparse and fragmentary survivals of Visigothic legislation on barbarian allotments recognisably respond to Roman efforts at reclamation: it allowed claims to be advanced for the extraordinarily long period of fifty years, thus significantly extending the period in which Roman landowners could seek to recover property.[57] The calamitous effects of the loss of family property, and the failure of his attempts to recover it, dominated Paulinus of Pella's meditation on his life. Writing close on half a century after these disasters, he accepted that he could not

---

[55] LC 12, 31, 54.2, 67. Note on the links between land registration and boundaries, see *Variae* 3:52.

[56] LJ 10.1.9; LC 12, 31, 67.

[57] CE 277.1. Note that there is no limitation to land unjustly seized or taken by force, as in comparable legislation elsewhere: the decree simply limits attempts to recover 'Roman third or Gothic allotments' to fifty years. There is no hint as to the potential contexts for such reclamations: but what would have occurred on the death of the initial Gothic guest? The remainder of this decree restates the general rule of prescription after thirty years, except in the case of fugitives. For the subsequent reception of the special fifty-year prescription in cases turning on land transfers between Goths and Roman see LJ 10.2.1 (restating Euric) and 10.1.14 (extending the initial ruling specifically about *sortes* to Roman property in general).

longer entertain hopes of recovery, and he gave thanks to God for the actions of the Goth who, wishing to acquire ownership of a small farm 'once wholly mine', sent 'a price of his own wishing, not indeed just, but accepted like a godsend'.[58] The experience of Paulinus's generation, which had borne the brunt of the first phase of barbarian settlements, was exceptional, and Paulinus himself was particularly vulnerable thanks to his involvement in the failed regime of Romulus Attalus and his family history. Paulinus's sons were able to seek favour at the Gothic court in Bordeaux, reclaiming property that was farmed by Gothic 'guests', and Sidonius could petition his friends at the Visigothic court for the return of his mother-in-law's property.[59] In Italy, Theodoric was clear that unjust seizures made by his followers should be returned, but found it convenient to uphold established time limits on litigation: responding to queries raised by two judges who had been dispatched to hear cases between Goths and Romans, he ruled that Roman land that had been improperly seized by Goths in his reign was to be returned, but cases predating his conquest of Italy were to fall on account of the thirty years' rule.[60] In the unique context of Vandal Africa, the constant lobbying of exiled African landowners inspired Imperial legislation that enshrined and extended rights of reclamation, discounting the period of Vandal rule from the normal thirty years' limitation.[61] Continuing Imperial hostility to the Vandal kingdom in Africa explains such legislation, but the case of the family of Bishop Fulgentius of Ruspe, arch-critic of the Vandal regime, shows that Roman landowners within Africa were able to advance claims and meet with success.[62] That Fulgentius's ancestors were able to recover at least some property under a barbarian regime systematically targeting

---

[58] Paulinus, *Eucharisticon*, lines 570–81. Is the interval between Paulinus's fall in 414/15 and the time of writing (c. 460) significant, corresponding as it does to the fifty-year limitation of Euric's code? The 'sale' of the farm is particularly intriguing, given that the farm was a former rather than a current possession of Paulinus's, it is difficult not to see a Gothic 'guest' here buying out the residual rights of a former Roman owner.

[59] Paulinus, *Eucharisticon*, lines 498–515 (note that when the *amicitia* of the king turned to *ira*, property was lost once again). Sidonius, *Letters*, 8.9, and note Sidonius's lament that he has 'yet to acquire the usufruct of a third at the price of a half', perhaps suggesting that what he sought was acknowledgement of his title over an estate granted out as *sortes*.

[60] *Variae* 1.18. For a specific case of restitution see *Variae* 8.28.

[61] Procopius, *Wars*, ed. and trans. H. Dewing (5 vols., Cambridge, MA, 1914–28), 3.3, says that this takes place in Spain under Honorius, but the closest surviving legislation comes in Valentinian III's attempts to compensate dispossessed African landowners (ed. Mommsen as an appendix to the Theodosian Code, as n. 15 above), as shown by Goffart, *Barbarians and Romans*, 66–7 n. 18, citing specifically novel 35 of 452, but also novels 13, 34 for context; Procopius wrote in the aftermath of reconquest when reclamation, specifically allowed by Justinian (n. 63 below) was a live issue. This legislation concerns expropriated property in general, not land granted out as *sortes* in particular; Vandal kings systematically expropriated senatorial landowners.

[62] Ferrandus, *Life of Fulgentius*, 1.4, trans. R. Eno (Washington, DC, 1992).

the wealth of the senatorial aristocracy and the Catholic church confirms that we should take the rulings that make up the bulk of our evidence for reclamation seriously.

The recurrence of attempted reclamations right across the barbarian west is striking, and should remind us that barbarian settlement was nowhere a once and for all transfer, but the subject of an argument and appeal over several generations. Ultimately, however, the passage of time hardened the loss of property into fact. This was the case even in Africa, where traditional time-limits were effectively suspended. Here, for all Justinian's encouragement of reclamation by the children or grandchildren of the dispossessed, a century or more of Vandal rule was a huge obstacle to successful claims, and other groups in provincial society felt that they had stronger claims; it is no surprise that there is little sign of extensive landholding on the scale of late Roman times in Byzantine Africa, and those sixth- and seventh-century figures whose interests extended across the Mediterranean into other Imperial provinces owed their position to their membership of a new court elite rooted in Constantinople.[63] Elsewhere, the residual claims of former Roman owners slowly fade as we move into the middle decades of the sixth century. Justinian's Pragmatic Sanction, in marked contrast to his African legislation, ignored the whole issue of prior Roman ownership and looked back to Theodoric's time in limiting claims to property in Italy; its object was to ease the disruption caused by the Gothic wars, not to undo barbarian settlement.[64]

Quite how the complex interplay between the title of Roman host and the control of barbarian guest that had typified the early stages of barbarian settlement unravelled remains obscure. But in a classic example of the elasticity of Roman legal forms and their ability to metamorphose to fit changing social contexts, prescription, which began as a potential defence against actions of reclamation, became a basis for claiming ownership. The establishment of title by long and uninterrupted enjoyment is often seen as indicative of 'vulgarisation', as the hierarchies of rights envisaged by Roman law were abandoned in the face of unlearned provincial practice that tended to equate title with the physical fact of occupation.[65] Here, as in the processes of division, clearance and compensation whereby barbarian guests were able to separate their interests from those of their Roman hosts and slowly establish outright and

[63] Justinian, Novel 36, ed. R. Schöll and G. Kroll, *Corpus Iuris Civilis*, III (Berlin, 1928); Procopius, *Wars*, 4.14. One thinks of the family of the Emperor Heraclius, the son of the governor of Africa who was able to mount a successful coup in 608–10: their interests depended on grants of office, not inherited land.

[64] Pragmatic Sanction, ed. R. Schöll and G. Kroll, *Corpus Iuris Civilis*, III (Berlin, 1928).

[65] Levy, *West Roman Vulgar Law*, 176–93.

unattentuated rights of possession, we can clearly witness a simplification of rights over property, but to see it as a vulgar deviation from a static classical norm is mistaken. Roman law was always a series of arguments and techniques used to order disputes, never a passive description of a given social structure. The unencumbered and absolute rights over property that we see emerging in the course of the sixth century were not the result of 'vulgar' provincials and barbarians deviating from established practice; they crystallised through the adaptation and extrapolation of traditional forms to interpret new social structures.

V

The wealth of legal material generated by such disputes over tenurial rights and wrongs in fact constitute the crucial proof that barbarian settlement was not a seamless administrative innovation that elicited little complaint from provincial landowners. In the rulings of barbarian kings like Gundobad and Theodoric, we hear the echoes of a chorus of complaint voiced in the practical language of the law-suit, and we see its effects. The output of the Burgundian, Ostrogothic and Visigothic courts is an impressive witness to the vibrant legal culture of the new kingdoms of the west, a continuity rooted in the education and expectations of the landowning classes. To be seen as legitimate by the provincial populace, authority had to be articulated and exercised in the appropriate terms, hence the reliance of barbarian kings on the expertise of Roman advisors, hence their responsiveness to the continued petitions of provincial landowners, hence their use of characteristically late Roman genres of legislative exhortation to make their will known and instruct their officials. But we should not be misled by these continuities in the idiom of authority: they were useful precisely as they helped cope with substantive change. Barbarian rulers and their Roman advisors had no alternative but to concede, and attempt to control and order, the transfer of land to the barbarian rank-and-file. To acknowledge this is not to return to older, and rightly discredited, views that see the fifth and sixth centuries in terms of migrations motivated by primal land hunger: the movements of barbarian armies were determined above all by the internal Roman politics in which barbarian rulers were now such key movers. But once, in the course of the fifth century, barbarian kingdoms began to emerge in the west, nothing was more inevitable than that those whose arms underpinned the new position of their kings should seek their reward. Here, established military customs governing the sharing of the spoils of victory may have played a role: after all, the Byzantine army which had reconquered Africa in the 530s was so outraged at Imperial orders which allowed 'the slaves and all other things of value' to be divided as booty, but insisted on the registration of the lands of the defeated Vandals as Imperial property, that it mutinied.[66]

The barbarian kings who built the first wave of successor states in the former Imperial heartlands of the west relied on the active collaboration of a critical mass of the landowning classes; hence they preferred wherever possible to use Roman honorifics, not claim ethnic kingship.[67] But they could not rule through Roman advisors alone; they were also dependent on both the continued support of their military followings. Compelled to recognise the social and political fact that their armies would acquire provincial land by hook or by crook, they had little alternative but to attempt to control that process in a manner that enabled them to present it as a bitter pill necessary for landowners to swallow if they were to continue to enjoy the rule of law and security of title. Roman fears focused on the very real possibility that settlement might end in the domination of a class of barbarian landlords, guests turned masters who might claim ownership over the lands of their former hosts and sit atop provincial society enjoying the income and produce of Roman estates. Where landowning elites were weak and barbarian rulers able and willing to impose their will through violence, this could happen: Victor of Vita shows Vandals taking over Roman villas in this manner in Africa, and Paul the Deacon imagined Lombard settlement as resting on Roman senators handing over a third of their income to their new masters, being thus reduced to the status of tributaries.[68] Land-division and the creation of barbarian allotments, as practised in the Burgundian, Ostrogothic

---

[66] Procopius, *Wars*, ed. Dewing, 4.14. Of course, Procopius's testimony is slippery as a representation of what actually happened in the mutiny: his tale here ascribes agency to the wives and daughters of former Vandal owners, who marry Roman soldiers and then shame them into claiming the land, in a tale run through with gender stereotypes. But it does draw on an expectation that the land of defeated foes could be treated as booty comparable to moveables and slaves; even if this expectation was influenced by the example of the barbarian settlements of the fifth and sixth centuries, it does show that land-division could be rooted in that notion that soldiers were entitled to a share in the spoils of war.

[67] Most recently, Andrew Gillett, 'Was Ethnicity Politicised in the Earliest Barbarian Kingdoms?', in *On Barbarian Identity*, ed. Gillett, 85–123; our terminology thus misleadingly normalises ethnic kingship.

[68] Vandal Africa: the stories of persecuted Catholics recorded by Victor of Vita concern a class of Catholics overseeing Vandal households or holding office at court, whose social context and religious response invites comparison with the ninth-century Cordoban martyrs movement in Islamic al-Andalus. Lombards: Paul the Deacon, *Historia Langobardorum*, 2.32, 3.16, ed. L. Bethmann and G. Waitz, MGH Scriptores Rerum Langobardorum (Berlin, 1878), seems to be thinking of a particular tenurial structure, that of the *casa tributaria*, witnessed on royal land in laws of Liutprand 59. This would underline the care with which we need to take this very late source, whose accounts of Lombard settlement constitute a mythical foundation charter for the eighth-century kingdom. But on Paul see now Walter Pohl, 'Per hospites divisi'. Wirtschaftliche Grundlagen der langobardischen Ansiedlung in Italien', *Römische Historische Mitteilungen*, 43 (2001), 179–226.

and Visigothic kingdoms, responded to these very real fears by giving guests a separate and separable stake in the countryside; barbarians who attempted to establish a stranglehold over Roman landowners rather than accepting an allotment were thus identified as the objects of royal ire.

The urgent and conflicting demands placed on barbarian kings were crucial determinants of the architecture of these primary successor states in the west. Barbarian elites quickly merged with the major landowners of the senatorial aristocracy, themselves eager to serve at barbarian courts in military as well as civil capacities. This process is well known, and rightly given a central role in the historiography, but it needs contextualising. For in the course of the fifth and sixth centuries, the hegemony of this nascent elite of militarised landlords was checked, and as a result state-formation in the early medieval west was to follow a unique path. Ancient agrarian Empires elsewhere in Eurasia were able to integrate military conquerors from their fringes within reconstituted elites; the structures of provincial administration and landownership were thus if not preserved at least adapted in the service of new masters. The necessity of conceding land to the rank-and-file of their armies made it impossible for barbarian rulers in the post-Roman west to preside over a comparable process. And those concessions of land prevented the emergence of a countryside structured by unmediated militarised landlord power. When we see Sidonius Apollinaris and his peers joking about the barbarity of the troops billeted on their estates, we might expect that fifth-century practices of hospitality might lead directly to the strengthening of the power of the top tier of the landholding elite, able to absorb bands of barbarian warriors as private armies and so secure their position through militarisation, whilst building careful alliances with barbarian leaders. But the forms of land transfer that emerged in the course of the fifth century nipped such possibilities in the bud. In their legislation, barbarian kings were insistent on the direct relationship between barbarian settlers and their king, a relationship implicated in and expressed through the special status of barbarian allotments. Insistence on the personal link between king and soldier, articulated by the munificence of gifts received from the king's hand, is a recurrent theme in the material collected in Cassiodorus's *Variae* and Sigismund's *Book of Constitutions*; in the latter, land allotments as special royal gifts are subject to very special rules of inheritance, and are not to be dissipated through sale, gift or bequest, so that they can continue to function as the focal point of a direct relationship between adult male warriors and their king.[69]

---

[69] These concerns, most fully expressed in the Burgundian laws, are echoed elsewhere e.g. in Salic law's famous discussion of inheritance of *terra salica*. I will discuss the implications of the process of settlement for gender relations in a forthcoming paper.

Barbarian settlement created a class of tax-exempt landowners, whose freedom and title was rooted in military service for the king of their people. Before we search for distant precedents in the forests of Germany as described by Tacitus or in an alleged Germanic warrior culture sustained by oral traditions first surfacing in high medieval vernacular literature, we should pause and consider that settlement in the former Roman provinces of the west transformed the internal structures of barbarian peoples. For in adapting from the economy of the wartrail to residence in the provincial countryside, the links within barbarian warbands and the structures of personal dependence that had bound them together were altered. Burgundian freedmen, thanks to the receipt of allotments, were able to become effectively independent of the masters in whose households they had previously dwelt. In Theodoric's Italy, we can even hear the voices of individual Goths, insistent that their military service gave them claim to a special freedom and guaranteed their continued independence of their richer neighbours. Anduit, an elderly veteran whose infirmity had allowed Gudila and Oppa to reduce him into slavery, successfully claimed that his military service meant that he should continue to enjoy 'the freedom of our army'; Costula and Daila were likewise confirmed as enjoying 'the freedom of the Goths' and so exempt from the 'onerous services' demanded from them by Gudila.[70] The tensions between Goths so evident here broke into the open following Theodoric's death, in a drawn-out political conflict between a Romanising Gothic elite crystallising around the extended royal dynasty and the military leadership.[71] Anduit, Costula and Daila claimed a specifically Gothic freedom rooted in military service for a king. This was a new kind of freedom, no longer enmeshed with concepts of citizenship and obligations towards the state, but rooted in military service and tax exemption and guaranteed by a personal relationship with a barbarian king.

This new social template was to animate the early medieval west. But its emergence was only possible because the mechanisms used to accommodate barbarian armies in the fifth- and sixth-century west had significant effects on existing structures of landownership. Of course, the impact of the barbarian settlements on Roman landowning is difficult to quantify, and the differential impact of settlement on different sizes of Roman landowners impossible to trace.[72] However, there is no

[70] LC 57; *Variae* 5.29–30.
[71] These conflicts have yet to receive a satisfactory examination; our understanding is dependent on the compelling but clearly disingenuous stories told by Procopius, *Wars*, 5.2–4.
[72] Our best estimate is that barbarian armies numbered tens of thousands but settlement took place over several generations, and barbarian armies included professional soldiers, the defeated followings of rival generals and displaced provincials, and not all barbarians received allotments.

real room for doubting that barbarian settlement marked a substantial transfer of resources away from the Roman landowning classes; its effects were particularly marked because settlements were in all probability geographically uneven, clustered in particular areas. We should not see the transfer of land to barbarians in isolation from the range of other factors tending to render large-scale and extensive landholding difficult to retain, not least the disruptive effects of disorder and warfare. Exile and expropriation for 'political crime' deserve particular attention. By the last third of the fifth century the crystallisation of political division severely limited the ability of the remnants of the senatorial aristocracy, Sidonius and his peers, to maintain the networks of friendship and obligation that had criss-crossed the provinces of the western Mediterranean; the Vandal conquest of Africa and the associated campaigns of expropriation here destroyed one crucial integrative mechanism. This context of fragmentation must have made barbarian settlement particularly difficult to negotiate for senatorial landowners; in a politically divided west, pressure could only be brought to bear on one barbarian court at a time, and entry into the service of one barbarian king encouraged the expropriation of properties on the other side of the new political boundaries which divided the former western Empire. The primary attempts at barbarian state-formation in the former Roman provinces, resting on coalitions of senatorial wealth and barbarian might, were to prove short-lived, and lasting political settlements came through the creation of looser, more open and flatter elites around the courts of the Merovingians in northern Gaul, the Lombards in northern Italy and the Visigoths in Spain. Geopolitics – the strategic advantages enjoyed by Justinian's Byzantium and the Merovingians when it came to mobilising barbarian military manpower from the long-standing Roman recruiting grounds along the Danube and Rhine frontiers – were central here, but the crucial result was the definitive, if inevitably temporary, end of large-scale landowning in the west.[73]

The systematic transfer of Roman property to barbarian settlers undermined the economic and social muscle of the senatorial aristocracy, and encouraged its disaggregation into a series of regional elites. The areas that had witnessed the densest barbarian settlement were precisely those whose detachment from the old networks that had bound the western Mediterranean heartlands of the Empire together was most apparent by the second half of the sixth century. The northern Italian plain, for example, proved unable to sustain an extensive political system of any kind in the second half of the sixth century. Lombard state-formation in the seventh and eighth centuries rested on the fact that the Lombard king was the only extensive landowner in the north, with royal gift-giving

[73] See now Chris Wickham, *Framing the Early Middle Ages: Europe and the Mediterranean 400–800* (Oxford, 2005), which appeared after this paper was completed.

to bind together small-scale elites whose horizons were limited to at most two or three cities and whose property interests were tiny by late Roman standards. The comparison with southern and central Italy, where aristocratic scale although diminished still sustained regional systems, is instructive. Here, middling landowners who in late Roman times had hung on to the coattails of their senatorial neighbours, and cemented their local position through civic patronage, were able to maintain their position relatively well: after 700, their networks of regional dominance, revolving around Rome, Naples and Benevento, begin to become visible. Historical differences between north and south and contrasting political experiences of course play a role in explaining differential rates of disruption, but it can scarcely be doubted that a century and more's worth of land transfers to successive barbarian armies in the north was a crucial cause of the extreme fragmentation so evident there.[74]

In southern Gaul, we see a similar dynamic, with collapse followed by a slow recovery allowing free-standing regional networks to emerge independent of distant courts by the decades around 700. Collapse is most dramatic in the former senatorial heartlands that were also – and hardly accidentally – where the Burgundian and Visigothic elites made their homes in the fifth century. Here, indeed, there was no equivalent to the Lombard court at Pavia, which by maintaining at least one system of extensive landowning was able to effect social and political reintegration in the seventh century. By the middle of the sixth century southern Gaul, socially and politically so closely bound to the Imperial court in the fourth century and able to sustain a series of regional political forums – barbarian courts at Toulouse and Lyon, a regional council at Arles – through the fifth, found itself distant from the seats of political power, on the periphery of a series of political systems whose heartlands were distant and essentially parasitic on the region.[75] Southern Gallic elites were unable to sustain a political system of their own: the failure of the would-be Merovingian king Gundovald is striking here. The well-known redefinition of the southern Gallic aristocracy in terms of a holy charisma rooted in episcopal office which mediated access to the court of heaven needs to be placed in this specific regional context of political marginalisation, rather than seen as a normative strategy of post-Roman survival or a manifestation of underlying continuity. Focused on saint's cults that legitimated family

---

[74] Fundamental on aristocratic scale in the north is Chris Wickham, 'Aristocratic Power in Eighth-Century Lombard Italy', in *After Rome's Fall*, ed. Murray, 153–70; for landowning in Byzantine Italy see Tom Brown, *Gentlemen and Officers: Imperial Administration and Aristocratic Power in Byzantine Italy 554–800* (Rome, 1984), whose emphasis is inevitably on Ravenna and Rome.

[75] Think of the Merovingians' relationship with Marseille, and also the importance of income from the land tax, only documented south of the Loire, for sixth-century Merovingian state-formation.

traditions of episcopal office in a handful of cities, the social topography of Gregory of Tours was wholly alien to that of his distant ancestor Sidonius Apollinaris, with its far-reaching networks of friendship. Those sixth-century Merovingians like Guntram who drew on Burgundian tradition were not based in the Rhone valley, but further north at centres such as Chalons-sur-Saone. It may well be that the very different elites of the Merovingian heartlands of northern Gaul, and of southern Spain where sixth-century Visigothic kings resided, surpassed those of southern Gaul in the course of the sixth century. In southern Spain, around Cordoba and Seville we can detect the survival of regional landowning networks with which sixth-century Visigothic kings attempted to align themselves: Theudis, for example, was able to gain the throne thanks to an armed retinue of 2000, largely recruited from the estates of the senatorial heiress he married.[76] In northern Gaul we can see impressive and extended systems of aristocratic landholding emerging around Merovingian courts by the time we begin to get a documentary record in the seventh century.[77] In the south, regional networks of landownership enabled their leaders to access court politics, and in the seventh century even to bid for power there, as the attempted usurpation of the Visigothic throne by Duke Paul of Narbonne, or the influence of Bishop Leodegar of Autun at the Merovingian court demonstrate.[78] Royal patronage here allowed the consolidation of landowning networks, and after 700 the failure of court politics in both Gaul and Spain as a result of internal conflict occasioned by the Carolingian and Islamic takeovers respectively enables us to see a series of local systems whose leaders enjoyed sizeable holdings: the will of Abbo *rector* of Provence details one such constellation.[79] These were formidable figures, but they stood at the apex of regional hierarchies, rather than defining an extensive system in the manner of their late Roman forebears.

VI

We began with Sarwa Gastimodus's epitaph, using a resolutely Roman medium to advertise his identity as a warrior and guest in early sixth-century Lyon. Let us end by returning there, and attempting to trace how changing identities were enmeshed with the structural transformations we

---

[76] Procopius, *Wars*, 5.7.

[77] See e.g. *Chartae Latines Antiquiores*, XIII, ed. H. Atsma and R. Marichal (Zurich, 1983), nos. 569, 571, XIV, ed. Atsma and Marichal (Zurich, 1984), no. 592.

[78] See *The Story of Wamba*, ed. and trans. J. M. Pizarro (Washington, DC, 2005); Paul Fouracre and Richard Gerberding, *Late Merovingian France: Hagiography and History* (Manchester, 1996).

[79] Abbo's will is edited, translated and discussed by Patrick Geary, *Aristocracy in Provence. The Rhone Basin at the Dawn of the Carolingian Era* (Philadelphia, 1985).

have been watching unfold. The identities that animated Sarwa's world were relational. To be a guest one needed a host, whilst the identification of barbarians as warriors presupposed a civilian population from which they were differentiated. Locked in a defining embrace, Burgundian and Roman identities thus played off and so transformed each other. The process of 'ethnogenesis', which took place as military followings of diverse origin acquired a common identity that defined a specific role in provincial society, thus effected more than those who learned to see themselves as 'Burgundians'. Roman identities were transformed, too. The constant appellation of provincial landowners, literally possessors (*possessores*), as Romans in the legal evidence, for example, served to define them in ethnic terms in contradistinction to their Burgundian guests; Roman identity, no longer tied up with notions of citizenship within a *res publica* which guaranteed the rule of law, became both far more 'ethnic' and far more immediate to the landowning classes, particularly the lower tiers whose horizons and identities remained resolutely local. And other modes of identification jostled with the binary ethnic division of provincial society. Kings increasingly referred to the totality of their subjects as 'our people', whilst the label 'barbarian', originally a Roman term for those who lacked the civilising benefits of law and self-restraint, was appropriated and transformed in Burgundian legislation.[80]

Ethnic distinctions also interacted with class identities. The horizons of the barbarian elite, enriched with gifts of royal land that were therefore unencumbered with any ongoing relationship with any host, differed from those of the humble holder of an allotment carved out from the estate of a Roman landowner who was therefore now a neighbour: Sarwa's identity as a warrior and a guest differed from that of his peers who entered into the highly cultured circles of senatorial patronage. One of Sarwa's contemporaries, Count Ansemund of Vienne, received a series of elegant Latin epistles from Bishop Avitus of Vienne, reflecting his integration into the cycle of banquets and politesse which animated the high society of the Rhone valley; he was to bequeath his property, in all probability acquired by royal gift, through a written instrument addressed to 'my brothers, the senators of Vienne'.[81] Royal legislation which it was Ansemund's job to enact, however, limited the ability of the majority of his fellow Burgundians to act likewise; allotments could not be disposed of as their owner pleased, and their very nature institutionalised a latent conflict of

[80] For discussion, Amory, 'The Meaning and Purpose of Ethnic Terminology'; the transformation of the label 'barbarian', paralleled in Ostrogothic Italy, is particularly striking.

[81] Avitus of Vienne, *Epistolae*, ed. R. Peiper, MGH AA 6.2 (Berlin, 1883), indispensable trans. and discussion by Danuta Shanzer and Ian Wood, *Avitus of Vienne: Letters and Selected Poems* (Liverpool, 1998), nos. 55, 80, 81; Patrick Amory, 'The Textual Transmission of the Donatio Ansemundi', *Francia*, 20 (1993), 163–83; the terminology of Ansemund's instrument corresponds to the language used of royal gifts rather than allotments in LC, as does Ansemund's freedom to bequeath it as he wishes.

interest over property at the heart of relations between Burgundian and Roman in the countryside.

If we are to understand the continued transformation of identities in its proper connection with the dynamics of social change, we need to trace the processing of these latent conflicts. When King Gundobad reiterated the basis of Burgundian settlement in his famous edict on allotments, he did so in response to the pleas of Roman possessors of land concerning the 'anxiety and disquiet' caused by a 'new and unjust strife and trickery'. Their complaint was in fact an old one: that Burgundians, by making enclosures and clearances to create land for themselves to cultivate, were impinging on established property rights in a landscape structured by long-established estate boundaries. Gundobad, in response, restated the remedies laid down in previous legislation, rooted in Roman law: in recognition of the rights of hosts over land cleared by their guests, and of shared rights by all landowners in common land, Roman landowners were entitled to a half of all clearances. Their right to claim half, moreover, pertained not only to forest used as pasture or cleared for cultivation, but also to buildings erected on newly cleared land.[82] In other words, the possessors' complaints centred on the creation of new farms – units of cultivation and residence – which destroyed valuable resources of pasture and wood, giving rise to strife and litigation. That those undertaking clearance deserved to enjoy the fruits of their labour as their property, and theirs alone, was undisputed, but they owed compensation to those whose interests had been effected.

Gundobad's legislation here evokes a landscape in transition, and a grid of property rights being adjusted to reflect new topographies rooted in new agrarian realities. Archaeology is now beginning to help us understand settlement change, with new building techniques used on often new sites with distinctive morphologies, and agrarian strategies adjusted in a new economic context of diminishing exchange that discouraged specialisation for the market.[83] The complex picture of a series of interlocking layers of

[82] LC 54.2, referring explicitly to earlier legislation; the trail of precedent runs from Roman law rules restated in LC 67, 31, 28, 12, to LRB 17.

[83] Archaeological work on southern Gaul has tended, as elsewhere, to focus on urban continuity, and on attempts to trace barbarian 'migration' in the material culture. For our region we lack the recent syntheses achieved for much of the Mediterranean, and northern Gaul (e.g. *Landscapes of Change. Rural Evolutions in the Early Middle Ages*, ed. Neil Christie (Aldershot, 2004), Helena Hamerow, *Early Medieval Settlements* (Oxford, 2002)). But for a methodologically innovative project on long-term changes in settlement and land-use, see *Regional Dynamics: Burgundian Landscapes in Historical Perspective*, ed. C. Crumley and W. Marquandt (San Diego, 1987); C. Crumley, 'A Diachronic Model for Settlement and Land-Use in Southern Burgundy', and W. Berry, 'An Experimental Model for Early Medieval Settlement in Southwestern Burgundy', in *Archaeological Approaches to Medieval Europe*, ed. K. Biddick (Toronto, 1984); recent work has focused on the Arroux valley around Autun, distant from areas most likely to be directly reflected in the legislation.

exploitation, and of interrelated zones of settlement relating to different kinds of property right suggested by the legal evidence, clearly needs properly relating to the material remains. In helping us see the human agency driving landscape and settlement change, and correlating social change with the redefinition of topographies and property, these laws illuminate a crucial passage of social change. Crucial to these changes was conflict over shared rights, where interlocking interests defined the relationship of Burgundian and Roman.

Those undertaking clearances that aroused such complaint enjoyed a collective identity as *faramanni*. Germanic words are very rarely used in the surviving Burgundian legislation, and the meaning of the term – literally 'those men who travelled together', it is used elsewhere to refer to the constituent parts of barbarian warbands as they broke apart to settle and is also witnessed as a personal name[84] – suggests that it is not a learned confection of those who drafted the laws, but the term used by Burgundian settlers cultivating the countryside to refer to themselves. In Gundobad's legislation, the *faramanni* are counterpointed to the possessors, Roman landowners amongst whom they nestled, but against whom they were defined. By the seventh century, however, the same Germanic vocabulary was used to articulate the self-consciousness of the weapon-carrying, landowning, elite whose interests defined a new social order: the chronicler known as Fredegar, whose interest in Burgundy probably reflects his origin in the region, could report the collective political or military action of this group as the activities of the 'Burgundaefarones'.[85] This identity, whilst it legitimated the power of the top tiers of the regional landowning elite, did so in terms of

---

[84] The most recent extended discussion of the term is that by A. C. Murray, *Germanic Kinship Structure: Studies in Law and Society in Antiquity and the Early Middle Ages* (Toronto, 1983), 89–97, which is a resolute search for an administrative and institutional definition which is ultimately impossible; other than the Burgundian evidence, the prime witnesses are Marius of Avenches's and Paul the Deacon's accounts of the Lombards' division into *farae* as they settled in northern Italy: *La chronique de Marius d'Avenches* (Lausanne, 1991), ed. Justin Favrod, s.a. 569; Paul, *Historia Langobardorum*, 2.9. See now Marios Costambeys, 'Kinship, Marriage and Gender in Lombard Italy', in *The Langobards from the Fifth to the Eighth Centuries*, ed. Paolo Delogu and Chris Wickham (San Marino, forthcoming).

[85] *The Fourth Book of the Chronicle of Fredegar with its Continuations*, ed. and trans. J. M. Wallace-Hadrill (Oxford, 1960), 4.44, 55; elsewhere he can refer to the same grouping as made up of the '*proceres* and *leudes*' or the army of the Burgundians, or simply talk of 'the Burgundians'. The significance of the terminology must be underlined by its use in personal names in at least one high-status landowning family of the seventh century, the founders of Faremoutiers; although active in the 'Frankish' kingdom of Neustria, around Meaux, their naming tradition must be seen in terms of a political and social alignment, and possibly family origins, with a Burgundian elite which was, in any case, closely enmeshed with that of Neustria by the seventh century.

their representation of a wider community of weapon-carrying free proprietors. Legal distinctions articulating aristocratic separateness, so typical of agrarian Empires, did not develop, precisely because even the richest landowners lacked the formal structures of domination enjoyed by their late Roman predecessors – who, after all, had negotiated direct with Emperors and warlords without reference to their poorer neighbours – and the coercive force to enforce their will on the countryside. Instead, in a distinctively western development, ethnic identities accessible to a relatively broad and open elite of landowners emerged. No longer possessors defined in terms of their legal title to their land, this class acquired a new identity which crystallised around the name favoured by a specific grouping who were far from being in a numerical majority: the *faramanni*. In a transformed countryside in which status was no longer defined in terms of the Roman property law, a new label rooted in collective endeavour and claiming free tenure through clean settlement articulated the community of the cultivating class as a whole. To Roman landowners seizing vacant land or clearing waste as they adjusted to the new economic and social realities, such an identity had much to offer.[86] In Fredegar's quite ahistorical account of Burgundian origins, this new social order found a foundation charter. Repeating the now traditional etymological derivation of 'Burgundian' from *Burg*, fortress, and the closely related account of Burgundian migration to fortresses beyond the Rhine, Fredegar went on to explain how, in the time of Valentinian I, they had been invited into Gaul by senators who wished to throw off the yoke of taxation.[87] Fredegar's story, written as Merovingian attempts to continue to levy the land tax were in their dying throes precisely because weapon-carrying free men claimed tax exemption, legitimated a social order of landowners whose freedom was exemplified by the absence of tax and expressed through public military action. This new identity was not the product of royal propaganda or clever historical narrative of the kind so well studied of late: the Burgundian kingdom had ended, conquered by the Merovingians, in the 530s. Rooted in the struggles of cultivators to lay claim to a new kind of freedom and new forms of control over land, it articulated a new social order. If we are to understand the peculiar importance of ethnic identity as a claim to political power in the early medieval west, we need to appreciate that ethnicity was

---

[86] For Roman landowners adopting such strategies see e.g. Sidonius, *Letters*, 6.10, Paulinus, *Eucharisticon*, lines 515–38. Note for Romans adopting barbarian names and lifestyles see also Sidonius, *Letters*, 6.4, on *Vargi*.

[87] Fredegar, *Chronicle*, ed. Bruno Krusch, MGH Scriptores Rerum Merowingicarum 2 (Hannover, 1888), 2.46; on changing views of Burgundian origins see Ian Wood, 'Misremembering the Burgundians', in *Die Suche nach den Ursprungen*, ed. Walter Pohl (Vienna, 2003), 139–48.

appropriated by fragmented and impoverished landed elites unable to maintain formal class privileges rooted in the law and implicated in the structures of the state. By allowing elites to claim to represent a wider community of landowners, ethnic identity legitimated loose structures of regional dominance rooted in the possession of land. Conflicts and compromises over land and freedom thus determined western Europe's distinctive post-classical historical trajectory.

Transactions of the RHS 16 (2006), pp. 75–94 © 2006 Royal Historical Society
doi:10.1017/S0080440106000466 Printed in the United Kingdom

THE ORIGINS OF THE ENGLISH HOSPITAL*

By Sethina Watson

READ 19 MAY 2006

The Alexander Prize Essay

ABSTRACT. The hospital was brought to England by the Normans and rapidly
absorbed into pre-Conquest frameworks of land-tenure, custom and alms. These
charitable houses became a recognised and popular type of house, distinct in
form and development from both monasteries and French hospitals. Although
its constitution was not written, the early hospital had a consistent arrangement,
physical in substance and purpose: it was a form of sited alms, with regular,
visible, dependent provisioning. Its customary systems of support were public
demonstrations (and thus repetitive commemorations) not only of the nature of
its endowment and alms, but also of the founder's intent and generosity.

In *c.* 1085 Archbishop Lanfranc, the (Lombard-born) Norman builder of
the monasteries of Bec, Caen and Canterbury, established two charitable
sites at Northgate and Harbledown in Canterbury. There are no texts of
Lanfranc's for his twin foundations, but Eadmer wrote twenty years later
of his work:

> I should not allow to pass unmentioned what he did for the poor, beyond the walls of
> the city of Canterbury. Outside the northern gate of that town he built (*construxit*) a stone
> house, fine and large, and added to it many small dwellings with an extensive courtyard,
> for the various needs and comforts of men. He divided this palace (*palatium*) into two,
> putting men suffering various infirmities in one part and ailing women in the other.
> He also arranged for them, from his own income (*de suo*), clothing and daily food, and
> attendants (*ministros*) and wardens (*custodes*) to see that they might want for nothing and
> that the men and women do not enter one another's areas . . . Further removed, beyond
> the western gate of the city, sheltered on the steep side of the hill, he built wooden houses
> and assigned (*delegavit*) them to the use of lepers, the men (as in other places) separated
> from the society of women. From his own income (*de suis*) he established that the lepers
> be supplied with all they might need according to the nature of their disease, and for this
> he appointed men whose skill, kindness and patience were such that, it seemed to him,
> none would dispute.[1]

Eadmer lacks a vocabulary for Northgate and Harbledown and his stilted
description suggests both the English author's own marvel and his attempt

---

* I am grateful to Benjamin Thompson, Barbara Harvey and Henrietta Leyser for their
inspiration, advice and discerning insight.

[1] Translated from Eadmer, *Historia Novorum in Anglia*, ed. Martin Rule (1884), 15–16.

to communicate the unfamiliar to a native audience. Although he does not have a word for it, Eadmer is recording the arrival of the hospital in England. The form spread quickly. Within a generation there were leper houses at Lewes, Rochester, Whitby, Colchester and Holborn, and poor houses at Kepier, Ripon, Norwich and York. By 1200 hospitals had been founded and supervised by bishops, monasteries, the crown, great and local lords, archdeacons and townsmen, and accommodated sick poor, the debilitated or languishing, travellers and pilgrims, lepers and the morbidly diseased, or distributed daily doles. Over 400 had been established, hundreds more in the following century, with the pace only waning *c*. 1260. More hospitals dotted the English landscape than monasteries, priories and cells of the Benedictine, Cluniac, Fontevrault and Cistercian orders combined.[2] By 1200 the typical English person would have been as familiar with the 'hospital' as they were with the 'monastery'; indeed the hospital's public nature – on the busiest roads, beside every middling town, open to even the lowliest lay person – suggests it may have been the more widely and intimately known by many.

Despite its popularity, scholars remain unclear as to what the English hospital was, especially in these early centuries. It remains uncertain, for example, whether the hospital differed from a monastery and, if so, how? Indeed, the very vigour, vitality and variety of hospital foundation is cited as the reason not to generalise about the 'hospital', and scholars instead advocate regional studies (with a social or theoretical theme) or case studies of individual (and typically later, grander and better archived) houses.[3] Antiquarian assumptions that early hospitals were religious houses, of monastic form, whose primary constitutional text was a rule, remain unchallenged.[4] That the surviving documents do not reflect this model only reinforces the hospital's already troublesome image, creating a widening chasm between the wealth of documentation (continuously augmented by new editions of *acta* or cartularies) and our ability to use it. That by 1300 some houses had elaborate liturgical services, some came under a rule, and others had neither, adds to the general lament that

---

[2] David Knowles and R. Neville Hadcock, *Medieval Religious Houses: England and Wales*, 2nd edn (Harlow, 1971), where hospitals constitute the most substantial section, 310–410.

[3] Carole Rawcliffe, *Medicine for the Soul: The Life, Death and Resurrection of an English Medieval Hospital* (Stroud, 1999), xiv; Nicholas Orme and Margaret Webster, *The English Hospital, 1070–1570* (1995), 11, 35–41; Sheila Sweetinburgh, *The Role of the Hospital in Medieval England: Gift-Giving and the Spiritual Economy* (Dublin, 2004), 20–5, 35.

[4] R. M. Clay, *Mediaeval Hospitals of England* (1909), 126–7; Miri Rubin, *Charity and Community in Medieval Cambridge* (Cambridge, 1987), 104, 153–6; Rawcliffe, *Medicine for the Soul*, 7, 30–1; Orme and Webster, *English Hospital*, 35, 49–56. P. H. Cullum, '"For Pore People Harberles": What Was the Function of the Maisonsdieu?' in *Trade, Devotion and Governance*, ed. D. J. Clayton *et al.* (Stroud, 1994), 36–54 (37).

the hospital possessed an undefined, unruly, shifting and quasi-monastic form.[5] Work has thus looked less to a shared constitutional framework than to the broader meaning of the hospital in the context of late medieval urban society. Theories of gift-giving and charitable or pious discourse have illuminated dynamics of power and contexts of need, interrogating notions of piety, charity and healing, and drawing complex pictures of the influence of prosperity and plight on late urban politics. Yet as their later milieux become more vibrant, hospitals themselves have become less known, and indeed less sought. As Miri Rubin has concluded: 'Hospitals existed between need, the disposition to acknowledge need and the perceived responsibility to alleviate need.'[6] Far from becoming clearer as a constitutional form, hospitals have become more spectral, a concept within social discourse.

No hospital is less known or less studied than the pre-1200 hospital, allegedly the most 'monastic', and largely neglected by scholars. Although English hospitals appear in the records haphazardly before c. 1180, they are not as a group ill-recorded. They have no chronicle tradition, and far fewer cartularies, but hospitals and their deeds pepper most major registers and archives in quantities comparable to monastic houses. Indeed, the *Victoria County Histories* have demonstrated just how rich, if perplexing, the documentary trail of even small houses can be.[7] But these texts are confusing and often unused by historians, since they provide little insight into the routines or events within the hospitals themselves. With the exception of work on leper houses in the context of perceptions of leprosy[8] these early centuries have been ignored in favour of the more enticing visitation texts and wills of the later middle ages. The period 1085–1200, however, witnessed the arrival of the hospital into every English county, and the foundation of hundreds of houses of a consistent and recognised form. It is here, before the documentary record becomes consistent that we must look for the constitutional origins of English hospitals. To understand what this might be, we must consider whether hospitals had their own form and identity, unravel England's distinct and peculiarly restricted pattern of textual constitution, and then reappraise

---

[5] Orme and Webster, *English Hospital*, 35; Sweetinburgh, *Role of the Hospital*, 21–2; Sally Thompson, *Women Religious: The Founding of English Nunneries after the Norman Conquest* (Oxford, 1991), 38, 52–3.

[6] Miri Rubin, 'Imagining Medieval Hospitals: Considerations on the Cultural Meaning of Institutional Change', in *Medicine and Charity before the Welfare State*, ed. J. Barry and C. Jones (1991), 14–25 (24).

[7] For example, *The Victoria History of the Counties of England* (1901–), *Chester*, III , 178–87; *Wiltshire*, III , 334–69.

[8] Notably, Max Satchell, 'The Emergence of Leper-Houses in Medieval England 1100–1250' (D.Phil. thesis, University of Oxford, 1998), and P. H. Cullum, 'Leprosy and Leper Hospitals in Medieval Guisborough and the North-East', *Cleveland History*, 76 (1999), 52–61.

the hospital within systems of alms and support in the eleventh and twelfth centuries. This analysis aims to challenge the prevailing picture of the hospital as a concept, a product of social discourses on leprosy and sin, charity or salvic strategies. It argues instead for the very physicality of the hospital.

Did the 'hospital' exist?

Two major models are currently used in the study of medieval English hospitals. The first draws from the system of listing in Knowles and Hadcock's *Medieval Religious Houses*, which assigns each house a 'type' (Almshouse, Clerics, Lepers, Poor, Pilgrims, etc.). The limits of this system are acknowledged even by the scholars who apply them.[9] 'Types' often blur: the most distinct type, leper houses, might contain non-lepers; hospitals for languishing poor received travellers. Each scholar must redefine a system of classification, an act typically of convenience to divide a mass of houses with a perplexing variety of uses.[10] This typology of hospitals contains one further flaw: it sidesteps the question of what it is that permits modern historians, or that permitted contemporaries, to consider a leper house in the same broad category as a large, liturgical hospital or a late fifteenth-century *maisondieu*. All of them had a charitable element, but then so did monastic houses – or even royal courts.

For the broader notion of 'hospital', scholars appropriate the model of religious houses. This has borne fruit for the later hospital, where the historiography of chantries, parishes and testamentary bequests have provided a rich landscape for the hospital and its will-evidence.[11] No equivalent work has advanced our understanding of the early hospital, whose classification as 'monastic' remains unchallenged. Early hospitals have been assumed to have emerged from monastic houses, either as an outgrowth of social demand on the services of the hospitaller and infirmarer, or as an inevitable reliance on the monastic form as the only available institutional model.[12] In both cases, the hospital is alleged not to have gained its distinctive form until the thirteenth century, when civic involvement elaborated its charitable and liturgical roles. Only Max Satchell has reconsidered this paradigm, updating the monastic model by drawing from Sally Thompson's discussion of post-Conquest nunneries to suggest a similar pattern of inchoate groups of lepers gradually formalised

[9] Martha Carlin, 'Medieval English Hospitals', in *The Hospital in History*, ed. Lindsay Granshaw and Roy Porter (1989), 21–39; Sweetinburgh, *Role of the Hospital*, 21–4.

[10] 'Type' has been used effectively by Satchell, 'Emergence of Leper-Houses', and Cullum, '"Pore People Harberles"', although their success may rest as much on their disciplined chronological and social frameworks.

[11] Notably the work of Cullum, Sweetinburgh and Rawcliffe (above).

[12] Clay, *Mediaeval Hospitals*, 3–6; C. H. Talbot, *Medicine in Medieval England* (1967), 170; Miri Rubin, 'Development and Change in English Hospitals, 1000–1500', in *Hospital in History*, ed. Granshaw and Porter, 41–59 (44–6).

into 'houses' through patronage and episcopal sanction.[13] There are many reasons to query the monastic affiliation, however; among them one question particularly demands attention: if the origins of hospitals were so strongly monastic in character and if that character became increasingly liturgical over the centuries, as scholars argue, then why did hospitals remain such a distinct category of house throughout the middle ages and, indeed, into modern historiography?

When Eadmer described Lanfranc's foundations, he clearly thought Northgate and Harbledown were something new. His description of St Gregory's priory, contained in the same section, was brief, precise and routine. Lanfranc, he noted, established the church (*ecclesia*) of St Gregory across the road from Northgate, endowed it with lands, tithes and rents, and installed canons there under a rule who should tend to the spiritual needs of the Northgate poor. In marked contrast, Eadmer lacked a word for the Northgate and Harbledown sites (*palatium* is particularly unusual). His lengthy description outlined the provision and location of sites in relation to the city, the construction of buildings, the organisation of space and provision of custodians. Unlike with St Gregory's, there was no internal religious provision, nor independent endowment. Instead, the material needs of the poor and lepers were supported directly from archiepiscopal income, and probably from the £140 annual payment that was confirmed by successive archbishops.[14] Eadmer's description contained the essential elements of any early hospital foundation, and encompassed the main features reiterated in subsequent charters, disputes and visitations of Northgate and Harbledown.[15]

The terminology for such charitable sites coalesced during the twelfth century. The word 'hospital' first occurs in Ranulf Flambard's 1112 foundation charter for Kepier, in which he established the parish church of St Giles with a *hospitali domo* (hospital house) attached.[16] 'Hospital' remained a descriptive rather than a constitutional term for most of the twelfth century, when these foundations were termed *domum hospitalem*, *domum infirmorum*, *domum leprosorum*, *domum pauperum*, *xenodochium* or *domum elemosinariam*, phrases that pair (much like Eadmer's account) the notation of the house or site with a description of aid or support. Terms could be interchangeable or irregular. Two charters issued 1148 × 51 for St John the Evangelist's, Brackley, for example, used different language for the same house: Earl Robert's charter referred to 'these my alms' (*haec*

---

[13] Satchell, 'Emergence of Leper-Houses', ii, 136–48; Thompson, *Women Religious*, 161–5, 195–210.

[14] The endowment was confirmed as Lanfranc's by Archbishop Richard of Dover, *English Episcopal Acta* (31 vols., 1980–) [hereafter *EEA*], II , no. 96.

[15] *Registrum Roberti Winchelsey*, ed. Rose Graham (2 vols., 1952–6), 827–31.

[16] William Dugdale, *Monasticon Anglicanum* (6 vols., 1817–30; repr. 1970) [hereafter *Monasticon*], VI , 732.

mea elemosina), whereas an agreement with the rectors of the parish used *hospitalis*.[17] The variability of terminology adds to the impression of the informality of the houses themselves. It also, again, underlies the refrain of the constitutional vagueness and irregularity of the hospital.[18]

The term *hospitalis* became increasingly common from *c.* 1130, used alongside and in *lieu* of other terminology.[19] By the third quarter of the twelfth century, new houses might be called *hospitalis infirmorum* or *hospitalis pauperum* (the hospital of the sick/poor).[20] By *c.* 1200 *hospitalis* had replaced *domus* as the common name for these houses, although other terms remained in use. When Maurice de Gaunt founded his almonry (*elemosinaria*) of St Mark's, Bristol, which established 1207 × 30 a chapel and the daily distribution of food doles, it was identified as *hospitalis*.[21] *Xenodochium* remained a formal term in law, but *hospitalis* had become the social label for houses of lepers, the sick, poor, travellers and of alms. And while contemporaries clearly struggled for a social terminology for hospitals, they did not appropriate the vocabulary of religious houses. The term *ecclesia* was rarely used in connection with a hospital, even when it had a chapel. Those few instances that did were usually established before *c.* 1150 and typically recognised a church with parochial or independent rights to which the hospital was subsequently attached.[22]

'Hospitals' were not a category of religious house. In popular imagination they were distinct from monasteries. Gervase of Canterbury's *Mappa Mundi* (*c.* 1200) listed '*Hospitalia*' separately from '*Domus religionis*', which were denoted by name (e.g. abbey, priory, deanery) and type (black monks, white canons, etc.).[23] In counties where he knew of no hospitals, Gervase provided the heading '*Hospitalia*' but left the list blank. Legal agreements recognised the hospital as a category of house distinct from a monastery, often employing the juridical term *xenodochium* to the hospital form. The priory of St Andrew's, Northampton, only agreed to the construction of a hospital beside their oratory of St Helen so long as the house was:

> built under this form, namely that in the aforementioned place there should in future come into existence no college, whether of monks, canons, Templars, Hospitallers or

---

[17] *Monasticon*, VI , 751, 752.

[18] Orme and Webster, *English Hospital*, 35, 39–40; Sweetinburgh, *Role of the Hospital*, 21–2.

[19] Thus St Leonard's, Newark, was a *hospitalis* for lepers in its 1123×35 foundation charter, *Registrum Antiquissimum*, ed. C. W. Foster and K. Major (10 vols., Lincoln, 1931–73), III, no. 920.

[20] *Registrum Simonis de Sudbiria*, ed. R. C. Fowler (2 vols., 1927–30), I , 210; *Monasticon*, VI, 972, no. 10.

[21] *Cartulary of St Augustine's Abbey, Bristol*, ed. David Walker, Gloucestershire Record Series X (1998), xxv–xxvi; *Calendar of Close Rolls* (1902–) [hereafter *CCR*], *1231–4*, 356.

[22] E.g., Kepier (above).

[23] Gervase of Canterbury, *Opera Historica*, ed. William Stubbs (2 vols., 1879–80), II , 418–40.

nuns; that is, that the house itself will at no time be changed into a church or the form
of a church, nor exceed the form of a *xenodochium*. [*sub hac forma constru(ctam) scilicet quod in
loco praenominato nullum in posterum fiet collegium, sive de monachis sive de canonicis sive de templariis
sive de hospitelariis sive de monialibus, ita est quod domus ipsa nullis temporibus in ecclesiam vel in
formam ecclesiae commutabitur nec formam xenodochii excedet.*][24]

When relocating the hospital of St Thomas from land belonging to
St Mary's priory, the archdeacon of Surrey extracted an agreement
that the priory would build nothing 'in the form of a hospital (*modum
hospitalis*)' on the old site, nor any other hospital (*aliud hospitale*) on the
streets of Southwark.[25] As late as 1355, when divisions between hospital
and church were blurring, the earl of Lancaster received royal licence 'to
build a monastery . . . out of that hospital which his father founded . . . and
to ordain in the monastery a college of a dean and canons secular'.[26] In
papal and royal decrees, hospitals were a distinct administrative category,
listed alongside – but separately from – 'religious houses' or 'abbeys and
priories'.[27]

What then were hospitals?

The limits of text

The English hospital continues to be defined in opposition to its records.
A monastic model under which hospitals followed a rule ensures that
scholars look to statutes and visitations for definitional discussions of the
'hospital'.[28] But these are largely post-1330; for the pre-1300 hospital we
must primarily rely on charters and ordinances, and for the pre-1200
hospital on few of those.

The working model of hospitals as religious communities under a rule
is drawn from work on French and Belgian hospitals. Before 1115 Ivo of
Chartres created a rule for the *leprosariam* at Grand Beaulieu de Chartres
which was shortly thereafter imported into St Gilles de Pont Audemer.[29]
From the 1170s networks of texts survive that suggest widespread efforts
in these regions to create religious rules for hospitals, a programme
extended by the Councils of Rouen (1212) and Paris (1214) under Robert
de Courson, which both required adequately funded hospitals to have a

[24] British Library Cotton Manuscripts Vespasian E.xvii, fo. 33v.
[25] Bodleian Manuscript Rawlinson D763, pp. 12–13.
[26] *Calendar of Patent Rolls* (1901–) [hereafter *CPR*] *1354–8*, 185.
[27] *CCR 1231–4*, 44, and *1254–6*, 438; *CPR 1292–1301*, 541; *Calendar of Charter Rolls* (6 vols.,
1903–27), *1300–26*, 131, 203; *Calendar Papal Letters* (1893–), I , 456; *The London Eyre of 1276*, ed.
Martin Weinbaum, London Record Society XII (1976), no. 298.
[28] Rubin, *Charity and Community*, 148–83; Orme and Webster, *English Hospital*, 49–64;
Rawcliffe, *Medicine for the Soul*, 30–1.
[29] S. C. Mesmin, 'Waleran, Count of Meulan and the Leper Hospital of S. Gilles de
Pont-Audemer', *Annales de Normandie*, 32 (1982), 3–19 (8–10).

rule.[30] From the late twelfth century a shared pattern of textual rules can be discerned. Many were long texts, drawing on Augustinian, Hospitaller and Dominican rules, with elaborate regulations for the organisation and daily duties of residents and directions for the spiritual devotions of brethren and sisters.[31] No comparable early texts survive for England, yet the French model continues to be imported for English houses, sometimes with the substitution of the Paris or Amiens statutes for 'incomplete' or 'missing' English texts.[32] The lack of such texts for England is ascribed to widespread loss; a surprising explanation given the pivotal role of bishops and their legislation in creating and preserving French texts. The English episcopacy is not otherwise known for a comparable failure to preserve records in the late twelfth and thirteenth centuries.

Early English hospitals are considered unknown and constitutionally inchoate because their statute tradition appears so confounding. Several early statutes are typically used to provide insights into this period, but these can be revealed as forgeries or misdated texts.[33] Thus the 980/1180 statutes of St John's, Bedford, the 1174 statutes of St Mary Magdalene's, King's Lynn, and the 1219 statutes of St John's, Bridgwater, are all spurious and probably late fourteenth century. Other texts are later than presumed: the twelfth-century statutes for Reading, Gloucester, Dudston and Norwich should all be re-dated to the late thirteenth or fourteenth centuries. With the unusual exception of Hugh du Puiset's brief Kepier rule, there are no statutes written for English hospitals until c. 1230.

A comparison with contemporary monasteries further highlights the distinctiveness of the hospital. Monasteries had customs that were unwritten, and which might be transmitted between houses by individual brethren or developed by the home community. When local customs were written down in the early thirteenth century, they were elaborate, detailed and sometimes controversial, clearly integral to the house and of long local practice.[34] But even these built on a tradition of textual rules to be read daily to the community (the Benedictine and Augustinian Rules) or used as agents of reform (the *Regularis Concordia* or Lanfranc's *Decreta*).

---

[30] Walter De Keyzer, 'L'évolution interne des léproseries à la charnière des XIIe et XIIIe siècles: le cas de l'évêché de Cambrai', in *Lépreux et sociabilité du moyen âge aux temps modernes*, ed. Bruno Tabuteau (Rouen, 2000), 13–20; *Statuts d'hôtels-dieu et de léproseries: recueil de textes du XIIe au XIVe siècle*, ed. Léon Le Grand (Paris, 1901), xi–xiii.

[31] *Statuts d'hôtels-dieu*, vi, xiii–xxii.

[32] Rubin, *Charity and Community*, 153–81, esp. 153 and 159n; Talbot, *Medicine*, 172–6.

[33] The discussion on patterns of survival, creation and content draws from S. C. Watson, '*Fundatio, Ordinatio* and *Statuta*: The Statutes and Constitutional Documents of English Hospitals to 1300' (D.Phil. thesis, University of Oxford, 2003), 240–96. For the texts themselves, *ibid.*, 301–58.

[34] For example, *The Customary of the Benedictine Abbey of Bury St Edmunds*, ed. Antonia Gransden, Henry Bradshaw Society XCIX (1973).

In contrast, English hospital statutes do not occur in any number until *c.* 1260, and then typically as visitation ordinances, or in conjunction with foundation. They are brief and bland. They do not record local customs or practices, but aim to prohibit extreme or contentious behaviours or to enforce widely accepted administrative practices, such as distinguishing basic common rights, enjoining presentation of accounts, and outlining procedure for election or appointment. Local detail was largely reserved for the house's endowment and the charitable uses to which it should be put. And while thirteenth-century legislation required monastic orders to standardise their customs and open local arrangements to wider scrutiny in chapters and visitations, there was no similar legislation for hospitals. Only Bishop Richard Poore of Salisbury drafted legislation (1217 × 19) requiring newly founded hospitals to have a rule. Despite the singular influence of his statutes, the chapter on hospital rules is not duplicated in any other diocese, including Durham, where Richard reproduced almost all of his Salisbury canons.[35] Until the papal proclamation *Quia Contingit* in 1311, there was no legislation directing the regulation of hospitals.[36] Nor were statutes the primary constitutive texts for English hospitals. Such texts, where they existed, might be forgotten or overhauled, and they were neither the first nor the primary documents solicited by visitors or courts seeking the hospital's constitution.[37] Statutes do not even form a diplomatically identifiable group. A hospital ordinance is rarely a textual rule, but rather a charter or agreement with inserted clauses outlining administrative arrangements, duties or personnel.

Visitations, inquisitions, court inquests, statutes or ordinances began with the same query: what was the foundation and endowment of the hospital? This was true of the 1185 legal controversy over St Cross, Winchester, which upheld the foundation charter as its *'institutio'*; and of Bishop Grosseteste's ruling over Brigg hospital, which used the founder's charter to determine the form and duties of the house.[38] When custodians, bishops or royal officials visited a hospital, they turned to the charters and public memory to uncover what the house was supposed to do and on the basis of what resources.[39] Archbishop Winchelsey's 1304 visitation of

35 *Councils and Synods, with Other Documents relating to the English Church*, II, ed. F. M. Powicke and C. R. Cheney (2 vols., Oxford, 1964), 92; Watson, 'Statutes and Constitutional Documents', 250–1, 260n.

36 *Corpus Iuris Canonici*, ed. Emile Friedberg (Leipzig, 1879–81), II , 1170–1.

37 A 1292 inquest into West Somerton hospital rejected the oath and rules, reinstating the terms of the founder's charters. British Library Harley Roll N20, outlined in Richard Mortimer, 'The Prior of Butley and the Lepers of West Somerton', *Bulletin of the Institute of Historical Research*, 53 (1980), 99–103.

38 *EEA*, VIII, no. 193; *Monasticon*, VI, 688.

39 *Register of William Wickwane*, ed. William Brown, Surtees Society XCIV (1907), 137–8; *CPR 1334–8*, 266–8.

Maidstone hospital stalled when he could not find a foundation ordinance
of the hospital, despite searching the writings, charters and instruments
of its archives. Unable to find 'an instrument among them concerning
the foundation, rule, or reason of the hospital', he wrote hurriedly to
the prior of Canterbury, requesting a search of the priory archives for
any deed relating to Archbishop Boniface's foundation and, particularly,
to any details of his endowment.[40] Winchelsey's letter explicitly equated
Boniface's 'gathering of lands' with the 'reason or rule' of the house, and
asked the prior to dispatch forthwith any charter that might illuminate
this.

Charters relating to foundation, preserved as a hospital's 'ordinance',
are a varied group. They have little in common with monastic foundation
charters, which have a relatively consistent diplomatic and a pious
language of intent that confirms for the support of a community of
religious a substantial and typically scattered collection of churches, lands,
tithes and rents.[41] In contrast, hospital foundation charters are simple,
succinct and, with the exception of a brief *pro anima* clause, peculiarly
devoid of pious language.[42] Echoing Eadmer's description, they outline
how the founder procured a site, designated a use or charity and provided
the means for this charity. Abbot Hugh of St Augustine's founded the
hospital of St Laurence, Canterbury, in 1137, purchasing nine acres of
land within his lordship beside the Dover road 'to make a hospital (*ad
faciendum hospitale*)'. 'To provide for the sick and the poor (*ad sustentationem
infirmorum aut pauperum*)' he assigned three cartloads of hay and, from his
demesne, tithes of his yearly crop on the right side of that road and the
tithe of corn and peas on the left.[43] In a charter of 1123 × 35 Bishop
Alexander of Lincoln wrote in his own hand, 'I have established beside
Newark a hospital for the sick paupers of Lord Christ and afixed certain
rents from my own possessions for both their clothing and food.'[44] He
listed £4 in rents from the mill-soke of Newark; ninety-six baskets (half
grain, half rye) from the bishop's yearly crop, £4 from his tithe of money
from the town and the tithes of all his own food and drink (excluding
wine), whenever he might be in Newark.

Over seventy such endowment charters survive for pre-1250 hospitals,
all stressing a similar pattern of creation; to these may be added over
100 parish and custodial agreements, and many later inquests and

[40] *Registrum Roberti Winchelsey*, 1326.
[41] Among many examples, V. H. Galbraith, 'Monastic Foundation Charters of the Eleventh and Twelfth Centuries', *Cambridge Historical Journal*, 4 (1934), 205–22, 296–8.
[42] Watson, 'Statutes and Constitutional Documents', 79–110.
[43] Bodleian Library Manuscript Top Kent d.3, fos. 5v–6r, printed in J. Duncombe and N. Battely, *The History and Antiquities of the Three Archiepiscopal Hospitals at and near Canterbury*, Bibliotheca Topographica Britannica XXX (1785), 440.
[44] *Registrum Antiquissimum*, III , no. 920.

monastic or civic accounts. The founder provided a site for the hospital, designated a form of alms to be carried out there and gathered an endowment to provide those alms. Like Lanfranc's annual payment of £140, this endowment was not meant to ensure independence, but quite the opposite, dependence: to reiterate daily, weekly or annually, the benefactor's creation and support of the site. The role of hospital founders has often been demeaned because their endowment was so small, especially compared to monastic founders. Indeed, before 1200 hospitals had minimal rents and their land-holding was often tiny and always local; before the mid-thirteenth century, hospitals did not receive churches or manors as endowment. What they had instead was a site, a small rental income and a form of dependent provision, typically physical and in kind.

This dependent income took several forms. Kings or bishops might prefer regular financial payments directly from sheriff, exchequer or episcopal revenue. When Bishop Reginald established St John's, Bath, he gave 'for the support of the poor of that place' annually a sheaf of corn from each acre of episcopal demesne and four marks from the charitable funds of the archdeaneries of Bath and Wells, two loads weekly of dead wood from his park and the right to keep two horses and two cows at pasture with his animals and 100 sheep on his land.[45] Most founders preferred a form of regular, physical provisioning, and tithes of crops, hay, local markets and mills were favoured. Because their value or size was usually unrecorded, these have seemed less significant than they often were: Abbot Hugh's tithes to St Laurence's, Canterbury, noted above, were in fact drawn from 630 acres of abbey land.[46] Since most twelfth-century founders were lords (lay, monastic or episcopal), their grants included freedoms or access for support: the right to draw firewood from the lord's woodland, to keep animals on the common or among the lord's animals, to graze pigs in his woodland or grind corn at his mill. Hugh du Puiset rebuilt Kepier hospital and supplemented Flambard's 1112 endowment (which included two sheaves of corn from fifteen demesne mills) with a thrave of corn from every carucate of the episcopal demesne, pasture for their beasts, fuel and timber, and grazing for their pigs through the whole of his forest, quit of pannage.[47] Lord Hugh de Hutton provided his hospital at Hutton (Yorks.) with a 4½ acre site, a hill with brush, a stream, the right to collect wood from woodland, to common pasture, freedom from tolls and fees, fifteen carts of peat from Hutton turbary and ten carts of heath from Hutton moor both

[45] EEA, X , nos. 80–1
[46] Calendar of Inquisitions Miscellaneous (7 vols., 1916–68) [hereafter CIM], II , 432.
[47] EEA, XXIV , nos. 51–3.

'where my men take them'.[48] John de Lacy endowed Castle Donington hospital with a messuage and three bovates, the tithes from his lordship and mills, pasture in his park, two cartloads of wood each week from his park and the tithes of all his fruits and from two of his manors.[49] Early hospital endowment was always local and characteristically dependent, in a form that publicly reiterated the benefactor's material and physical support.

Few of these endowments were recorded in foundation charters before c. 1180. Indeed, before c. 1180 foundation charters were rarely written for hospitals; those few that survive are brief, non-prescriptive and of a randomness of form that suggests they were neither integral nor important to the shaping of the hospital. Early systems of provision come down to us in post-1180 charters, typically those entrusting custody of the hospital to a monastic house. Of charters recording foundation arrangements for pre-1180 hospitals, the disproportionate number of agreements detailing custodial or jurisdictional arrangements (including confirmations) suggests that the foundation and provision of early hospitals were recorded in text primarily when prompted by the interests of a third party. And many of these may be incomplete. Roger of Gloucester's arrangement with Llanthony priory over his Dudston hospital did not mention the two daily loaves, annual load of hay, tree for fuel and pasture which the priory was required to supply. His provision was publicly known, however, since it formed the acknowledged model for a c. 1225 endowment for St Bartholomew's, Gloucester.[50]

So what gave the hospital its form and constitution? Before the thirteenth century, religious customs were exceptional; indeed, as the constant concerns about custody attest, rarely was there even a formal community in a hospital. Until Poore's 1217 × 19 Salisbury statute (itself of limited application) and the 1311 Quia Contingit, there was no legislation dictating the form or regulation of hospitals in England. Yet somehow hundreds of hospitals were established from the late eleventh century

[48] Cartularium Prioratus de Gyseburne, ed. W. Brown, Surtees Society LXXXVI, LXXXIX (1889–94), nos. 330–1.

[49] CCR 1237–42, 223, 411; Calendar of Inquisitions Post Mortem (1904–), V , 156; CIM, II , 277.

[50] His charter specified an endowment 'that the same thirteen leprous brothers dwelling there should be provided their necessities in food and clothing' (ut ipsi tredecim fratribus leprosis ibidem commorantibus in victu et vestitu necessaria provideant), and mentioned that he had made an agreement to provide food for fuel and repair of the buildings. The support was detailed in a lost priory ledger book. 'Charters of the Earldom of Hereford, 1095–1201', ed. David Walker, in Camden Miscellany XXII (1964), 1–75, no. 27; A Calendar of the Registers of the Priory of Llanthony by Gloucester, 1457–1466, 1501–1525, ed. John Rhodes (Gloucester, 2002), 50n.2(g); M. H. Ellis, 'The Bridges of Gloucester and the Hospital between the Bridges', Bristol and Gloucester Archaeological Society Transactions, 51 (1929), 169–210 (193).

along similar lines, with a framework that was recognised and upheld in legal contests, inquests and visitations from at least 1185. While the textual tradition of English hospitals is haphazard in its diplomatic and internal record, the form of a hospital was consistent. It was a site, a designated form of alms and an endowment (regular, dependent and often physical) to supply those alms.

Instead of a written constitution, the early hospital had a designated use and an endowment, publicly dependent upon the founder or his chosen agent. The early hospital was given constitutional form through repetitive acts of payment or provision, as established by the original endower, the founder. Its constitution was written not in text, nor in a form of religious life, but in its regular, public provisioning. This was less the abstract quality of charity than the physical transfer of alms. The constitution of an early hospital was written in the local landscape, in the repetitive gift and in custom.

A legal and constitutional form of alms

The origins of this constitutional arrangement can be witnessed in Domesday Book. Here 'alms' and 'almsland' denoted several forms of tenure, including land granted to a religious community and land held of a manor church by its priest for his own support. It also included a form of lay tenure whereby an individual held land from a lord in a form of mercy, at the lord's will for the almsman's use, the tenant specifically unable to sell the land, transfer it or pass it as inheritance without the lord's consent.[51] These almslands were typically parcels of land within a manor, most commonly of half a hide. This was half the size of the standard parcel of land held by royal or manorial priests, suggesting it was considered a basic unit of income or support. Although both the tenure of almsland and a number of the almsmen and women holding such land pre-dated the Conquest,[52] many of the Domesday instances had been given by the Conqueror and his queen. Matilda had given half a hide of land in alms to both Doda and Alward in Dorset and Devon respectively, and the king's almsmen included several Frenchmen.[53] This system of landed support was similar in form and size of holding in many

---

[51] Cited here from *Domesday Book* (Phillimore edition) [hereafter *DB*], Herts.17.15; Linc.7.55. Two sons held parcels of such lands (Wilts.19.4; Devon.1.11). For land held by the church 'in alms' in the twelfth century, and perhaps drawing from distinctions in tenure defined in Normandy under the influence of church reform, see John Hudson, *Land, Law, and Lordship in Anglo-Norman England* (Oxford, 1994), 90–2, 104–5. Its use in charters and codification under the common law during the time of Henry II is considered by Benjamin Thompson, 'Free Alms Tenure in the Twelfth Century', *Anglo-Norman Studies*, 16 (1994), 221–43 (223, 236–9, 242).

[52] *DB*, Wilts.18.1, Camb.32.32

[53] *DB*, Dors.56.20, Devon.52.30, Bucks.57.7, Herts.1.9.

counties throughout England. It was also practised by other lords; Azelin, for example, held a hide of land in Ratton from the earl of Arundel.[54]

This tenure was relatively infrequent and personal, suggesting that many almsmen and women may have been known personally to their benefactor, but some at least held their land from open-handed charity. The king had designated almslands in Leicestershire and Warwickshire that might be held by lay individuals.[55] The only labelled 'cripples' in Domesday, Edric *mancus* and an unnamed '*quidam loripes*', were almsmen held over from King Edward's reign; in Warsop 'a certain blind man (*quidam caecus*)' held one bovate in alms.[56] The 951 × 55 will of King Eadred decreed that twelve (clearly anonymous) almsmen be chosen from each of his estates and sustained in perpetuity as an act of Christian charity.[57] Some almslands were provided with customary duties attached: Thorkell the priest was permitted to retain land in alms from the king 'for which he performed mass every week on Monday for the souls of the King and Queen', and a village held as almsland of the king paid annually for his soul two pigs and 100 loaves with ale to the church there.[58] Almsland in Domesday does not offer a social origin of hospitals, since these holdings were attached to a person not a house or site, and the conditional, personal tenure would make it unlikely that the holdings themselves developed into hospitals.[59] Domesday does offer a legal, tenurial and constitutional model for hospitals, however, whereby an income (here, landed) was designated by the lord to be held at his will for the material support of a charitable recipient (of the lord's own choice), with attendant obligations or duties of his own determination.

Customary payments from royal shire income were also designated for alms in Domesday, such as the 20s from the revenues of Northamptonshire.[60] Most such payments appear later, in the pipe rolls, where the personal alms extended via land in Domesday take the form of financial payments from royal revenues. Individuals received payments in alms of either 30s 5d or occasionally half that amount, 15s 2½d. At Colchester in 1156 and 1157, Ralph the Lame, Terric the Almsman, Simon the Blind and Tursten the Sick were among a group of men who each

---

[54] *DB*, Sussex.10.31.

[55] *DB*, Warw.43, Leics.8 and 13.33.

[56] *DB*, Devon.1.11, Bucks.57.6, Notts.1.25.

[57] *Select English Historical Documents of the Ninth and Tenth Centuries*, ed. F. E. Harmer (Cambridge, 1914), 34 and 64.

[58] *DB*, Bedf.57.21, Gloucs.W5.

[59] Cullum has observed that almsland, noted in Domesday, predated the priory and hospital that were subsequently founded in Pontefract; she suggests this with Eadred's will may offer an early model for royal charity. P. H. Cullum, 'Hospitals and Charitable Provision in Medieval Yorkshire, 936–1547' (D.Phil. thesis, University of York, 1989), 15–17.

[60] *DB*, Nhants.B36.

received a customary payment of 30s 5d.[61] The amount is important, since 30s 5d is 365 *denarii*, or 1 penny for each day of the year. It is a common sum in the pipe rolls: the amount paid to local royal servants such as the chaplain or vintner of Windsor castle; more important servants received multiples of this sum, such as the custodian of the king's house at Windsor who received 60s 10d and another 10s for his clothing.[62] 365 *denarii* was clearly an amount reckoned to supply a basic provision.

During the twelfth century, the number of named almsmen on the pipe rolls declined and payments to established hospitals increased. In 1156 payments of 30s 5d were made to both the infirm of St Albans (the hospital of St Julian's) and of St Edmunds (the hospital of St Peter's) and £4 11s 3d (three times 30s 5d) to the *hospitalis* in Norwich. Royal hospital foundations duplicated this equation. Henry I endowed his hospital of St Bartholomew's, Oxford, with annual payments of £19 15s 5d (thirteen times 30s 5d) and 65s (thirteen times 5s) for clothing from the sheriff's revenues.[63] This move from personal alms to the support of a site (a hospital) permitted the king to shift provisioning from a person to a system of support. St Giles, Holborn, had been founded before 1118 by Queen Matilda, with a site and a customary payment 'for the food of the sick' of 60s from her land of Queenshythe. Henry II added annual payments direct from the exchequer on the feast of St Michael of another 60s 'to buy the lepers' clothing' and 30s 5d 'to buy light for them'.[64] The pipe roll may reflect changes occurring more widely. A payment for the bishop of Ely occurs on the pipe roll *in elemosinis constitutis* between 1162 and 1164, but occurs in 1171 and 1172 as '£8.8s. in appointed alms to the hospital of Ely via the demesne manors of the bishopric'.[65]

By the twelfth century, four ingredients were typically required to create a monastery: a church, a resident community or convent, a Rule of life to which they were held and, increasingly, a domestic architecture to provide for their common life. In every century during the middle ages, none of these was required for a hospital, although elements became more common and popular, notably chapels from *c.* 1170 and codes of behaviour and a limited domestic architecture from *c.* 1240. Instead, hospitals had three constitutive ingredients, as first outlined by Eadmer: a site with a building, a regular income and a designated use for that income (that is, specified alms).

[61] *The Great Rolls of the Pipe . . . AD 1155–8*, ed. Joseph Hunter (1844), 72, 132, and see *ibid.* 134. A similar pattern without named individuals can be seen in *The Pipe Roll of 31 Henry I* (1833, repr. 1929), 126.

[62] *Pipe Roll 31 Henry I*, 100, 126–7; *Pipe Roll (1155–8)*, 18, 71, 151.

[63] *Pipe Roll (1155–8)*, 35, 74, 82, 93, 125, 149.

[64] *Monasticon*, VI, 635–6.

[65] W. M. Palmer, 'The Hospitals of St. John the Baptist and St. Mary Magdalene at Ely', *Proceedings of the Cambridge Antiquarian Society* (1935), 76–108, no. 2.

A hospital was a form of sited alms. Its constitutive ingredients were acts of the founder or almsgiver: procuring the site, gathering a basic endowment or system of support and designating its use. This was a sited, impersonal version of the alms tenure in Domesday and on the pipe rolls. In both, the benefactor did not fully relinquish the source of those alms: the regular payments or material provision reiterated both the gift and the dependency of the house, in origin, form and provision, on the founder's generosity and intent. From the earliest hospital charters, the endowment's use (i.e. the alms) were designated by the *ad* clause, which was recognised in subsequent centuries as the statement of a hospital's constitution.[66] When a bishop visited a monastery, he already knew its rule and the pattern of behaviours or observances to which the convent should conform; when a visitor or inquest arrived at a hospital he/they had to first establish, through charters or local report, the hospital's endowment and its use. This was what Winchelsey sought when he searched the Maidstone archives and dispatched his plea to Canterbury priory for details of Boniface's original endowment.

A hospital's alms were different from those given to monasteries. Grants to monasteries could have strings attached, but their impact was limited by law. Monastic gifts established broader systems of income and aimed to further the financial stability, even independence, of the abbey while fostering a relationship with the benefactor. Once a founder had selected his monastery's order, he had limited say in how the convent might live: his grant in alms was a one-off gift to 'purchase by a happy commerce eternal things with temporal, abundant heavenly gifts with earthly ones'.[67] It fostered a self-directing religious community that in turn generated alms primarily in the form of the *Opus Dei* (liturgy and prayer). In contrast, the alms of a hospital founder were physical in form and intent: they proclaimed dependence and stressed not the conceptual gift to God, but the routine material transfer of support. The regular provisioning through food, firewood or customary payment *was* the meaning of the endowment. Its repetitive, customary and public performance acted as both a reiteration of this constitution and the means of ensuring constitutional stability. A hospital's constitution was performed or repetitively re-enacted rather than recorded. Twelfth-century hospitals did not thus require charters or textual statements, and many were not committed to vellum until the early thirteenth century. At this time Isabella confirmed her ancestor's endowment of St Margaret's, Huntingdon, which included £8 'in established alms', and Queen Isabel outlined the complex provision of tithes, corn, hay, wood, pannage and

[66] Watson, 'Statutes and Constitutional Documents', 54–75.
[67] From a charter of Henry I, cited in Thompson, 'Free Alms Tenure', 224n. For a discussion of monastic gifts, *ibid.*, 225–7, 242.

pasture attached to St John's, Berkhamstead, when she granted the house to the hospital of St Thomas of Acre.[68] The early hospital was not to do, but to receive. As even the most religious of hospital foundation charters, Hugh du Puiset's 1184 × 89 deed, stated:

> we have built that house beside the bridge of Sherburn near Durham ... with certain benefits assigned to the same hospital for its maintenance ... that there from the benefits and possessions charitably gathered to the same hospital, the hunger, thirst and nakedness of the same lepers, and other failings and wretchedness by which they are incessantly afflicted, should be relieved. [69]

Hospital foundation charters appeared in large numbers and more regular form from *c.* 1180, embraced by founders as an opportunity to elaborate their wishes and with them the hospital's form and duties. The *ad* clause, where the use of endowment was specified, provided the mechanism. Originally a simple directive such as 'to support the poor or sick', it was expanded during the twelfth century, first to specify more precise recipients of alms, as *c.* 1160 at St Mary's, Newcastle, '[*ad*] to harbour the poor and sick clerics and pilgrims passing through', but becoming by the end of the century an opportunity to elaborate duties and organisation.[70] Bishop Gilbert Glanville founded Strood hospital in 1193:

> [*ad*] to receive and preserve the poor, weak, infirm, both those known dwelling [there] and those travelling from distant [places], that they should be fittingly provided in their bed, food and drink until they should die or leave again in safety and, with those dying or leaving, other passing poor or weak should be perpetually substituted. [*ad recipiendos et con[serva]ndos pauperes, debiles, infirmos, et sibi minime sufficientes, tam notos commorantes quam a remotis transeuntes ut in lecto, cibo, et potu eis congrue providea[n]tur, donec vel decedant, vel cum incolumitate recedant illisque decedentibus vel recedentibus alii pera[grantes] pauperes et debiles imperpetuum substituentur.*] [71]

By the mid-thirteenth century, a hospital was expected to have a textual statement of its constitution. Bishop Nicholas Farnham was perturbed that Northallerton hospital, founded by his predecessor in *c.* 1200, had no charter. He composed one in 1244, judging that although 'certain goods had been gathered to the same hospital for the work of the poor passing through or dwelling there (*ad opus pauperum transeuntium sev ibi commorantium*)', the deaths of his predecessors must have prevented an ordinance being drafted; it therefore fell to Farnham 'to balance for the hospital its capacity [i.e. alms] with its possessions [i.e. endowment]'.[72]

---

[68] *Monasticon*, VI, 652; *Calendar of Charter Rolls*, III, 399–400.

[69] *EEA*, XXIV, no. 145.

[70] *Early Deeds relating to Newcastle upon Tyne*, ed. A. M. Oliver, Surtees Society CXXXVII (1924), 9, no. 1. For the '*ad*' clause generally, Watson, 'Statutes and Constitutional Documents', 100–7.

[71] *Registrum Roffense*, ed. John Thorpe (1769), 637.

[72] *The Register, or Rolls, of Walter Gray*, ed. James Raine, Surtees Society LVI (1872), 180–1.

The move to a textual constitution, and the use of the *ad* clause to elaborate the hospital's constitution, changed the hospital from a system of simple, repetitive support. With a new mechanism to direct, founders became more precise, abstract and detailed in their demands. The arrival of a textual constitution in charter-form transformed hospitals, but still within the legal framework of an endowment and use specified by the founder.

The hospital as a sited form of alms unravels a series of problems that beset the study of hospitals and their deeds. First, how the overwhelming varieties or 'types' of hospital can be part of a single form of house. Since every founder could specify the use of their alms, in increasing detail once texts were used, the varieties of alms were conceptually limitless, although many fell into socially familiar categories or fashions. The apparent variety of hospitals thus shared one simple constitutional model. Secondly, a hospital founder could designate the precise use not only of his own endowment, but of any future income. Forbidden to a monastic founder, clauses requiring future income to be used to feed additional poor or house more long-term sick were common in charters of hospital founders.[73] Thirdly, hospital founders could dictate strict terms upon which they would assign their alms. Bishop Bartholomew of Exeter provided the lepers of St Mary Magdalene with five marks of silver paid directly from his *camera* on four public liturgical (and financial) holidays, with tithes and profits from his corkwood, so long as they remained chaste and honest, admitted no more than thirteen to the house and did not wander freely without his licence. 'If the said lepers should not observe these things', he warned, 'we wish that the aforesaid alms be assigned to any good use of alms by arrangement of the bishop and chapter and town of Exeter.'[74] Finally, the dependent, material nature of alms, settled on spaces often with no fixed community and limited management, also created the main challenge for early hospitals: reliable oversight. Concern to ensure that a hospital and its endowment was adequately maintained pushed founders and patrons to turn successively to monasteries, chaplains, bishops and civic bodies in an attempt to secure their alms.

Conclusion

The arrival of the hospital in England presented an appealing alternative to existing systems of personal or diffuse alms. Instead of one almsman ensconced on part of a manor, a hospital was placed on a very public site in an important and politically symbolic town, affording a more open

---

[73] *Registrum Antiquissimum*, III, nos. 792–3.
[74] *EEA*, XI, no. 98. See also, 'Charters of the Earldom of Hereford', no. 27.

and public display of charitable lordship.[75] Its minor endowment was part of its design, as the early hospital was supposed to be dependent, its systems of support public, visible and daily. The move to public, sited alms also appealed to the local community. Hospitals provided succour based upon need rather than person; they also permitted participation in a regular act of alms by those who were not holders of large landed estates. Although the founder established the use of the house, local benefactors could give alms in support of this use. These could be more dramatic gestures of provisioning, such as Bath priory's gift to the hospital of St John, which they had agreed to oversee 'just as their own alms', of a sheaf of corn annually from each acre of their demesne, and the tithe of all bread, cheese, salt and meat within the convent; or the chapter and town of Exeter, which gave respectively fourteen loaves from their commons and a portion of their market tolls each week.[76] However, most such gifts were small annual rents or regular payments by lesser local lords or townsfolk. The local community took an active interest in their hospitals, filing complaints if they deteriorated, testifying at inquests and visitations, and eventually assuming day-to-day administration of many houses.

The hospital was quickly absorbed into an existing Anglo-Saxon framework of lordship, alms and custom. This not only supplied a legal framework for the English hospital but shaped its distinctive social form as a house of local alms. Even Lanfranc's twin foundations were noted not for the grand civic gesture they were perhaps intended to be, but for their simple acts of alms. William of Malmesbury noted the call to alms as Lanfranc's defining public exhortation, and as his fervent practice and innovation:[77]

> So he brought bread and shoes for the poor and all that was needed to keep them alive and clothed. He was too wise and sensible to deal with them by giving them money. He knew that such people, when their purses are stuffed, endure hunger with a dry mouth.

In these early centuries, England did not develop the pattern of hospitals that have been identified in France and Flanders, with larger, independent communities under a textual rule and with a form and oversight mirroring those of religious houses. Some individuals imitated aspects of continental practice in England. Rahere, inspired by a hospital in Rome, founded St Bartholomew's, London; Hugh du Puiset, motivated by the model of French princeship, built the large, conventual hospital of Sherburn and supplied the unique Kepier rule; and Richard Poore, a colleague of

[75] The correlation between leper houses and episcopal or honorial seats has been noted by Satchell, 'Emergence of Leper-Houses', 121–7.

[76] EEA, X, no. 80; EEA, XI, no. 98.

[77] William of Malmesbury, Gesta Pontificum Anglorum, trans. David Preest (Woodbridge, 2002), 46.

Robert de Courson, introduced legislation requiring rules in Salisbury hospitals. It is curious, however, how limited an impact these bold actions had. They inspired no evident English imitators and were themselves quickly absorbed into local structures of hospital constitution, notably into systems of alms and chartered arrangement as witnessed in both Durham and Salisbury.[78]

Finally, the distinctive publicisation of private alms that underlay the legal framework of the hospital explains the peculiar constitutional grey-area that English hospitals inhabited. A hospital was recognised in law as a legal body whose possessions and rights could be defended, but it was not a living body, capable of redesigning or reforming itself or even of change. They were always accountable to the original intentions of their founders, to the degree that their support could be rescinded and transferred should they fail to uphold their appointed alms. Hospitals were a recognised type of house, administered and used by the laity in ways more common and intimate than were monasteries. Widely known and popular, the hospital may have been less influenced by the monastery than vice versa. For the elements of hospital constitution – the founder's alms, his intentions for their use and the hospital's accountability to that fixed form – may underpin many of the critiques increasingly visited upon monasteries from the late fourteenth century.[79]

---

[78] Watson, 'Statutes and Constitutional Documents', 249–62.

[79] Benjamin Thompson, 'Monasteries and their Patrons at Foundation and Dissolution', *Transactions of the Royal Historical Society*, sixth series, 4 (1994), 103–25.

Transactions of the RHS 16 (2006), pp. 95–115 © 2006 Royal Historical Society
doi:10.1017/S0080440106000429   Printed in the United Kingdom

TRUST AND DISTRUST:
A SUITABLE THEME FOR HISTORIANS?

By Geoffrey Hosking

READ 20 MAY 2005

ABSTRACT. In the last twenty years or so, sociologists have shown that trust is an especially problematic but also especially important feature of modern societies, in which traditional and familiar social ties have been broken up and reconfigured in new patterns. On the whole, however, sociologists do not attempt a historical analysis, contenting themselves with the distinction between modern and pre-modern societies. With few exceptions, historians, who could give a more differentiated account, have not shown much interest in trust. Even those who deal with themes like religion, ethnicity, gender and the family tend to interpret them through power relationships rather than trust relationships. There are very good reasons, though, why historians should tackle the theme of trust. In this essay it is argued that the manner in which trust works in any given society is vital to the understanding of most social phenomena. An account is attempted of certain crucial junctures in European history when the radius of trust has broadened relatively rapidly. Finally the essay offers some suggestions as to why a perceived 'crisis of trust' has arisen, both in the contemporary western world and in the global economy, and what might be done about it.

Trust is one of the most pervasive – and perhaps for that reason least noticed – aspects of social life. We need to display trust in order to live at all. As the German sociologist Niklas Luhmann remarked, 'A complete absence of trust would prevent [one] even getting up in the morning.'[1] Life confronts us every day with unfamiliar situations and people we have never met before. We constantly have to take decisions without being able to gather all the information we would need to take them in a completely rational manner. Which of us, before boarding an aircraft, checks every rivet, joint and fuel duct in it? Or even the qualifications of the engineers responsible for maintaining and repairing those parts? The answer is obvious. Yet our lives depend on the impeccable working order of those parts, the skill and conscientiousness of the engineers. The fact is, we take them on trust because everyone else does so, because planes do not usually crash, and because to do otherwise would require us to have both time

[1] Niklas Luhmann, *Trust* (Chichester, 1979), 4.

and skills we do not possess. We do not 'decide' to board an aircraft: we just do it. Every day we exercise trust in a myriad such unnoticed ways.

Trust is necessary, then, in order to face both the known and the unknown, whether another human being, or simply the future and its contingent events. It offers us a way of reducing uncertainty. It lies somewhere between hope and confidence, and involves an element of semi-calculated risk-taking. It is simply essential to any kind of social life. As Georg Simmel has said,

> Without the general trust that people have in each other, society itself would disintegrate, for very few relationships are based entirely on what is known with certainty about another person, and very few relationships would endure if trust were not as strong as, or stronger than, rational proof or personal observation.[2]

Trust also makes an essential contribution to our cognitive equipment. It forms a constitutive part of the way in which we conceive the world. We learn about the world first of all from our parents, and later through our contacts with partners, friends, colleagues and people with whom we feel an affinity. Since we cannot learn everything by personal experience, we take on trust much of what they tell us. At an even deeper level, their discourse, their ways of mentally constituting the world in which they live becomes a usually unnoticed but firmly embedded part of our own world-picture.

Over the last twenty years or so, sociologists have been taking an increasing interest in trust, because of the way the modern world fragments communities but also diversifies choice and offers us the opportunity to take up relationships with distant people and impersonal institutions. Anthony Giddens, for example, writes that 'In circumstances of uncertainty and multiple choice, the notions of trust and risk have particular application. Trust . . . is a crucial generic phenomenon of personality development, as well as having distinctive and specific relevance to a world of disembedding mechanisms and abstract systems.' In Giddens's vocabulary the term 'disembedding mechanisms' refers to the processes in modern life which detach us from our immediate locale, family and friends, requiring us regularly to interact at a distance and with people we have never met before. In these circumstances trust offers a

> 'protective cocoon' which stands guard over the self in its dealings with everyday reality. It 'brackets out' potential occurrences which, were the individual seriously to contemplate them, would produce a paralysis of the will . . . Trust is a medium of interaction with the abstract systems which both empty day-to-day life of its traditional content and set up globalising influences.

---

[2] Georg Simmel, *The Philosophy of Money*, ed. David Frisby, trans. Tom Bottomore and David Frisby, 2nd enlarged edn (London, 1990), 178–9.

Modernity, then, changes the nature of trust, but does not eliminate the need for it.[3]

On the contrary, the issue of trust is crucial today. In the decade and a half since the end of the cold war, most nations and a good many international organisations have been looking for ways to reconcile bitterly divided communities, to create and maintain peace. 'Truth and reconciliation commissions' have endeavoured to enable former oppressors and their victims to live in the same society without tearing each other apart. 'Peace-keeping' has become the principal business of many national armies, and that sometimes seems to mean creating a peace where there was none to keep. In the Balkans, the former Soviet Union, Angola, Indonesia and elsewhere international organisations have been seeking ways to promote social cohesion and the stability which encourages economic growth. Failure in this endeavour is far more dramatic and 'interesting' than success, and gets itself better reported in the media, so that the ordinary newspaper-reader or television-watcher gains the impression that promoting trust is hopeless, and we are certainly not well informed on the ways in which success is sometimes achieved.

In advanced western societies trust is also a serious problem: there is growing public distrust of the institutions, official and professional, in which we used to place our confidence, and as a result, there is more litigation, more overworked teachers and demoralised social workers, greater reluctance to help the police, greater recourse to private health care and the like. Michael Power has shown that both governments and the public have become more distrustful of professional people and try to check on their performance by means of inspections, audits and the meeting of targets.[4] Robert Putnam has suggested that since the 1960s membership in associations of civil society in the USA has drastically declined, and that as a result the peaceful and mutually trusting interaction of citizens necessary to democracy may be under threat.[5] In her Reith Lectures of 2002 Onora O'Neill argued that the decline in trust is undermining some of our most cherished ideals – like freedom of the

[3] Anthony Giddens, *Modernity and Self-Identity: Self and Society in the Late Modern Age* (Cambridge, 1991), 3. Among other important recent sociological studies are Anthony Giddens, *The Consequences of Modernity* (Cambridge, 1990); Luhmann, *Trust*; Barbara Misztal, *Trust in Modern Societies* (Cambridge, 1996); Francis Fukuyama, *Trust: The Social Virtues and the Creation of Prosperity* (London, 1996), and also his *The Great Disruption: Human Nature and the Reconstitution of Social Order* (London, 1999); Piotr Sztompka, *Trust: A Sociological Theory* (Cambridge, 1999).

[4] Michael Power, *The Audit Society: Rituals of Verification* (Oxford, 1997).

[5] Robert D. Putnam, *Bowling Alone: The Collapse and Revival of American Community* (New York, 2000).

press – and cannot be restored unless we are prepared to balance our freedoms and rights with equivalent responsibilities.[6]

I became aware of the problem of trust through trying to understand the history of Russia. It seemed to me that what distinguished Russia from other European countries was its means of conducting government and preserving internal peace. Right into the twentieth century it had both a very strong state and very strong local communities, but between them there was very little, other than patron–client networks, which depended on persons rather than institutions and laws for their operation.

Local communities functioned on the basis of 'joint responsibility', a system that both preserved internal peace and provided a way of interacting with higher authorities. It grew out of the needs of both state and peasant community. The state needed to be able to collect taxes, recruit soldiers and apprehend criminals; the peasant community needed to ensure its own survival in a harsh climate and on relatively infertile soils. The state made its needs known, but usually it was the village that took the essential decisions about how taxes should be apportioned, which young men should be sent to the army and how criminals should be discovered and brought to justice. That saved the state and its local agents a lot of trouble, a very important matter when Russia was claiming European great power status with very scanty resources. To decide how to discharge its duties and how to handle the communal aspects of economic life, the village had a 'democratic' general assembly, the *skhod*, consisting of all heads of households – nearly always older men – who took decisions by discussion and consensus. The basis of that consensus was ultimately *pravda*: everything that is true, just, morally right, in accordance with God's law or with accepted custom. Similarly, peasant courts, which consisted of the 'best people' – usually the most trusted or experienced householders – of the village or *volost'* (canton) would deal with civil disputes and petty criminal offences as far as possible in a way that reflected *pravda* and that removed causes of possible future conflict in order to preserve the peace.

To ensure that taxes could be paid, many villages periodically awarded extra land to households that were growing, and took it away from those that were shrinking. The more land a household held, the higher the taxes it had to pay, and vice versa. Arable land, then, was conceived as a communal resource, available to all who needed it; similarly, access to timber, meadows, watercourses.

'Joint responsibility' profoundly affected the peasants' outlook on law, property and authority. Everyone had an interest in everyone else's welfare. If your neighbour did not pay his taxes, you would have to help make up the shortfall. If your neighbour's son absconded from the

[6] Onora O'Neill, *A Question of Trust* (the BBC Reith Lectures 2002) (Cambridge, 2002).

army, or was found to be unfit for military service, your son might have to serve instead.

As a result, it was accepted that, if a household got into difficulties, the others should rally round and help. It might be the illness or death of a family member, it might be a fire or bad weather. In any case, bread would be put aside for a starving family, herbs or other medical help would be provided for the sick, neighbours would lend a hand with the reaping at harvest time. This kind of mutual aid was not altruism, but common sense in the circumstances.

It sounds attractive, but it had its dark side too. Villagers kept a close watch on each others' lives and constantly exchanged information – gossip, to put it more simply. Heavy drinking, stealing or marital discord could wreck the economic life of a household and so drag its neighbours into extra expense or labour. Furthermore, extremes of wealth were regarded with suspicion: a poverty-stricken household was a burden on the rest of the community, while a wealthy one was probably engaged in sharp practice or criminality which might threaten the orderly life of the village. As a popular saying had it, 'Wealth is a sin before God, and poverty is a sin before one's fellow villagers.'[7]

'Joint responsibility' is by no means unique to Russia. All European and many Asiatic countries had similar institutions for centuries. What is distinctive about Russia is that modernisation did not weaken those institutions, but actually strengthened them. From the seventeenth to nineteenth centuries, when analogous customs in most European countries were giving way to institutions and laws based on the principle of individual personal responsibility, the Russian state exploited 'joint responsibility' more systematically, because it was such a convenient way to collect taxes and recruits, and no other sinews of power were available.[8]

I would argue that 'joint responsibility' continued in modified form even under the Soviet regime. In place of institutions and laws that embodied the principle of legal responsibility and equality before the law, the Soviet regime perpetuated personalised power systems that made heavy demands on the population. Recent research has shown

---

[7] Quotation from B. N. Mironov, *Sotsial'naia istoriia Rossii perioda imperii* (St Petersburg, 1999), i, 330. My account of *krugovaia poruka* and its effects draws on V. A. Aleksandrov, *Sel'skaia obshchina v Rossii (xviii-nachalo xix veka)* (Moscow, 1976), chs. 2–3; M. M. Gromyko, *Traditsionnye normy povedeniia i formy obshcheniia russkikh krest'ian xix veka* (Moscow, 1986); Stephen P. Frank, 'Popular Justice, Community and Culture among the Russian Peasantry, *Russian Review*, 46 (1987), 239–65; Alena Ledeneva, 'The Genealogy of *krugovaia poruka*: Forced Trust as a Feature of Russian Political Culture', in *Trust and Democratic Transition in Post-Communist Europe*, ed. Ivana Marková, Proceedings of the British Academy, no. 123 (Oxford, 2004), 85–108.

[8] On the abandonment of 'joint responsibility' in other European countries, see Jerome Blum, 'The Internal Structure and Polity of the European Village Community from the Fifteenth to the Nineteenth Century', *Journal of Modern History*, 43 (1971), 543–76.

that at the workplace in the Soviet enterprise, at the dwelling place in the communal apartment, and in the labour camps, systems of 'joint responsibility' reasserted themselves. Each person's welfare depended on how his colleagues performed, and deviations from the norm were regarded with suspicion. Mutual surveillance became even more marked, because a communal apartment is more claustrophic than a village, and because it was backed up by a formidably inquisitive security police. One of the reasons for the ubiquity and savagery of Stalin's terror was that people denouncing their neighbours were often convinced they were morally justified in doing so.[9]

The post-Soviet period, however, saw a disastrous clash between the customs of 'joint responsibility' and the institutions of the Americanised market economy, depending as they do on contract, property, the rule of law, transparent corporate governance and the public provision of social welfare and infrastructure. Structures of social solidarity inherited from the USSR, however primitive and under-productive they may have been, did more or less guarantee a basic minimum for everyone, no matter how poorly educated they were, or how bad their health. Now those structures were fatally undermined without the benefits of a genuine market or the rule of law being put in their place. The gap was filled by 'oligarchs', who played roughly the same role as the mafia in nineteenth-century Sicily: they regulated the economy in their own interests by creating extensive monopolies, protecting their clients and enforcing contracts where necessary through their private armies.[10] The result was a disastrous drop in productive output, extreme social inequality, the degradation of the health and education systems and a steep rise in the mortality rate.

Thinking about this Russian disaster led me on to broader questions about how societies and economies function. The vital question, it seems to me, in Russia as elsewhere, is the reason why people trust one another – and why they distrust one another. In other words, we need to supplement the abundant accounts we have of power structures with an account of trust structures. If we do not study systematically the structures of trust and social cohesion, we risk missing essential features of a society and are likely to make serious mistakes in dealing with it.

That is what the International Monetary Fund and other international financial institutions have done in Russia, Mexico, Indonesia and

    [9] Geoffrey Hosking, 'Forms of Social Solidarity in Russia and the Soviet Union', in *Trust*, ed. Marková, 47–62.
    [10] David E. Hoffmann, *The Oligarchs: Wealth and Power in the New Russia* (Oxford, 2002); Joseph Stiglitz, *Globalization and its Discontents* (London, 2002), 160–2; Diego Gambetta, 'Mafia: The Price of Distrust', in *Trust: Making and Breaking Cooperative Relations*, ed. Diego Gambetta (Oxford, 1988), 158–75.

elsewhere. It took for granted that the forms of trust associated with modern financial and fiscal institutions, contract and the rule of law could easily be established by a few simple reforming steps. But in those countries most people placed their trust in quite different ways, incompatible with modern institutions. They depended for their economic well-being on personal patrons, whether in government structures, in private firms or in local communities: those patrons carried out a modest redistribution of wealth in favour of their clients and thus smoothed out some of the glaring social inequalities, though in a rough and ready manner which left many people still extremely deprived. The IMF demanded that, since official procedures were corrupted by such patronage, markets be deregulated, state budgets be balanced by cutting expenditure and the stability of the currency be maintained. These policies entailed curtailing social services, education, health care and pensions, without which many people's capacity to contribute to the economy was degraded. Where there is no trust in institutions, the deregulation of markets tends to mean that individuals will use what assets they can seize to provide for their own security at everyone else's expense, and if necessary defend them by creating private armies. The result is capital flight and extreme social inequality, which are not only inhumane, but undermine the potential for further economic development.[11]

Our own modern legal and financial institutions have grown out of centuries of gradual relocation of the focus of trust. Their origin often lies with arrangements initially improvised in order to foster familiarity and trust. The English legal profession was born in the Inns of Court and Chancery in London, where apprentice practitioners learned their trade from their seniors, and also ate their dinners together. The latter practice was presumably intended to promote conviviality and mutual confidence, as well as the exchange and discussion of experience. Since attendance was expensive, especially for those who lived outside London, its members had the comforting consciousness of belonging to an elite club. That is one of the ways in which mutual trust is built up, and the motive is evidently still at work: to the present day aspiring barristers must dine thirty-two times over at least eight terms in order to qualify.[12]

Similarly, both insurance companies and stock exchanges originated in seventeenth-century London coffee houses, where merchants, shipowners and bankers would gather to exchange news about commodities, technical novelties and commercial voyages. At establishments such as Jonathan's or Garraway's in Exchange Alley in the City, buyers and sellers of securities

[11] Stiglitz, *Globalization*, esp. 160–2.

[12] J. H. Baker, 'The English Legal Profession, 1450–1550', in *Lawyers in Early Modern Europe and America*, ed. Wilfred Prest (London, 1981), 16–41; Richard L. Abel, *The Legal Profession in England and Wales* (Oxford, 1988), 38.

could be brought together and matched. Not far away, Edward Lloyd's Coffee House specialised in marine insurance and Tom's and Causey's in fire insurance. With the help of the latest information and of various colleagues' estimates of it, those involved could better assess the price one should pay for particular goods and services, and the risk one was assuming in undertaking certain types of transaction. The informal bonhomie of such establishments was very helpful, perhaps indispensable, in generating the mutual confidence necessary for commercial and financial operations.[13] In recent decades this kind of background trust has become acknowledged as an essential aspect of 'social capital'. Institutions based on it reduce uncertainty and cut transaction costs; they thus play a crucial role in economic growth.[14]

Yet when economists write about insurance companies and other modern financial institutions, they do so without seeming aware that the trust which makes them effective has been created by historical evolution, and cannot be conjured up mechanically in institutions which lack that evolution.

The fragility of institutions not based on such historically developed trust is brought out in an excellent study by Craig Muldrew, who reminds us that today, when the values of free competition are constantly preached, 'we must understand that the full realisation of such values, without a concurrent emphasis on trust, sociability and the redistribution of wealth, would be the creation of a world of Hobbesian insecurity and debtors' prisons'.[15] He provides ample evidence for his assertion in a rich study of credit relations and the way they gradually became embedded in English social structure in the sixteenth to eighteenth centuries. He shows that from the mid-sixteenth century trade expanded at a much faster rate than the supply of coinage, so that it inevitably depended on the growth of credit. Such credit was sometimes entered in account books, but much of it was given orally, in the presence of witnesses. The calculation of whether one could offer credit and, if so, how much derived from one's assessment of the standing and hence imputed trustworthiness of the potential debtor. For the consumer, then, much of social life consisted in displaying one's creditworthy credentials in the form of dress, behaviour, the furnishing of one's house and/or shop, the nature of one's relations with others and so on. All traders had to enter into this intricate web of calculation, since, as Daniel Defoe remarked, 'He that gives no trust and

[13] Ranald C. Michie, *The London Stock Exchange: A History* (Oxford, 1999), 20; P. G. M. Dickson, *The Financial Revolution in England: A Study in the Development of Public Credit* (Aldershot, 1993), 590.

[14] Douglass C. North, *Institutions, Institutional Change and Economic Performance* (Cambridge, 1990).

[15] Craig Muldrew, *The Economy of Obligation: The Culture of Credit and Social Relations in Early Modern England* (Basingstoke, 1998), 333.

takes no trust, either by wholesale or by retail... is not yet born, or if there were ever such, they are all dead.'[16]

Another historian who has alerted us to the importance of understanding the origins of modern economic practice is Margot Finn. In her study of the evolution of credit practices in eighteenth- to early twentieth-century England she suggests that the modern concept of economic man as an autonomous individual motivated by material interest and bound by contract emerged only slowly from a quite different set of representations. She shows that for most of the eighteenth and nineteenth centuries a lot of retail trade was carried on through credit, which 'made a degree of mutual trust integral to buying and selling'. Retailers and purchasers were 'bound... in networks of mutual lending that encouraged all parties to surround their contractual agreements with a scaffolding of extra-legal customs, obligations and expectations'. Since not all transactions could take place between people who knew each other well, 'creditors sought constantly and unsuccessfully to read debtors' personal worth and character from their clothing, their marital relations, their spending patterns and their perceived social status, attempting to assign stable cash values to consumers in markets continuously buffeted by the vagaries of credit'. Those anxious to consume but lacking the necessary wherewithal would take care to project a personality that 'drew upon the perceived verities of social capital rather than upon the monetary values of the cash nexus alone'.[17]

One famous literary example of the paradoxical results of such a financial-social calculus is Rawdon Crawley, from Thackeray's *Vanity Fair*, who 'lived comfortably on credit. He had a large capital of debts, which, laid out judiciously, will carry a man along for many years, and on which certain men contrive to live a hundred times better than even men with ready money can do.'[18]

Muldrew and Finn have shown that modern impersonal, rational *homo economicus* has emerged from a complex evolution of expectations embedded in societies which were hierarchical, clientelistic and 'prejudiced', and whose members were extremely attentive to nuances of personal behaviour.

It remains true that most historians have not yet built trust as a crucial determining factor into their studies of social evolution. There are, however, two whose work I have found very useful in trying to understand the role trust has played in past societies, by directing our attention away

[16] From Daniel Defoe, *The Compleat English Tradesman*, quoted in Muldrew, *Economy of Obligation*, 95.
[17] Margot C. Finn, *The Character of Credit: Personal Debt in English Culture, 1740–1914* (Cambridge, 2003), 21, 95, 320.
[18] Thackeray, *Vanity Fair*, ch. 17.

from vertical power-based relationships articulated in juridical documents to horizontal, community-based relationships articulated in non-verbal customary practices. They are Susan Reynolds, for the middle ages, and Peter Blickle, for the early modern period.

Susan Reynolds contends that in our accounts of what most historians call 'feudal society' we have tended to overemphasise power relationships and the boundaries between hierarchical social categories. We have been unduly influenced by lawyers seeking retrospectively to justify authoritarian social relationships by drawing up documents based on Roman or canon law, which drew too sharply the demarcation between rulers and ruled. She suggests that parishes, village communities, guilds and lay fraternities had their own forms of internal solidarity which were not necessarily laid down in written form. Writing of guilds and fraternities, she argues that

> they relied first and foremost on affective bonds, modelled on the ideal of sibling relationship or monastic community, reinforced by oaths, and maintained by the collective jurisdiction over their members that all collective groups tended to assume . . . They would drink together, swear solidarity and pledge themselves to mutual good works. Above all, they would do for one another the one act of mercy that everyone needed, by giving each other honourable burial and a helping hand into the next world.[19]

As for villages, she proposes that they

> acted collectively in running their agriculture, their parish churches and fraternities, their local government and perhaps a good deal more besides. Many of the groups seem to have consisted of peasants, both free and unfree, who were united partly by subjection to the same lordship, but partly by their common rights and duties as farmers, parishioners and neighbours.[20]

In general, between 900 and 1300, she asserts

> that lay society and government depended in a mass of different ways on the collective activities of a wide range of people; that this activity was undertaken as a matter of course in support of government, as well as in opposition to it; and that in all its aspects it reveals a very homogeneous set of values, which combined acceptance of inequality and subordination with a high degree of voluntary cooperation.[21]

The implication of her account is that trust, directed both horizontally and vertically, played a greater role in medieval society than we have commonly realised.

Writing of a later period, Peter Blickle likewise finds the terms used to describe social change in early modern Europe – feudalism, absolutism, capitalism – insufficient. He proposes a fourth to complement them: communalism. Most villages as well as towns, he points out, had their own

---

[19] Susan Reynolds, *Kingdoms and Communities in Western Europe, 900–1300*, Oxford, 1984, 77–8.
[20] *Ibid.*, 152.
[21] *Ibid.*, 332.

standardised institutions and procedures for keeping the peace, promoting the common weal, distributing dues and obligations and ensuring that each household had its own subsistence – what the Germans called *Hausnotdurft*: sufficiency according to its size and function. Certain values underlay these practices: tradition, right behaviour, fairness, natural law, God's law. At most times these values could be promoted in cooperation with feudal lords or the agents of the absolutist state, but at certain times both rural and urban communities acted together to defend them from encroachment by superiors, either through collective petitions or on occasion through armed resistance.[22] Blickle specifically argues that communalism 'harmonised extremely well with the New Testament notion of love for one's fellow man' and so played a major role in generating the rural and urban unrest in southern and western Germany in the 1520s. 'What made the reformation so dangerous was the fact that theologians were playing dangerously with the social movement of communalism, and this compelled the princes to take a stand against the communal reformation.'[23]

'Communalism', then, implies that, in Blickle's words,

> the community has the right to determine its own internal regulations, its own administration and judicial institutions, that the fulfilment of everyday needs and the preservation of peace within and without are communally organised and that all members of the community are equally obliged to observe the legal norms which they entail and are also empowered to enforce them as rights rooted in the locality.[24]

Compared with social scientists, historians have two great advantages when approaching questions of trust. The first is that they do not examine economies, political structures or social welfare systems in isolation: they are interested in whole societies. Western economists working in the former Soviet Union in the 1990s were probably excellent economists, but they did not seem able to place their economic counsel in a wider context, to see that measures which promote growth in one society will stifle it in another, or even endanger the social fabric. An economy is part of a web of inter-relationships which make up society as a whole. Historians are better placed than most social scientists to study the entirety of that web.

---

[22] Peter Blickle, 'Kommunalismus: Begriffsbildung in heuristischer Absicht', in *Landgemeinde und Stadtgemeinde in Mitteleuropa: ein struktureller Vergleich*, ed. Blickle (Munich, 1991), 5–38; see also his 'Introduction' and 'Conclusions', in *Resistance, Representation and Community*, ed. Blickle (Oxford, 1997), 1–4, 325–38. Other papers in this volume develop these themes at some length; see especially Hugues Neveux and Eva Österberg, 'Norms and Values', 155–215.

[23] Peter Blickle, *Communal Reformation: The Quest for Salvation in Sixteenth-Century Germany*, trans. Thomas Dunlap (New Jersey, 1992), 181, 184.

[24] Peter Blickle, 'Kommunalismus, Parlamentarismus, Republikanismus', *Historische Zeitschrift*, 242 (1986), 535.

Secondly, historians locate their studies in the flow of time. A social problem is not like a chess problem, where the previous moves needed to reach the position on the board are irrelevant to the solution. Societies are composed of people whose mentality and outlook have been constituted by their previous life experience and that of those around them. Their future actions will be strongly, perhaps decisively, influenced by that experience. It is vital, then, when studying any society, to know what social actors' past was and to understand how they reacted to it.

In principle, then, historians could be useful in providing an insight into the different ways in which trust functions in different societies, and in which social cohesion is or is not sustained. Yet actually, when I look at what most of my colleagues are doing, with exceptions mentioned above, I have to admit that the generation of peace and stability is not high among their priorities. To take just one simple example: far more studies have been written of the breakdown of the Weimar Republic before 1933 than of the establishment of the German Federal Republic after 1945. Yet the latter is the more unusual and remarkable story, and understanding it at least as important to us today. Nowadays we have histories of many things: war and revolution, political power, ethnic and national identity, economic development, the family, gender, religion and so on. But not of trust – and its opposite, distrust – which partly underlie all these phenomena.

Trust is not an invariant entity, present in different societies at the same level and in the same forms. On the contrary both its incidence and its social forms vary greatly. Some societies seem peaceful and stable, and their members relate to each other without acute or chronic distrust for generations; other societies are riven by apparently unceasing distrust, so that conflict between individuals or groups is always either present or latent, ready to break out at the slightest provocation. No society can survive, however, on a diet of total distrust. As Adam Smith once said, 'Society . . . cannot subsist among those who are at all times ready to hurt and injure one another . . . If there is any society among robbers and murderers, they must at least . . . abstain from robbing and murdering one another.'[25] Furthermore, the transition from widespread trust to widespread distrust can take place remarkably quickly during, for example, an economic crisis, or a period of ethnic strife. As the post-Yugoslav wars broke out in the early 1990s the Croat writer Dubravka Ugrešić noted with alarm 'the terrifying speed with which all [her] colleagues change colour, flag, symbols, the genres of oral and written confession with which they cleanse themselves of Communism and Yugoslavism' in order to take up their new identity of Serbs and Croats,

25 Adam Smith, *Theory of Moral Sentiments* (Oxford, 1976), 86.

denouncing each other.[26] The result was a drastic hardening of identity and narrowing of trust, characteristic of a community faced with great danger.

The opposite can also be true; as John Plumb remarked in the preface to one of the few historical works which explicitly aims to explain the onset of social cohesion: 'Political stability, when it comes, often happens to a society quite quickly, as suddenly as water becomes ice.'[27] The association of freezing is perhaps unfortunate, but the physical metaphor of a critical stage where social molecules rearrange themselves quite rapidly in a different and more stable configuration is suggestive and I think appropriate for certain junctures in the history of societies.

The valuable work that sociologists have done on trust is not strongly based historically. They usually study only the modern world, and they confine themselves to a broad distinction between forms of trust in pre-modern and modern societies. Anthony Giddens, for example, posits that in pre-modern societies trust reposed in kinship and local community, and was backed up by tradition and by a religious cosmology. Kinship and local community offered 'a nexus of reliable social connections', which inevitably involved tension and conflict between persons, but were 'very generally bonds which could be relied upon in the structuring of actions in fields of time-space'. Tradition offered continuity and habit which removed the necessity for complex calculations in unfamiliar contingencies, while religious cosmology provided a framework for explaining events and situations and suggesting responses, as well as 'moral and practical interpretations of personal and social life . . . , which represented an environment of security for the believer'. Together these mechanisms presented a way of coping with risk and uncertainty. In general, then, traditional trust was personal, moral and limited in radius.[28]

In modern societies, on the other hand, according to Giddens, the interchanges of kinship and local community have been largely replaced by more long-distance, impersonal and instrumental interchanges which take place in the context of institutions having their own procedures and practices. Trust is projected over extended time and space and is placed in systems; it 'takes the form of faceless commitments, in which faith is sustained in the workings of knowledge of which the lay person is largely ignorant'. Religious cosmology and tradition have largely been supplanted by 'reflexively organised knowledge, governed by empirical observation and logical thought and focused upon material technology

---

[26] Dubravka Ugrešić, *The Culture of Lies*, trans. Celia Hawkesworth (University Park, PA, 1998), 42.

[27] J. H. Plumb, *The Growth of Political Stability in England, 1675–1725* (London, 1967), xvii.

[28] Giddens, *Consequences of Modernity*, 100–6.

and socially applied codes'. Modern trust, in short, is impersonal, instrumental and much broader in radius.[29]

Giddens's generalisations about pre-modern and modern societies are useful rules of thumb, but, as historians will realise, the nature of kin, of local community, religions and traditions has been almost infinitely diverse. For the historian perhaps the most useful sociological approach to trust is that adopted by the Polish sociologist Barbara Misztal, who treats it as a 'habitus', in Bourdieu's sense, that is, as a constituent of a socially learned environment, and therefore as something whose nature changes from one society to another. She sees trust as 'a protective mechanism relying on everyday routines, stable reputations and tacit memories, which together push out of modern life fear and uncertainty as well as moral problems'.[30] Actually, in my view trust is not quite as effective as that, but Misztal's emphasis rightly suggests that the historian has an important function, in elucidating how routines, reputations and memories have been generated in particular societies, and what their effect is on people's perceptions and behaviours.

Everyday routines and habits are a crucial aspect of trust. They reduce social complexity, enabling us to function 'on auto-pilot' for much of our life, and so they save our effort and attention for the unfamiliar and challenging. Families, friends and work colleagues develop familiar practices which simplify mutual interaction and construct a community identity, consisting of those people with whom we feel most at ease and with whom we communicate most readily.[31] By the same token those practices delineate boundaries separating the 'in-group' from the 'out-group'. Trust and distrust exist in mutual symbiosis.

Memory bolsters and enlarges the sphere of routine and habit. It creates and sustains the sense of collective identity. It 'reduces the complexity and restricts the uncertainty of our social environment. Individuals seek to impose legibility on the irregularities in institutions and values, and thus provide for the comprehension and continuity of their historical experience.'[32] For that reason, all societies, even those which aim to build a wholly new world, like France after 1789 or Russia after 1917, seek a past to attach themselves to and create myths, symbols and rituals which evoke that past – as France did under Napoleon and Russia under Stalin.[33]

[29] Ibid., 88, 109.
[30] Misztal, Trust, 102.
[31] Ibid., 105–11.
[32] Ibid., 139–56; quote on 139.
[33] Maurice Agulhon, Marianne into Battle: Republican Imagery and Symbolism in France, 1789–1880, trans. Janet Lloyd (Cambridge, 1981), 32–4, 182–4; Richard Stites, Revolutionary Dreams: Utopian Vision and Experimental Life in the Russian Revolution (Oxford, 1989); David Brandenberger, National Bolshevism: Stalinist Mass Culture and the Formation of Modern Russian National Identity, 1931–1956 (Cambridge, MA, 2002).

The good reputation of a leader, a military commander, a business company, a lawyer or doctor likewise generates trust, by enhancing the probability that expectations will be met and thereby creating a stable environment. Reputation is built up gradually, from an accumulation of events and actions. In a face-to-face society, it is the subject of frequent gossip and exchange of opinion; in societies where contact is less direct it is formalised in procedures like letters of reference or checks of creditworthiness.[34]

There is not only one kind of pre-modern configuration of trust, then, but a great variety of different kinds, corresponding to different social structures. Their nature can change quite fast. Breakdowns of trust are especially abrupt, and the historical literature is full of them. However, in the spirit of Plumb, as quoted above, I would like to suggest six conjunctures in European history, when I believe trust broadened relatively rapidly, to create new kinds of social cohesion. Very often these were societies in which significant economic growth had recently taken place, but which faced particular threats or dangers, which could be adequately met only by creating institutions embodying new and broader forms of trust.

1. Athens of the late sixth century, like other Greek communities, had been basically a tribal society. However, its growing wealth and the diverse networks of trade it had built up increasingly divided the rich and the poor from each other, especially since those who fell into debt became slaves to their creditors. This polarisation not only generated serious social conflict, but also weakened the city's defences, since slaves could not serve in the army. Customs and forms of trust appropriate to tribal society, where there was no such gap between rich and poor, were sapping the vitality of a great trading city. The reforms of Solon redrew the property-owning map by forgiving debt, freeing indebted slaves, redeeming their land and forbidding future debt bondage. Those of Cleisthenes, some decades later, reconstituted the tribes on a geographical basis, so that they formed the constituencies for a new kind of rule, the polis or city-state, governed by its own citizens, rather than by tribal leaders or tyrants. These reforms represent the stage when Athenian society moved from the forms of trust associated with tribal society to those appropriate to a city-state, where one had to accept, tolerate and work with people quite outside one's kin, of very different wealth and social status. They laid the foundations for Athens's prosperity and her extraordinary culture over the next couple of centuries.[35]

34 Misztal, Trust, 120–39.
35 Philip Brooks Manville, The Origins of Citizenship in Ancient Athens (Princeton, 1990); Christian Meier, The Greek Discovery of Politics (Cambridge, MA, 1990); Simon Hornblower, 'The Creation and Development of Democratic Institutions in Ancient Greece', in Democracy: The Unfinished Journey, 508BC–AD 1993 (Oxford, 1993), 1–16.

2. Rome of the first century BC was in a state of chronic crisis caused by the incapacity of city-state institutions to cope with governing what by then had become a far-flung empire. A few oligarchs enriched themselves through colonial plunder, while much of the population was poverty-stricken. A former soldier might return after giving of his best in Rome's wars to discover that an oligarch had bought up his farm and evicted his family. Much of the power in the state had devolved to military leaders who each took a province as a base and used their wealth to provide for these impoverished soldiers, turning them into clients in private armies. Those warlords were powerful because the soldiers invested their trust in them. When Augustus seized power he outbid the warlords by converting the army from a citizen one into a professional one, using his own immense wealth and that of the Roman treasury to pay for it as well as to endow needy veterans with their own land. He also provided famine relief, municipal works and public entertainments for Rome's own poorest inhabitants. Both soldiers and citizens were able to redirect their trust towards him. Acting as a kind of super-patron, he was able – without admitting it – to supersede the city-state and erect administrative and financial structures capable of governing the empire. His super-patronage enabled Rome finally to bridge the gap between city-state and a huge and diverse territorial empire. This was the basis for the *pax Romana* of the next two centuries or so.[36]

3. The city-states of late medieval Italy were wealthy thanks to industry and trade, especially the maritime ones, Venice and Genoa. But they were faced with a breakdown of public order caused by the weakening power of the Holy Roman Emperor. To protect themselves against destructive aristocratic feuds they formed their own self-defence associations, taking oaths of mutual protection. These associations gave them an intense attachment to their 'commune'. The loyalty and mutual trust thus generated enabled them to experiment with new economic institutions, such as deposit banking, the bill of exchange and the *compagnia*, precursor of the modern corporation. Italian cities also pioneered the floating of long-term loans against the provision of annuities for borrowers. These innovations not only made trade easier; they actually increased it considerably by making it less dependent on coinage. They stimulated the provision of credit – the economic version of trust – and thereby engendered economic growth beyond the bounds set by the limited supply

[36] Michael Crawford, *The Roman Republic*, 2nd edn (London, 1992), chs. 9, 15; P. A. Brunt, *The Fall of the Roman Republic and Related Essays* (Oxford, 1988), 68–81, 240–81; J. B. Campbell, *The Emperor and the Roman Army, 31 BC–AD 235* (Oxford, 1984), 157–76.

of coins.[37] (We should note, of course, that the increased use of credit in an economy also renders it more liable to panics, crises and depressions. Trust is ubiquitous, but it is also fragile.[38])

4. In the fifteenth to seventeenth centuries Italy was replaced as the focus of international credit by the Netherlands, first of all centred in the city of Antwerp, then Amsterdam. Its pre-eminence rested on the growing prosperity of the Dutch economy, especially in agriculture, fishing, shipping and the Baltic maritime trade. Like the Italians, the Dutch had a strong sense of solidarity focused on their municipalities. We may hypothesise that this solidarity was generated by the long defensive battle against the sea, and by the gradual reclaiming of polder land, for which purpose special citizens' associations were set up. This solidarity was certainly intensified by religious conflict with Spain, followed by the long war of independence – nearly eighty years altogether. During this period, which one might have expected to be especially unstable, the Dutch cities developed and extended the technique first devised in Italy: floating large public loans paid back in the form of annuities, which had a first claim on their tax revenue. These proved very attractive to potential lenders, since municipal councils and provincial estates represented the real wealth of the country, and they could not afford to let their credit be undermined. Lending to them was, therefore, more reliable than lending to absolute monarchs. As a result the United Provinces raised a long-term debt which considerably exceeded their annual income.[39]

5. Mid- to late seventeenth-century England suffered from instability engendered by the attempt to impose a European-style absolute monarchy on a nation some of whose structures of trust were intensely local, while others were already supra-national, linking the home-country with overseas colonies. When William III seized power in 1688, the great landowners and city merchants bound him to a constitutional style of rule in which they consented to being seriously taxed in order to establish trustworthy forms of public credit, in return for gaining control over parliament, the army and navy and the fiscal system. For the first time the Italian and Dutch method of raising public loans was fully applied at the level of a large European monarchy, and it could only be done by a constitutional monarchy, whose parliament could render credible the

37 Lauro Martines, *Power and Imagination: City States in Renaissance Italy* (New York, 1980), III; Robert D. Putnam, *Making Democracy Work: Civic Traditions in Modern Italy* (Princeton, 1993), 121–51; Carlo M. Cipolla, *Before the Industrial Revolution: European Society and Economy, 1000–1700*, 3rd edn (London, 1993), 160–4, 179–82.

38 Charles P. Kindleberger, *Manias, Panics and Crashes: A History of Financial Crises* (Basingstoke, 1996).

39 James D. Tracy, *A Financial Revolution in the Habsburg Netherlands: Renten and Renteniers in the County of Holland, 1515–1565* (Berkeley, 1985).

promise to make repayment the first charge on the public revenues. The result was what the historian John Brewer has called the 'military-fiscal state', far more efficient than its great rival France at raising both taxes and loans, so that with more modest resources it was able to mobilise much greater economic power for war-making purposes.[40] Forms of trust came into being which subsequently underlay both the nation-state and the capitalist economy.

6. After 1945 it was clear that the kind of solidarity which focused on the nation-state, while it had mobilised unprecedented human resources, had also brought unparalleled destruction and death to millions in Europe and Asia. It seemed imperative to set up international institutions which would prevent nationalism getting out of hand again and enable nations to work together – to create in fact global structures of trust. That was the purpose of the United Nations, the Bretton Woods currency agreement, the International Monetary Fund, the World Bank and the General Agreement on Tariffs and Trade. The USA also distributed Marshall Aid, mostly in the form of grants, to European countries, to help them overcome post-war economic dislocation and establish stable constitutional political systems. Meanwhile the Europeans themselves were beginning to create supra-national institutions, first the Coal and Steel Community, then Euratom, then the European Economic Community, which has evolved into the European Union of today. The express aim of its founders was to break down distrust between nations, and thereby to eliminate war as an instrument of state policy and also to lay the basis for a more prosperous world.[41]

In each of my six examples of trust-broadening, operations involving money played a key role. This is not accidental. It may make sense to regard money as the key symbol of the modes of trust existing in any given society. This was the major insight of the sociologist Georg Simmel, in his work *The Philosophy of Money*, first published just over a century ago. Money makes possible the exchange of infinitely diverse goods and services, which are an essential part of the life of any society. It can take many forms, from sheep or corrie shells through coins and bills of exchange to electronically mediated credit. But it always both presupposes a measure of social trust – consensus that a monetary unit has a certain value and will continue

[40] Dickson, *Financial Revolution*; Niall Ferguson, *The Cash Nexus: Money and Power in the Modern World, 1700–2000* (London, 2001), ch. 4; Douglass C. North and Barry R. Weingast, 'Constitutions and Commitment: The Evolution of Institutions Governing Public Choice in 17th Century England', *Journal of Economic History*, 49, no. 4 (Dec. 1989), 803–32; John Brewer, *The Sinews of Power: War, Money and the English State, 1688–1783* (London, 1989); Patrick K. O'Brien, 'Fiscal Exceptionalism: Great Britain and its European Rivals from Civil War to Triumph at Trafalgar and Waterloo', in *The Political Economy of British Historical Experience, 1688–1914*, ed. Donald Winch and Patrick K. O'Brien (Oxford, 2002), 245–66.

[41] Tony Judt, *Postwar: A History of Europe since 1945* (London, 2005), esp. ch. 8.

to have it – and also confirms and extends that trust. One might add that money, being neutral, precisely calculable and infinitely fungible, represents the ideal symbol of the impersonal and instrumental forms of trust that exist in the modern world. This was the characteristic of money which led Karl Marx to complain that 'The bourgeoisie, whenever it has got the upper hand, has put an end to all feudal, patriarchal, idyllic relations . . . and has left remaining no other nexus between man and man than naked self-interest, than callow cash payment.'[42]

Another feature of my six examples is that in all except the second a broader institutional basis was created for the input of ordinary people into public life and politics. Even in the Roman case it could be argued that the taming of the warlords of the late republican period, even by autocratic means, made it easier for both patricians and plebs to feed their aspirations and grievances into the political process. As societies become more complex, it is evidently crucial that they find a way of involving people of different status and function in tackling common problems. Without that involvement, certain categories of the population feel permanently excluded, without a legitimate and acknowledged way of influencing their own life chances. In that way trust is undermined and social conflict, potential or actual, is built into the system.

To conclude, then, I believe that one of the major challenges standing before historians today is to delineate the forms of trust which have existed in the past and to use those forms to interpret the discourses and practices of any given society. Without such interpretation we lack tools to understand cardinal features of social structure, since trust is crucially involved in fundamental social phenomena.

Let me finally essay one speculative hypothesis. As we have seen above, at least four of the six historical conjunctures where social cohesion has rapidly crystallised was preceded by an act of economic generosity or of extremely enlightened economic self-interest which had the effect of rather suddenly broadening the radius of economic trust.

Today's global economic order was a great achievement in its time, after 1945. It now operates, however, in such a manner that it manifestly undermines trust between different nations, and especially between the affluent western (in part east Asian) world and the rest. Just as one example: the affluent nations, and the international financial institutions they dominate, expect developing ones to operate a free market policy and to open their economies fully to international trade. But they protect the vulnerable sectors of their own economies – agriculture, textiles, steel – from the competition which such free trade implies.[43] Both within and between nations, the systems of trust I have outlined above will only

[42] *Manifesto of the Communist Party* (Moscow, n.d.), 52.
[43] Stiglitz, *Globalization*.

operate successfully provided they are not seen to promote blatant injustice. Rebellions and wars break out when trust is clearly seen to be abused. A history of trust is of necessity also a history of distrust.

If we want to create a more stable global order and a more prosperous global economy, the world's rich nations need to attempt some act of economic generosity or enlightenment, analogous to those outlined above, whether it lies in debt forgiveness, aid, redistribution of income or the opening of frontiers to trade and labour. Either globalised trust becomes more real, or distrust continues to break out in ever more virulent forms at the next level down, the nationalist movement or the international religious fraternity. That is the pattern the history of trust suggests, and it is being played out before us today.

Using the concept of trust also helps us to understand the greatest obstacle to such steps of economic enlightenment. Nowadays in advanced western societies we place our trust in institutions connected with the operations of money, and these will only work well where there is continuous economic growth. Where we used to look to family, local community or religious institutions to help us face life's risks, today we depend on state welfare, savings banks, insurance policies and pension funds. On the whole, it must be said, this works better, or at least more predictably. But it has a downside. Since insurance companies and pension funds are obliged to invest where they can find the highest return, 'shareholder value' dominates the outlook of business enterprises. When it falters our pensions are at risk. It is extremely difficult for national economies run on this basis to act generously or even with intelligent foresight towards the world around them.

The more we place our trust in institutions whose *raison d'être* is monetary operations, the more we reshape our social lives according to the standards set by those operations. Because money is a universal and neutral instrument with a precise, calculable value, it tends to reduce all our social actions to a series of quantitatively conceived means without ends and without autonomous significance.[44] It favours those who, in Oscar Wilde's words, 'know the price of everything and the value of nothing'. That is the situation we increasingly find ourselves in today in the globalised world. Even relationships between sub-units of companies and institutions tend to be mediated in monetary terms, and therefore justified in those terms too. For that reason the practices of accountants, auditors and corporate lawyers determine much of the routine of our professional lives, imposing on us forms to fill in, reports to write and targets to meet, for it is they who will pronounce on whether or not we are providing 'value for money'. In this way, as Onora O'Neill showed in

[44] Simmel, *Philosophy of Money*, 431.

her Reith Lectures, efforts to bolster trust in practice generate distrust.[45] We feel that 'the imitation of activity is squeezing out real activity' – to quote the Russian philosopher Alexander Zinoviev, who ironically was describing the Soviet planned economy, not contemporary globalised capitalism.[46] Activities which cannot be codified and assessed in the appropriate auditorial and juridical templates are perceived as lacking in genuine substance.

In brief, then, I believe that examining the way trust has worked in different societies can provide a way in towards investigating problems which are otherwise difficult to conceptualise adequately. That is a good reason for suggesting that historians should ask more systematic questions about the operations of trust. This essay has aimed to offer a few hypotheses as an impulse towards asking those questions.

[45] See also Power, *The Audit Society*, and Kieron O'Hara, *Trust from Socrates to Spin* (Cambridge, 2004), ch. 9.

[46] Alexander Zinov'ev, *Ziaiushchie vysoty* (Lausanne, 1976), 191–3.

Transactions of the RHS 16 (2006), pp. 117–41 © 2006 Royal Historical Society
doi:10.1017/S0080440106000442   Printed in the United Kingdom

WITCHCRAFT AND THE WESTERN IMAGINATION*

By Lyndal Roper

READ 28 JANUARY 2005

ABSTRACT. This essay proposes a new view of demonology, arguing that it was not just a set of theological and legal writings but could also form part of a literature of entertainment. Demonologists frequently used literary techniques such as the dialogue form, hyperbolic set-piece descriptions of the dance or the Sabbath, told stories to pique the reader's interest, and employed humour, salaciousness and horror. Their work intersected with that of artists, influenced by classical images of witches, who began to produce elaborate panoramas of the Sabbath. The cultural legacy of demonology was immense. Through the *Faustbuch* of 1587, which borrowed from demonological treatises, demonology influenced drama and even figured in the development of the early novel.

I

Jan Ziarnko's image of the Witches' Sabbath accompanies one of the strangest works to be inspired by the European witch-hunt, the *Tableau d'inconstance des mauvais anges et démons* (1612), by Pierre de Lancre (Figure 1). At the heart of the book, where de Lancre describes the Sabbath, the reader can fold out Ziarnko's extraordinary detailed poster-size image, the visual counterpart of de Lancre's literary evocation of the sights, sounds and smells of the Sabbath. We read of the ritual meal where witches eat bread made of black flour, ground from the bones of unbaptised children, or they stew 'unbaptised baby hearts, the flesh of the hanged, and other horrible decaying carcasses'. Piling on the metaphors in sentences that barely pause for breath, de Lancre describes a Sabbath which resembles a giant marketplace of rotten, stinking organs and liquids in a literary tour de force which seems to have little to do with conventional demonology.[1] Ziarnko's tableau, produced for the second edition of the work in 1613,

---

* This essay is dedicated to the memory of Gareth Roberts. I am grateful to Robin Briggs, Stuart Clark, Jonathan Durrant, Ruth Harris, Clive Holmes, Erik Midelfort, David Parrott, Amy Wygant, the various audiences who heard and commented on earlier drafts, and especially to Nick Stargardt for their help in writing this essay.

[1] 'On y voit de grandes chaudieres pleines de crapaux et impres, coeurs d'infants non baptisez, chair de pendus, & autres horribles charonges, & des eaux puantes, pots de graisse et de poison, qui se preste & se debite a cette foire, comme estant las plus precieuse & commune marchandise qui s'y trouve.' Ziarnko's image faces 118, Pierre de Lancre, *Tableau*

Figure 1 Jan Ziarnko, 'Description et figure du sabbat', in Pierre de Lancre, *Tableau de l'inconstance des mauvais anges et démons*, 2nd edn (Paris, 1613) [British Library 719.i.11], facing p. 118. By permission of the British Library.

maps each chilling detail, and there is even an alphabetic key so that the viewer can locate every horror. Word and image join in a single assault

---

de l'inconstance des mauvais anges et démons, 2nd edn (Paris, 1613); and for a brilliant discussion of the text see Margaret M. McGowan, 'Pierre de Lancre's *Tableau de l'inconstance des mauvais anges et démons*: The Sabbat Sensationalised', in *The Damned Art. Essays in the Literature of Witchcraft*, ed. Sidney Anglo (1977).

on readers' senses as they confront the nightmare world of the demonic gathering. The description of the Sabbath forms the climax of de Lancre's work, and it brings together the themes that fascinated him throughout his literary career. He had been involved in hunting witches in the border region of Labourd, and the idea of illusion, the changeability of all things and the limits of belief obsessed him in all his writings.[2]

With De Lancre's description of the Sabbath, demonology was hijacked for literary effect. Yet extravagant as his creations appear to be, they exploit a possibility that had always lain at the core of writings about witches and the Devil from the fifteenth through the seventeenth centuries. Demonology is often regarded as a science of evil, a corpus of publications that systematised belief about witches, providing the intellectual underpinning of the witch-hunt. Stuart Clark, who has done more to illuminate this body of writings than any scholar, has pointed out that demonology was never a genre with defined boundaries, but derived its cultural authority from its capacity to infiltrate differing kinds of writing.[3] In this essay I shall take Clark's argument a step further, proposing that demonology did not limit itself to mapping the witchhunter's intellectual belief-structure, but contributed to a new literature of entertainment. The cultural legacy of demonology reaches through the Faust of 1587 and beyond, to the origins of the German novel.

Commonly viewed as a branch of theology, philosophy and metaphysics, historians tend to regard demonology as a set of arguments that provided the intellectual framework for witchcraft belief, and which presented the world as a set of binary opposites, of good opposed to evil, white to black and male to female. But demonology was also a Pandora's box, an imaginative resource which inspired drama, art, literature and other cultural forms, occasionally in directions which led to moral ambiguity and doubt. One reason why it has been so difficult for historians to appreciate the role of entertainment, creativity and humour in the literature of demonology has been the knowledge that beliefs about witches that were formalised in works like these led to the deaths of hundreds of individuals. It is hard to see such works as anything other than dangerous and pathological.

---

[2] Pierre de Lancre, *Tableau de l'inconstance et instabilité de toutes choses* (Paris, 1607; 2nd edn Paris, 1610); *idem, L'incredulité et mescreance du sortilege plainement conuaincue* (Paris, 1622). The confessions on the other side of the Spanish border in the same panic were also very elaborate: see Gustav Henningsen, *The Salazar Documents. Inquisitor Alonso de Salazar Frias and Others on the Basque Witch Persecution* (Leiden, 2004); Gustav Henningsen, *The Witches' Advocate. Basque Witchcraft and the Spanish Inquisition (1609–1614)* (Reno, 1980); Julio Caro Baroja, *The World of the Witches*, trans. Nigel Glendinning (1964).

[3] Stuart Clark, *Thinking with Demons. The Idea of Witchcraft in Early Modern Europe* (Oxford, 1997).

Such an approach to writings about witches would be misconceived, however. Beliefs trigger aggression only when they fit with other anxieties and conditions; often, they lie dormant in the mind, the contents of which are very far from being a set of coherent arguments. This is one reason why witch-hunting was characteristically episodic, striking particular areas at moments of crisis, and leaving others untouched. From the outset, demonology teased the imagination. Its intellectual problematic, too, circled around the issue of the nature of the imaginative faculty, the realm of illusion and the power of the senses, all questions central to the nature of art itself. Not for nothing did the most famous fifteenth-century work of demonology, the *Malleus Maleficarum*, embark on a long disquisition on sensory illusion, how perception works, changeability and fantasy in its opening pages:

> For fancy or imagination is as it were the treasury of ideas received through the senses. And through this it happens that devils so stir up the inner perceptions, that is the power of conserving images, that they appear to be a new impression at that moment received from exterior things.[4]

II

The close connection between literature and demonology is evident in the fact that Jean Bodin's treatise on witchcraft was translated just a year after its appearance in the original French by the German poet and literary genius Johannes Fischart of Strasbourg. Fischart had already translated Rabelais's masterpeice *Gargantua and Pantagruel*, extending and elaborating the original to produce a German prose epic in its own right, twice the size.[5] Bodin's original had been composed in French rather than Latin, and it and *The Six Books of the Commonwealth* were his only works composed in the vernacular: clearly, *Démonomanie des sorciers* aimed at a wide market. It has an appendix designed to demolish the arguments of the witch-sceptic Johannes Weyer, but intellectual ambition often seems little more than a

---

[4] Early on in the work, he considers why it is that a man can walk along a narrow beam when it is stretched across the street, but cannot do so if it were suspended over deep water: 'because his imagination would most strongly impress upon his mind the idea of falling': Heinrich Kramer and James Sprenger, *The Malleus Maleficarum*, trans. and ed. Rev. Montague Summers (1928; New York, 1971) [hereafter cited as *Malleus*], 13 (pt I qu. 2). There is a long passage on fascination, the gaze and perception. The discussion of the imagination is on 50 (pt I qu. 7).

[5] Jean Bodin, *Vom Außgelaßnen Wütigen Teuffels heer Allerhand Zauberern/ Hexen vnd Hexenmeistern/ Vnholden/ Teuffelsbeschwerern/ Warsagern...*, trans. Johann Fischart (Strasbourg, 1581) (other editions are known from 1586 and 1591); the French original appeared at Paris in 1580 as *De la Démonomanie des sorciers*. Francois Rabelais, *Affenteurliche und Ungeheuerliche Geschichtschrift von...Herrn Grandgusier, Gargantoa und Pantagruel*, trans. Johann Fischart (Strasbourg, 1575). See Stefan Janson, *Jean Bodin, Johann Fischart: De la démonomanie des sorciers (1580), Vom ausgelaßnen wütigen Teuffelsheer (1581) und ihre Fallberichte* (Frankfurt am Main, 1980) (= Europäische Hochschulschriften 352).

fig-leaf to conceal Bodin's desire to titillate, to explore the exotic and to reveal the intimate workings of the imagination. Bodin relates the dreams of his 'friend', almost certainly the author himself, which featured red and white horses; and the 'friend' was visited nightly by a good spirit advising him how to act in daily life.[6] We hear what Bodin discovered about the art of 'tying the codpiece knot' so as to cause impotence, when he was lodging at the house of a French noblewoman whose name he piquantly refuses to disclose. We read of witches in Africa, and lycanthropy in Europe. And we discover how Bodin had been a guest at another household during travelling assizes when a visiting beggar, in reality a witch, had cursed the entire household, him included.[7] This book is far more than an intellectual treatise, and Bodin by turns fascinates us with his candour about his own experience, dreams and emotional dilemmas; sweeps us away with a flood of anecdotes and uncanny stories; and dazzles us with a welter of brilliant demolitions of sceptical arguments. Nor is he above the crudely salacious. So we are told how

> In a convent there was a dog people said was a demon, which lifted up the dresses of the nuns to abuse them. It was not a demon, in my opinion, but a normal dog. At Toulouse there was a woman who indulged in this abuse, and the dog tried to violate her in front of everyone.[8]

Writing like this is pornographic, drawing on staple anti-monastic, misogynist fable with little relevance to Bodin's ostensible argument. But it was just the kind of thing that would appeal to Fischart, the author of a poem in which the author imagines himself a flea, crawling around women's private parts.[9]

Yet Bodin also stands four-square in the tradition of demonology. His chosen four-part structure, with a final book devoted – broadly – to the trial and punishment of witches, was loosely modelled on the design of the infamous *Malleus Maleficarum* of 1486, by then a classic a century old. The *Hammer of Witches*, written by the infamous Dominican Heinrich Kramer, has been credited by some with having caused the witch craze, though

---

[6] Jean Bodin, *On the Demon-Mania of Witches*, trans. and abridged Randy Scott (Toronto 1995), 59–62, bk 1 ch. 2. See, on this passage, Robin Briggs, 'Dubious Messengers: Bodin's Daemon, the Spirit World, and the Sadducees', in *Angels in the Early Modern World*, ed. Peter Marshall and Alex Walsham (Cambridge, forthcoming).

[7] Bodin, *Démonomanie*, fos. 7r–14 v; Bodin, *Vom Außgelaßnen*, 61–82, bk 1 ch. 2 (dreams); Bodin, *Démonomanie*, fos. 58r–9v (codpiece); Bodin, *Démonomanie*, fos. 94v–104r; Bodin, *Vom Außgelaßnen*, 343–64, bk 2 ch. 6 (lycanthropy); Bodin, *Démonomanie*, fos. 123v–127v; Bodin, *Vom Außgelaßnen*, 426–30, bk 3 ch. 1 (alms).

[8] Bodin, *Démonomanie*, fo. 162r–v; Bodin, *Vom Außgelaßnen*, 537–8; translation from Bodin, *On the Demon-Mania of Witches*, 169, bk 3 ch. 6: Bodin continues to elaborate on this theme; some of his material comes from Weyer. Boguet recycles these stories about dogs, though in brief: Henry Boguet [*sic*], *An Examen of Witches* (French 1590), trans. E. A. Ashwin, ed. Rev. Montague Summers (1929).

[9] Johann Fischart, *Flöh Hatz, Weiber Tratz*, ed. Alois Haas (Stuttgart, 1967; 1982).

it appeared in Latin a hundred years before the major European witch-hunts. It was certainly well known and widely available. Ostensibly an intellectual treatise designed around a series of questions, objections and responses, its appeal has little to do with the force of its arguments. These, as many readers have pointed out, are self-contradictory, illogical and frequently just get dropped as something else captures Kramer's interest.[10] The technique of larding demonology with anecdote was exploited by the *Malleus*, and though it lacks Bodin's flashes of introspection, it also bears the stamp of personal experience. Written in the wake of a failed witchcraft persecution, Kramer was coming to terms with defeat. He responded by magnifying the threat posed to Christian society by witchcraft; and when he referred to what he had seen with his own eyes, he underlined the role of clerics like himself in the ongoing struggle. So he writes about the witch in a place called 'N' who stole a Host and buried it in a pot, and whose crime was discovered when a child's crying was heard. Kramer concludes by advising his fellow priests that women should only receive communion with their tongues well out, and their garments well clear, so that they cannot misuse the sacrament.[11]

The *Malleus* has a picaresque quality that foreshadowed later writings. The rekindling of interest in witchcraft that took place after 1560, when a new and larger wave of persecution began, helped the genre take off, as a clutch of writers like del Rio, Boguet, Daneau, Binsfeld and Rémy developed its potential. Their works are heterogeneous in style – Bodin's rhetorical brilliance has little in common with del Rio's exhaustive categorisation of all the different kinds of magic, or with Guazzo's plodding compilation – and yet they form a recognisable body of work, partly because they are all parasitic on one another. Boguet deals with trials in Franche-Comté but he plunders Rémy's account of Lorraine for all the stories he can find; Bodin borrows liberally from Weyer, whose work he is supposedly attacking, and Guazzo sews stories from Bodin, Rémy and the others into a seamless whole. Some of the borrowings even run counter to confessional belonging. Nearly everyone, Protestant

---

[10] See, for example, Sydney Anglo, 'Evident Authority and Authoritative Evidence: The *Malleus Maleficarum*, in *The Damned Art*, ed. Anglo (1977).

[11] *Malleus*, 116–17, pt II qu. 1 ch. 6. On Kramer, and on his role as sole author, see, in particular, the indispensable introduction, text and notes of *Der Hexenhammer*, ed. Wolfgang Behringer and Günter Jerouschek, trans. Wolfgang Behringer, Günter Jerouschek and Werner Tschacher (Munich, 2000), which is superior to the unreliable translation of Summers; Eric Wilson, 'Institoris at Innsbruck: Heinrich Institoris, the *Summis Desiderantes* and the Brixen Witch-Trial of 1485', in *Popular Religion in Germany and Central Europe, 1400–1800*, ed. Bob Scribner and Trevor Johnson (Houndmills, Basingstoke and London, 1996); Anglo, 'Evident Authority and Authoritative Evidence'; P. G. Maxwell-Stuart, *Witchcraft in Europe and the New World, 1400–1800* (2001); Walter Stephens, *Demon Lovers. Witchcraft, Sex and the Crisis of Belief* (2002); Hans Peter Broedel, *The Malleus Maleficarum and the Construction of Witchcraft. Theology and Popular Belief* (Manchester, 2003).

or Catholic, cited the Dominican *Malleus*. Bodin draws on the Protestant Daneau; while the Jesuit Martin del Rio makes understandably heavy weather of a story he has drawn from Luther about a 'heretic woman' who gave birth to a baby 'vested and tonsured like an ecclesiastic'.[12] They found a ready market across Europe, especially in German-speaking areas: just about every major work of demonology from these decades was published in German or found a German publisher for a local Latin edition.[13]

Not only were the stories predictable; so too were the topics to which the demonologists turned. Practically every demonologist felt compelled to consider the question of whether demons could sire children, and whether changelings were demonic.[14] The outlines of the witchcraft story had become standardised too, with seduction, pact, dance, baptism and Sabbath forming so recognisable a sequence that by the time Guazzo penned his *Compendium*, it was possible to offer an illustrated guide to

[12] Euan Cameron, 'For Reasoned Faith or Embattled Creed? Religion for the People in Early Modern Europe', *Transactions of the Royal Historical Society*, sixth series, 8 (1998), 165–84; plagiarism of Lutheran Gödelmann's attack on Paracelsus by Del Rio, 170, in bk 6. Evidently, Del Rio also knew the demonology of the Calvinist Daneau well enough to set him and Gödelman right on points of detail: Martin del Rio, *Investigations into Magic*, ed. and trans. P. G. Maxwell-Stuart (Manchester, 2000), 135, 213; example taken from Luther, 44.

[13] The market for the *Malleus* was partly among those who had enjoyed a classical education and who read for pleasure – the *Malleus* itself was not translated into German. It was aimed at the upper end of the popular vernacular market, often published in large format. The other classics of demonology were mostly translated into German and went through several editions, as their printing histories show: Lambert Daneau's *De Veneficis* was published in Cologne in 1575 and 1597 with a German version appearing in Frankfurt and Cologne in 1576 (VD16: D77–80); Grillando's *De Sortilegiis* appeared in Latin in 1592 in Frankfurt (VD16: G3344); Jean Bodin's was printed in a Latin translation at Basel in 1581, with Fischart's German translation printed in Strasbourg in 1581, 1586 and 1591; and 1592 in Frankfurt (*Verzeichnis der im deutschen Sprachbereich erschienenen Drucke des XVI. Jahrhunderts* (25 vols., Stuttgart, 1983–2000) (VD16: B6266–72); Rémy's *Demonolatry* was published in Lyon in 1595 in Latin and issued in the following year at Cologne and Frankfurt; a German translation appeared in Frankfurt in 1598 as *Daemonolatria. Das ist Von Unholden und Zaubergeistern*... (VD16: R1090, R1091, R1092, R1093) and was extremely influential in the Holy Roman Empire, possibly even more so than the *Malleus*: Schulte, *Hexenmeister*, 141–3; Peter Binsfeld's *Tractat Von Bekantnuß der Zauberer und Hexen* appeared in German in 1590 (VD16, nos. B5531, B5532); Johannes Georg Gödelmann's Latin work of 1591 appeared in German as *Von Zauberern Hexen und Unholden* translated by Georg Nigrinus at Frankfurt in 1592 (VD16, nos. G2486, G2488); James IV's *Daemonologia* was published in Latin in Hanau in 1604; Martin Del Rio's *Disquisitionum Magicarum Libri Sex* was reprinted in numerous editions in Cologne and Mainz; Pierre de Lancre's work appeared in German in 1630 as *Wunderbahrliche Geheimnußen der Zauberey*... (s.l.) (VD17 12:640907L; there was another edition of the same year, VD17 23: 238328W). Boguet's *Discours des sorciers* was published in at least three editions at Lyons; I have found no records of a German publication of it or of Guazzo's *Compendium* (though copies of Boguet's *Discours des sorciers* and of his *Discours execrable des sorciers*, Rouen, 1603 exist in German libraries); Guazzo's treatise was published in 1608 in Milan and republished there in an extended edition in 1626.

[14] See Lyndal Roper, *Witch Craze. Terror and Fantasy in Baroque Germany* (2004), 98–104.

Figure 2 Cutting up bodies of criminals, Francesco Maria Guazzo, *Compendium maleficarum* (Milan, 1626) [British Library 719.h.8], 149. By permission of the British Library.

witchcraft: his text is adorned with a series of woodcuts of witches in all the familiar lurid scenes, the witches tricked out in contemporary fashionable clothing with Devils to match. These images linger on the repellent: we see children butchered by well-dressed matrons, or pious-looking burghers spitting on the cross. Some owners even had these cheap woodcut images hand-tinted to enhance their appearance (Figures 2 and 3).[15]

Like the images, the stories seem to revel in the gory. Kramer tells us of the midwife of Dann in the diocese of Basel who killed more than forty young children by sticking needles into their skulls as they came out of the womb, or relates a story he heard from 'the Inquisitor of Como' about 'a certain man' who found a congress of women killing his child, drinking its blood and devouring it.[16] Later demonologists readily exploited this kind of writing. Nicolas Rémy describes how two witches disinterred the bodies of two infants, cutting off the right arm, so that 'the finger-tips of

[15] Francesco Maria Guazzo, *Compendium Maleficarum* (Milan, 1608), 106 man and woman roast child; 149 cutting up bodies of criminals. Many of the woodcuts are re-used, some several times: see for example 26, 43; 107, 109.
[16] *Malleus*, 140, pt II qu. 1 ch. 13; 66, pt I qu. 12.

Figure 3 Spitting on the cross, Francesco Maria Guazzo, *Compendium maleficarum* (Milan, 1626) [British Library 719.h.8], 34. By permission of the British Library.

that dismembered limb used to burn with a blue sulphurous flame until they had entirely completed the business which they had in hand; and when the flame was extinguished the fingers would be just as whole and unimpaired as if they had not been providing the tinder for a light' – a ghoulishly vivid description of the so-called Hand of Glory.[17] He goes on to describe children being ripped from the bodies of pregnant women, and the cooking of infant flesh, concluding with a hint of embarrassment, 'But this is perhaps more than enough about a particularly unpleasant subject.'[18] Such writing is certainly designed to shock and appal, and the savouring of vivid details suggests it is also part of the text's attraction, like the horror film and hard-core pornography, which continue to draw on images of violence and dismemberment as entertainment. Then, as now, the subject-matter of witchcraft offers fertile possibilities for such forms

---

[17] Nicolas Rémy, *Demonolatry*, ed. and trans. Montague Summers (1930) 100 (bk II ch. iii); on the hand of glory, see, e.g., A. Roger Ekirch, *At Day's Close* (2005) 41–2: hands of executed criminals were used as candles by thieves to ensure that the household slept while they engaged in robbery.

[18] Rémy, *Demonolatry*, 103 (bk II ch. iii).

of pleasure; what gave it an especial frisson to sixteenth- and seventeenth-century audiences was the possibility that it might be true.

The demonological treatises make infuriating reading because they mix authority of very different kinds. Personal experience, jurists, theologians, the Bible and classical authors are all cited alongside one another as if they offered equivalent proof of the reality of witchcraft. The *Malleus* adopted this technique, and it is to be found in most other demonolgical writers. Classical references were of course part of a general tendency of this period to recuperate the heritage of antiquity; but the possibilities this literature opened up for witchcraft writings were electrifying. For where the Bible offered meagre pickings to those interested in witches – Saul and the Witch of Endor, the injunction in Exodus 'Thou shalt not suffer a witch to live' – the classical tradition featured sorceresses, enchantresses and witches, from Circe to Medea, whose cultural resonances were far broader. Though the *Malleus* carefully distinguishes between classical 'myth' and writers it regards as historians, classical literature provided a treasure-trove of exotic stories about witches that could be mentioned in the same breath as trials in which Kramer had himself participated. So, in one typical passage, Kramer piled up material on witches who could unbewitch from Aquinas and St Bonaventure, adding a story about an unnamed bishop and love magic from the time of Pope Nicholas, going on to mention his own experience in Reichshofen where such crowds flocked to a particular witch that it was worth the local count's while to set up a toll-booth to collect money from the travellers, before embarking on a long story about a 'certain market merchant' of Speyer who was bewitched.[19] These stories in turn became part of demonological tradition, and can be found in Bodin, Guazzo, Boguet and del Rio, where, by the time they were writing, classical references were a badge of learning accepted across Europe. But the result of the mixture of classical references with contemporary cases was disturbing, for it linked the humdrum, poor witch of the time to the much more ambiguous figure of classical literature, snake-haired goddesses or glamorous creatures like Circe. These were sorceresses who resembled alchemists, able to shapeshift or transform one substance into another.[20]

The range of metamorphoses the classical figure of the witch could undergo is evident in a host of images and literary inventions, and in a wide range of contexts, including court masques and *ballets de cour*.[21] One of the most interesting is the remarkable cycle of nearly thirty epic

[19] *Malleus*, pt II qu. 2, 155–64.
[20] Gareth Roberts, *The Languages of Alchemy* (1997).
[21] See Margaret M. McGowan, *L'art du ballet de court en France (1581–1643)* (Paris, 1963): classical witches, such as Circe or Medea, featured; and Stephen Orgel, *The Jonsonian Masque* (Cambridge, MA, 1965), esp. 130–47.

paintings commissioned by Marie de Medici from Rubens and completed between 1626 and 1631, just over a decade after Jan Ziarnko's etching. Unlike a memorial to a male which might be arranged around a series of battles, this cycle is primarily structured around the female life cycle: Marie's marriage, the birth of her son Louis XIII and her maturity and widowhood on the death of Henri IV. The political conflicts of her life and regency are subsumed within the life-cyle narrative. Marie's political significance was centrally determined by her status as wife and mother, and Rubens's bravura modelling of female flesh makes this an extraordinary combination of monumentalism and voluptuousness.[22]

Yet tucked away in this hymn to feminine power are at least three images of witch-like figures. In the Council of the Gods, a fleeing witch-figure with snake-hair can be found on the extreme right, a lighted torch visible through her leg. Near the middle of the cycle, the Felicity of the Regency is crammed with images of fertility and fecundity; three bound figures representing Ignorance, Calumny and Envy are sprawled in the foreground, Envy with the wasted body of the old witch. And in the Conclusion of the Peace, there is a viper at the very centre held by a blind-folded male Fury, while Fraud and Envy cluster alongside, Envy in the form of an old woman with sagging breasts, while on the right, another vice in the shape of an old hag clutches a snake. These are not real witches, but allegorical representations of the dangers faced by the queen.[23] They have a particular pointedness in a cycle that is dedicated to the feminine. They also allow Rubens to make painterly allusions, for the iconography of the nude witch had been made instantly recognisable by the work of artists such as Dürer and Hans Baldung Grien. In imagery like this, the witch-figure can allude to the Furies of Greek Myth, the snake-headed Gorgon of legend, or the emblematic convention of representing Envy as an old hag. The very flexibility of the imagery can even hint at the subterranean connection between snake-headed goddesses and fertility: in sixteenth-century Augsburg, local humanists interested in the town's pre-Roman past unearthed a goddess with snake-hair called Cisa which they identified both as a Medusa and as a goddess of fertility.[24] The witch may be the emissary of Satan, but her significance in paintings or relics like this extends far beyond the clichés of demonology.

---

[22] See *Rubens' Life of Marie de Medici*, ed. Jacques Thuillier and Jacques Foucart, trans. Robert Erich Wolf (New York, 1967), esp. 85–6, 88–9ff; and see plates.

[23] Though the witches may not only have been allegorical: there were rumours that an astrologer who controlled a Devil had predicted Henri IV's death; see McGowan, 'Pierre de Lancre's *Tableau*', 182. On the cycle, see Ronald Forsyth Millen and Robert Erich Wolf, *Heroic Deeds and Mystic Figures. A New Reading of Rubens's Life of Marie de Medici* (Princeton, 1989); Svetlana Alpers, *The Making of Rubens* (New Haven and London, 1995).

[24] See Lyndal Roper, 'The Gorgon of Augsburg', in *Women's Communities*, ed. Susan Broomhall and Stephanie Tarbin (forthcoming).

The figure of the witch was beginning to take on a life of her own. Like the proud owners who had their woodcuts colour-brushed, turning cheap print into collector's item, the demonologists of the sixteenth and seventeenth centuries began to embellish their works with self-consciously writerly techniques. They invented lively dialogue, and tested their literary skills on set-piece descriptions, in particular, of flight, the dance and the Sabbath. These were also the subjects which had established themselves as artistic genre scenes. Sometimes, as in Jan Ziarnko's image of the Sabbath that accompanied de Lancre's text, the point was to clarify the didactic message. But just as de Lancre's writing is bursting with extravagant hyperbole, so too the Sabbath, flight and dance scenes became an opportunity for the artist to show off his skill, presenting half-nude bodies falling from different persectives, using the etching techniques to cram in as much detail as possible, and structuring a complex pictorial panorama where each appalling incident vies for the viewer's attention. Matthaeus Heer's vast etching of Walpurgis Eve (c. 1620) packs every kind of depravity into one broadsheet, aiming at as encyclopaedic an effect as the literary demonologists. Others, like Jacques de Gheyn, strove to recreate the grisly mood of the Sabbath, featuring remote, wild landscapes. These visions, like the literary descriptions, were designed to tease the imagination and stick in the mind.

De Lancre was certainly not the first to exploit the literary potential of the Sabbath. The *Malleus* does not feature a Sabbath, and Kramer does not dwell on the sensation of flight; but Bodin penned an extended passage on the hideous music played at the diabolic dance in his work of 1580. By the time we get to Rémy (1595) we have extensive descriptions of the dreadful sound of the fiddle and bagpipes to be heard at Sabbaths. Descriptions of dancing, which were at first little more than references to the dance, soon expatiated on how Devils danced back to back, condemning the 'whirling dance' of the witches, which made 'people wild and raging, and women to miscarry', or castigating those witches who 'run masked about the streets in their Carnivals of pleasure' (Figure 4)[25] Like other moral campaigners, including the authors of the Devil-books, demonologists often titillated as much as they condemned.[26]

III

The most significant German artistic production of the era of the witch-hunt was the printed story of Faust, which appeared in Frankfurt in 1587 and was based on a popular story about the real Dr Faustus, an

[25] Bodin, *Démonomanie*, fo. 88v; Bodin, *Vom Außgelaßnen*, 308; Rémy, *Demonolatry*, 63.
[26] On the genre of the Devil-books and moralism, see Lyndal Roper, 'Drinking, Whoring and Gorging', in *Oedipus and the Devil* (1984).

Figure 4 Sabbath Dance (H), detail, Jan Ziarnko, 'Description et figure du sabbat', in Pierre de Lancre, *Tableau de l'inconstance des mauvais anges et démons*, 2nd edn (Paris, 1613) [British Library 719.i.11], facing p. 118. By permission of the British Library.

intellectual who reputedly sold his soul to the Devil. It soon became a classic. The year before, another Frankfurt publisher had produced a bumper *Theatre of Witches*, packing seventeen treatises by different authors into a single volume. This publishing venture was evidently modelled on a *Theatre of Devils*, published by another Frankfurt house in 1569 and containing a series of moral tracts laced with humour. Each sin is given its own Devil, from the He-Man Devil to the Trousers Devil, which had lampooned the new fashion for Turkish-style trousers. Hoping to cash in on the vogue for witchcraft-tales, the publisher, Nicolas Basse, and the editor, Abraham Saur, plumped for a motley bunch of demonologists. Some were known sceptics, like Johannes Weyer; some, like Johannes Gödelmann, were sceptical about some aspects of the witch-hunt; others, like Lambert Daneau, were believers. Broadly Protestant, it ranged from Ulrich Molitor's old fifteenth-century treatise on witches through the ghost stories of Lavater to the strange meditations of Paulus Frisius on the

Devil and illusion.[27] But Basse was surely counting on the entertainment value of these works to sell them too.[28]

Again, we find a stream of stories buried in the treatises, even Tannhäuser making an appearance.[29] August Lercheimer writes of how

> I myself heard from a sorcerer of how he together with others from 'N' in Saxony flew on a coat for more than a hundred miles to Paris for a wedding uninvited; but how, when a murmur went up about who these uninvited guests were and where they had come from, they quickly made off.[30]

He was not the only person to be gripped by this fantastic version of the flying carpet story. The passage was lifted almost verbatim the next year by the author of the Faust book, where it forms part of the fabulous anti-Catholic tour the Devil gives Faust. The duo travel to the wedding in Paris on their magic coat, but the Faust-book goes one better, describing all the cities of Germany over which they pass. When they get to Rome, Faust cannot contain himself, exclaiming 'Pfuy! Why didn't the Devil make me a Pope too?' because he saw

> all his equals, that is conceit, pride, arrogance, immoderation, gorging, drinking, whoredom, adultery and all the godless being of the papacy and his tools, so that he was moved to say afterwards 'I thought I was a pig or sow of the Devil, but he must keep me for longer. These pigs of Rome are fattened, and all ready to roast and cook.'[31]

This is not a witch's flight, but the passage owes a good deal to the idea of flight elaborated in demonology, as well as to anti-papist propaganda, moralistic Devil-books, and even to the tradition of travel-book descriptions of cities which goes back to one of the first classics

---

[27] Abraham Saur, *Theatrum de veneficis* (Frankfurt am Main, 1586), Nicolaus Basse, *Theatrum diabolorum* (Frankfurt, 1569), Sigmund Feyerabend (VD16: F904); and on the publishing history of these books and the allegations of piracy which surrounded them, Frank Baron, *Faustus on Trial. The Origins of Johann Spies's 'Historia' in an Age of Witch Hunting* (Tübingen, 1992), esp. 69ff. The title page and foreword of *Theatrum de veneficis* have it both ways: Basse's carefully judged preface opens with a conventional attack on *Zauberer* and is no call to take up arms against the persecution of witches (fos. iir–iiiv); but there is a prominent motto at the start, 'Richtet recht ihr Menschen Kinder' from Psalm 57 which is, in context, a barely coded warning to judges that many executions for witchcraft were unjust.

[28] Basse clearly had developed a niche market in printing works of demonology, for he had published a German version of Daneaus's treatise on witchcraft, together with Molitor's work, (which also stresses the role of illusion in witchcraft), in 1576 (VD16: D80); the German translation of Bodin in 1592 (VD16: B6272); a selection of witchcraft treatises in Latin including the *Malleus* in 1580 (VD16: M8383); and would publish Johannes Georg Gödelmann's *Von Zauberern Hexen und Unholden* in 1592 (VD16: G2488).

[29] Abraham Saur, 'Eine kurtze/ trewe Warnung...', in Saur, *Theatrum*, 209–10.

[30] Lercheimer, 'Ein Christlich Bedencken', in Saur, *Theatrum*, 279. Lercheimer's passage on the magic coat is in a section which is mixed up with stories about Faust, so the borrowing was suggested by the context.

[31] *Historia von D. Johann Fausten. Text des Druckes von 1587. Kritische Ausgabe*, ed. Stephan Füssel and Hans Joachim Kreutzer (Stuttgart, 1988), 60–70.

of print, Hartmann Schedel's *Chronicle of the World*.[32] A work like the Faust-book could directly plagiarise demonology, opening up its imaginative possibilities and expanding the writer's subjects. The teasing scepticism evident in Basse's selection fostered this use of its material, but demonology's own potential to stimulate the imagination fuelled a distinct baroque sensibility.

The fascination with language, stories and the imagination was not the only feature that gave demonology such potential as entertainment. Demonology also allowed authors to experiment with character types. Bodin exploited this to the full, referring throughout his book to the case of the accused witch Jeanne Harvillier to provide a kind of narrative thread binding the work together; Boguet copied the technique, opening with a leaden version of the story of the possessed girl Loyse Maillat in an attempt to enliven his text with human interest. There were, of course, certain kinds of individual whose cases particularly attracted literary attention of this kind: Jeanne Harviller and Loyse Maillat were young girls, not the old women who in fact formed the majority of victims of the witch-hunt.[33]

The records of witches' trials could themselves become literature. Nicolas Rémy packs his text with countless individuals culled from the trial records that had 'beaten at his brain' for expression – in his work, demonology comes close to paraphrase of criminal trial records as he summarises scores of individual cases. De Lancre also includes trial material from the Labourd region; and August Lercheimer, from whose tract the flying coat story was taken, concludes with criminal protocols of six widows. He includes them to show how women could make confessions which were untrue and impossible, but, as the title page of the whole volume shows, advertising the 'confessions, examinations, test, trial records and punishment of some executed witches', they were also thought to appeal to buyers.[34] Popular presses produced cheap broadsheet accounts of witch trials to accompany executions. Typically, these were set out as a narrative of an individual's seduction and fall into the clutches of the Devil, and illustrated, cartoon-style, by woodcuts depicting each scene. The blocks were standard, often re-used to illustrate another execution with only the names changed. Such a focus on the individual, and her fate, also posed the question of what kind of person could sink so low. It was the very attractiveness of these young women as character types, their dreadful descent into sin and their terrible subsequent history that suggested dramatic possibilities.

[32] *Ibid.*, 60, and see 197.
[33] Boguet, *An Examen of Witches* (1929), 34; Bodin, *Démonomanie*.
[34] The tract by Reinhard Lutz in the volume also contain lengthy descrptions of witches burnt at Schlettstadt, together with trial material (1–11); so also does Abraham Saur's treatise.

The most remarkable example of the cross-over from demonology
to drama is Marlowe's *Dr Faustus* of 1588, written a year after the
Faust-book was published in German. In one sense, it is perhaps a
short step from printing a trial record (as the *Theatre of Witches* did),
which is itself a dialogue, to transposing stories about witches and
demons into dialogue form. Works of demonology, like many polemics,
occasionally experimented with the use of the dialogue as a didactic
device: Lambert Daneau, the Calvinist demonologist, had produced a
dialogue on witches which was translated into English and German
the year after its publication, while George Gifford later employed the
same technique to lambast cunning folk and satirise popular credulity
about witchcraft.[35] Drama, however, also stretched the limits of belief.
Demonology from its inception was obsessed with the boundaries between
illusion and reality; and the very same issues were raised by the spectacle
of the theatre.

The uneasy relationship between theatre and reality occasionally
produced confused reactions in the audience. In Exeter, a performance
of Marlowe's *Dr Faustus* ended in pandemonium when it was discovered
that 'there was one devell too many amongst them, and so after a little
pause desired the people to pardon them, they could go no further with
this matter, the peple also understanding the thing as it was, every man
hastened to be first out of dores'. Theatrical experience was so powerful
that it became real.[36] By contrast, in 1661 in Augsburg, the fifteen-year-
old chimney sweep Johann Lutzenberger confessed, like Faust, to making
a pact with the Devil. He said a man dressed in black had given him
and his companions nuts, pears and handfuls of coin. Lutzenberger was
certain his benefactor was the Evil One. But when his companions were
interrogated, they said they thought the strange man had come from
the *Comedi*, a carnival character: they were sure this was theatre, not
witchcraft.[37]

Drama offered a host of ambivalent ways of presenting the witch that
drew not only on demonology and pamphlets but on classical culture.
Marston's *The Tragedy of Sophonisba*, 1604–6, offers us a classical witch,

[35] Lambert Daneau, *A Dialogue of Witches*, trans. attributed to T. Twyne ([London], printed
by [T. East? for] R. W[atkins], 1575); for German editions see VD16: D77–80; George
Gifford, *A Dialogue concerning Witches and Witchcraftes* (1593).

[36] E. K. Chambers, *The Elizabethan Stage* (4 vols., Oxford 1923), III, 424, undated report. I
am grateful to David Harley for this reference. See also Jonathan Barry, 'Hell upon Earth
or the Language of the Playhouse', in *Languages of Witchcraft. Narrative, Ideology and Meaning
in Early Modern Culture*, ed. Stuart Clark (Basingstoke, 2001), for the Rev. Arthur Bedford's
attempt to rid the theatre of reference to devils: he clearly believed such mentions were
dangerous, though his campaign and indefatiguable recording of such instances also proves
they were common currency.

[37] Stadtarchiv Augsburg, Urgichten, Johann Mattheus Lutzenberger 1661; Strafbuch des
Rats 1654–99, 136, 22 Mar. 1661.

a truly terrifying old yellow hag who tricks the villain into satisfying her repulsive lust. By contrast, the *Witch of Edmonton*, first performed in 1621, presents an ordinary seventeenth-century English witch, Elizabeth Sawyer, whose case also featured in a pamphlet by Henry Goodcole. She is an old woman with one eye and the drama features a Devil Dog. The play is unusual because it is sympathetic to her as a figure who is unjustly accused. Middleton's *The Witch* borrows wholesale from the witchcraft sceptic Scot, filching its lists of demons and cauldron ingredients from *The Discoverie of Witchcraft*.[38] As Anna Bayman has recently argued, London's print market was volatile, and metropolitan audiences were tiring of credulous witch pamphlets:[39] one reason may have been their saturation in the far more thrilling versions of witchcraft offered in the plays of Shakespeare, or the gory dramas of Webster. Here witchcraft has avowedly moved into the sphere of imagination, and many of these works presumed a knowing agnosticism amongst their London audience.

IV

In its exploitation of terror and titillation, of belief and scepticism, demonology often also depended on humour. Here writers drew on a medieval tradition of laughing at the Devil. The *Malleus* contains the unforgettable passage about male members which 'eat oats and corn', going on to describe how

> a certain man tells that, when he had lost his member, he approached a known witch to ask her to restore it to him. She told the afflicted man to climb a certain tree, and that he might take which he liked out of a nest in which there were several members. And when he tried to take a big one, the witch said: You must not take that one; adding, because it belonged to a parish priest.[40]

This is clearly Dominican propaganda, a knowing, sexy *fabliau* directed against their competitors, the parish clergy. The story is meant to be funny, not to be understood as the literal 'truth'.

Humour and the demonic go together in a joke from Schwäbisch-Hall recounted in a prose work by Georg Widmann. One night, the Devil spies a salt-maker with a cauldron full of hot boiling water; and putting his large nose through a slit in the salt house, he says 'How about this for a nose?' The salt-steamer promptly tips the cauldron of hot salty water over the Devil's nose, saying 'How about this for a flow?' For answer, the Devil picks up the salt-maker and throws him over the river and the cauldron

[38] *Three Jacobean Witchcraft Plays*, ed. Peter Corbin and Douglas Sedge (Manchester, 1986).
[39] Anna Bayman, '"Large Hands, Wide Eares, and Piercing Sights": The "Discoveries" of the Elizabethan and Jacobean Witch Pamphlets', *Literature and History* (forthcoming).
[40] *Malleus*, 121 (pt II qu. 1 ch. 7).

over the Gensbühl hill, retorting 'How about this for a throw?'[41] The nose is a penis, and the competition is over who can ejaculate furthest: the Devil seems to be getting the worst of it until the cheeky salt-steamer meets his come-uppance.

Comic stories about the Devil had a venerable lineage, going back to oral tradition; and tales about peasants and trickery that even surpasses the Devil were classics of print.[42] These elements found their way into the published Faust of 1587. For example, Faust meets a peasant one night in town with a cart laden with animal feed, and gets into mock negotiation with him, asking what price he will accept to let him eat his fill. The peasant, playing along with the whim of the drunken, well-heeled townsman, agrees a figure – only to gape with astonishment when Faust opens his mouth and consumes half the load. Or Faust sells a pair of fine horses to a horse-dealer, warning the new owner never to ride them through water. The curious horse-dealer cannot resist trying this at the first opportunity – and finds himself sitting on two bales of straw. Furious, he rushes off to complain. Finding Faust sleeping, he takes him by the leg, and, to his horror, the limb comes off in his hand. Faust cries 'Murder!' and the terrified horse dealer flees the scene. Here, tradition is turned on its head: the trickster is an urban educated sophisticate, and his dupes are peasants and that canniest of swindlers, the horse-dealer.[43]

Humour did not exclude tragedy, and the full ambiguity of the Faust figure and of evil emerges as it slides imperceptibly from the burlesque to the tragic mode. In Faust, the Devil is at first a conjuror with a sense of humour; and finally a terrifying force that literally destroys Faust, leaving his blood and brains spattered about the room. Faust himself is at once the debauched drunkard, the sophisticated intellectual, the solicitous visitor who gives his pregnant hostess miraculous Italian grapes, and the fraudster. But he is also the man who, terrified of his own end, begs his beloved student companions to eat and drink with him one last time, and

---

[41] *Deutsche Schwänke*, ed. Leander Petzoldt (Stuttgart, 1979), 190, from *Georg Widmanns Chronica*, ed. Christian Kolb (Geschichtsquellen der Stadt Hall, 2) (Stuttgart, 1904), 91.

[42] Collections of stories featuring fools and peasants had long been popular – there were *Dil Ullenspiegel* (1515), *Claus Narr* (1572), *Das Lalebuch* (1597). In Wolfgang Büttner's *Sechs hundert/neben vnd zwentzig Historien/ Von Claus Narren* (Eisleben, 1572), someone tries to match-make Claus with a rich, ugly old woman. Claus retorts that if she is ugly, the Devil should have her, for when he is sick of her he will surely find another poor devil to pass her off onto (fo. L3r–v): apart from this misogynist tale, the Devil features little. There were also the Alsatian Martin Montanus's many collections, including such classics as his *Gartengesellschaft* of 1559 (Martin Montanus, *Schwankbücher*, ed. Johannes Bolte (Bibliothek des Litterarischen Vereins Stuttgart 217) (Stuttgart, 1899). In one of these, a widow marries a man who promises her he will keep her well and she will have no need to work; but this dream lover turns out to be an over-sexed devil, who 'rides her to death' (ch. 85). Some of the motifs of Montanus's stories echo fairytales, but on the whole, witchcraft does not feature much.

[43] *Historia von D. Fausten*, 86–7.

then sends them off to bed, knowing he must face the Devil alone.[44] He stands for all of us. This is what makes him such a compelling figure for Marlowe's drama.

V

The aesthetic of the German baroque is distinguished by its virtuoso shifting from one mode to another, from tragedy to comedy to theology. In demonology, jokes, drama and prose, we find this characteristically promiscuous mixture of sexual titillation, interest in character, fascination with the bizarre and humour of a wonderfully explosive, bodily kind. All these elements contributed to the next metamorphosis of the literature of the diabolic, as the early German novel that took shape in the second half of the seventeenth century.

The growth of a reading public had created a market for printed stories, and by 1650, with witch-hunting in decline, tales of witchcraft featured amongst the anthologies that canny authors compiled to turn a penny. The *Hundstägige Erquickstunden* of 1650 – stories for those dog days – included many stories about witches, drawn from the works of demonologists, classical sources, and others. It was self-consciously designed to amuse, 'to drive away melancholy', and its twelfth chapter dealt with witchcraft at length, moving straight on to discuss hermaphroditism.[45] In 1668, Johann Praetorius built on its success when he published his *Blockesberges Verrichtung*, a collection of fabulous tales about witchraft and the uncanny.[46] Here we read about lesbian witches in Africa who lure the respectable wives who take their fancy; of Lilith and the Jewish spirits that grow on menstrual blood, enjoy sex with young men and stalk the chambers of women in childbirth. Praetorius also furnishes

[44] *Ibid.*, 118–24.

[45] *Hundstägige Erquickstund. Das ist / Schöne / Lustige Moralishe und Historische Discurß vnd Abbildungen* (Frankfurt, Joh. Gottfried Schönwetter, 1650): the title page makes it explicit that the aim of the collection is to drive away 'Das schwäre Gemüht der Menschen zuerfrischen / die Melancoleyen zu vertreiben' – a nice irony, since it was widely held by those who took witchcraft seriously that melancholy might lead one to fall into the clutches of the Devil and incline one to witchcraft. The twelfth chapter (427–574) has an extensive section on witches which eventually moves on to hermaphrodites.

[46] Johann Praetorius (= Hans Schultze), *Blockes-Berges Verrichtung* (Leipzig and Frankfurt, Johann Scheiben (Leipzig), Friedrich Arnst (Frankfurt), 1668): see 291ff on Africa, 313–71, for the famous passage on flight and the Sabbath from which Faust drew. The first edition does not include the frontispiece. This was included in the second edition. See the modern reprint, *Blockes-Berges Verrichtung*, intro. Hans Henning (Leipzig, 1968). Praetorius also makes great use of the Devil-books, as well as Bodin, Meder, Gödelman, Rémy, Binsfeld and Grillando. The book is also sprinkled with games and anagrams, many sections spelling out BLOCKSBERG and so on. Praetorius made his living through writing and was very prolific. Much of his books consist in reprinting the works of others; the *Blockes-Berges Verrichtung* is a miscellany which even contains a treatise in Latin.

vivid and gruesome descriptions of the witches' Sabbath, material which
Goethe later drew on for his own *Faust*. All this owes a great deal to
works of demonology written fifty years or more before at the height of
the witch craze. We meet old friends, like the journeyman who watches
his widowed mistress go each night when all are abed to a certain place
in the stable where she reaches out for her pitchfork. Suspecting her, he
copies her action – and finds himself at a Sabbath, a story that is also
reminiscent of Hans Baldung Grien's haunting woodcut, 'The Enchanted
Groom' of 1544.[47] Praetorius's sources are the works of demonologists
like Bodin, Rémy, Kramer and Grillando; but he exploits them for their
entertainment value, making good use of the *Hundstägige Erquickstunden*
and setting stories culled from demonologists alongside ghost stories,
local fables and puzzles. A prolific author, Praetorius also invented the
wonderful character Rübenzahl, whose adventures were often pirated
from older works, such as the printed *Faust*. A collected *Daemonologia
Rubinzalii* was published in 1661, its title a tongue-in-cheek reference to
demonology that would have been unthinkable a generation before.[48]

The second edition of the *Blockesberges Verrichtung* is illustrated with
a dramatic woodcut of the Blocksberg itself, which owes more than
a little to earlier panoramas of witchcraft. But instead of providing a
moral commentary on the inescapable punishment of witchcraft, death
by burning, this image stuffs every salacious tidbit about demons, pagan
belief and witches into one pastiche (Figure 5). Again we see witches flying
to Sabbaths on goats, while another tumbles precipitously downwards,
her hair loose and her dress raised to reveal her legs. At the bottom of the
image, a giant winged Devil defecates into a chamber-pot, a motif that
seems to have been pinched straight from Lutheran propaganda about
the diabolic origins of the monks, where She-Devils sitting on gallows
defecate monks.[49] At the centre of the image, witches perform the anal
kiss on a giant goat, while long lines of assorted pairs of Devils and

[47] Praetorius, *Blockes-Berges Verrichtung,*'Die zauberkundige Witwe und ihr Hausknecht',
which is similar to Del Rio, *Investigations*, 95–7; and on the Baldung Grien image, see, for
an interpretation linking the image to fantasy and to sleep, Linda C. Hults, 'Baldung's
Bewitched Groom Revisited: Artistic Temperament, Fantasy and the "Dream of Reason"',
Sixteenth Century Journal, 15, 3 (1984), 259–79.
[48] Johannes Praetorius, *Daemonologia Rubinzalii* (Frankfurt, 1661), which even reproduces
the story about Faust and the horse-seller, but replaces Faust with his hero Rübenzahl, 329,
and includes plenty of material about ghosts, Silesian legends and superstition. Praetorius,
as someone who lived from his writing, had to have an eye for what would sell.
[49] See, on such images in Reformation anti-monastic propaganda, R. W. Scribner, *For
the Sake of Simple Folk: Popular Propaganda for the German Reformation* (Cambridge, 1981; rev. edn
Oxford, 1994), 85–7.

Figure 5 Johann Praetorius, *Blockes-Berges Verrichtung...*, 2nd edn (Leipzig, 1669), 4. By permission of Suhrkamp Insel Verlag.

witches wind their way in a snake-like spiral around the picture, playing phallic-looking bagpipes and horns.[50]

---

[50] Interestingly enough, the publishers of a work by Georg Spitzel in 1687 included an engraving which was a barely disguised re-hash of Praetorius's frontispiece (Gottlieb Spitzel, *Die Gebrochne Macht der Finsternuß / oder Zerstörte Teuflische Bunds- und Buhl-Freundschafft*

The image is framed by the Blocksberg or Brocken, the mountain which was fabled as the setting for Walpurgis Night, when witches from all over Germany would gather for a huge Sabbath. Praetorius begins his work with a naturalistic description of the mountain, devoid of vegetation and shrouded in mists. Now, instead of Faust's fantastic journeys with Mephistopheles, witchcraft furnishes information for a real tourist guide, and Praetorius provides a real-life account of his ascent to the summit of the Blocksberg; and the main character of the book is not the witch or even the Devil, but the mountain itself.[51]

Happel's *Curiosities of the World*, a baggy, multi-volume epic, published in 1683 and another forerunner of the picaresque German novel, also includes an entire section devoted to the diabolic and miraculous, and boasts, amongst its section on geology, a long description of the Blocksberg, where it is 'generally believed that every year, on Walburg's night or May 1, the witches hold their gatherings'.[52] Happel describes how the mountain is always wreathed in fog, and discusses the uncanny nature of the views over great distances that it affords; but he explains this naturalistically: 'the cause is that while one is surrounded by cloud, there is clear and bright sunshine both below and above'. Yet then he shifts gear, appending a story about a medical doctor who found himself on the Brocken at a spring, and sticking his hand beneath it to discover the source of the perishing coldness of the water, found pellets of silver; once off the mountain, he could never find the treasure again.

Happel draws on some chestnuts of demonology. We meet the wonderfully titled 'Diabolic Postal Service', which tells of the Dutch merchant who encounters a man at an inn in Livonia (Figure 6). The stranger boasts he can fly to his house in the Netherlands and back in an hour. Naturally the merchant bets that he cannot; but the stranger reappears within the hour, bearing a silver spoon from his house and the ring off his wife's finger.[53] The speedy stranger is the Devil, a motif that is indebted to the stories of witches who fly to Sabbaths while their husbands sleep. This tall tale is illustrated by a woodcut of a fabulous diabolic cart, horses, reins, diabolic outriders, and all flying through the air; the ultimate comic transmutation of the witch on her goat.

Demonology had become entertainment. By the 1690s, a clutch of old French demonological classics were being reprinted, this time not for

---

mit den menschen... (Augsburg, 1687), 207, but in a work which was a serious contribution to demonology. Spitzel did believe that some of witchcraft was illusion, though he was convinced the Devil was active in the world and that witchcraft was real.

[51] Praetorius, *Blockes-Berges Verrichtung*, introduction, fos. iir–xivr.

[52] Eberhard Happel, *Gröste Denkwürdigkeiten der Welt, oder sogenannte Relationes curiosae* (5 vols., Hamburg, 1683–90) (vol. II has two parts), II, pt 2, 140–1.

[53] *Ibid.*, III, 472 (Teuflische Post); this section contains such stories as Zauberische Liebe, Verfluchte Chrystall-sehen, Teufflische Bocksfahrt.

Figure 6 Eberhard Happel, *Gröste Denkwürdigkeiten der Welt, oder sogenannte Relationes curiosae* (5 vols., Hamburg, 1683–90) [British Library 446.b.5], III, 472. By permission of the British Library.

their worth as intellectual treatises, but for fun.[54] Witchcraft had become part of a popular market for stories; the witch, a character of fiction.

The figure of the witch can even be traced in the novels of Hans Jakob Christoph von Grimmelshausen, the best-known of all the seventeenth-century German writers, whose style epitomises the baroque. His fictional anti-hero Courasche, the woman who survives all that the Thirty Years War can throw at her, is no witch but a tough, sexually experienced harridan. She stands for the moral bankrupcty caused by the Thirty Years War, yet she has the classic attributes of a witch, sexual licentiousness and old age. At one point in the novel she even purchases a familiar, who makes her tavern business boom, for no one can resist her diabolic beer. Courasche has escaped the typology of the witch to become a character in her own right. And yet, it was the interest in character type evident in trials and demonology that provided the materials from which an emblematic figure like Courasche could emerge.[55]

---

[54] See, for example, the works of Jean Bodin, Nicolaus Rémy and others, published in a multi-part series entitled *Beschreibung Teuffelischer Zauber- und Hexen-Poßen; Der bösen Geister und Gespensten Wunder-seltzahme Historien und Nächtliche Erscheinungen; Der Gespensten Gauckel-Wercks Dritter Theil* (Hamburg, Frankfurt and Leipzig, 1693, 1698).

[55] Hans Jakob Christoph von Grimmelshausen, *Lebensbeschreibung der Erzbetrügerin und Landstörzerin Courasche*, ed. Klaus Haberkamm and Günther Weydt (Stuttgart, 1971), 85–90 (ch. xvii).

VI

The baroque aesthetic in literature is widely treated as an inferior form of art, or even regarded as pathological. Yet the picaresque manages to celebrate the variety of life, encompassing the gross, the tragic and the comic in one gargantuan whole, and presenting without embarrassment, the closeness of pleasure to pain or of sex to comedy. By the close of the eighteenth century, these varied modes had begun to part company, as the witch of nursery tale finally separated from the *Faust* of drama.

There is a difference between fantasy and reality. Men like Rémy were implicated in the deaths of hundreds of people, and though his work breathes a disconcerting empathy for the women whose individual souls he hoped to save, he acted on his murderous impulses. It is for the historian to consider not just the subversions and interesting possibilities that art and literature offered, but the more difficult issue of the relationship between such violent, ribald fantasies about sex and women – often with a vicious streak, as in depictions of old women – and the horrors of witch-hunting. What makes fantasies and beliefs trigger violent action is not just the beliefs or the fantasies themselves, but a set of historical circumstances – which in the late sixteenth century and early seventeenth century included religious tensions, legal systems and dearth.

This tour of the cultural legacy of the figure of the witch has taken us from demonology to drama, image and the novel. As we follow her progress from the demonology of the late fifteenth century through the flowering of writings about the Devil in the 1570s and beyond, we trace the gradual disenchantment of the figure of the witch and the final domestication of the Devil. From the outset, demonology fired the imagination, and, like other moralist literature, it consistently threatened to entertain its audience at least as much as it instructed. Demonologists knew their markets – or their publishers did – and the possibilities of set-piece description, writerly flair and a damn good story were always there to be exploited. Humour was not incidental to this, for audiences were gripped as much by laughter as by terror. By laughing at the Devil, sixteenth- and seventeenth-century people's belief in him was not one whit diminished. Humour, it might be claimed, is a means of warding off evil, just as the way to get rid of the Devil, according to Luther, was to fart at him.[56]

But laughter, of course, also tends to tease belief. What drove demonology from the very beginning was its obsession with the issue of truth and illusion, and that is why so many of the stories that demonologists loved also stretched credulity, and are funny. What was true, and what

---

[56] See Heiko Oberman, 'Teufelsdreck: Eschatology and Scatology in the "Old" Luther', *Sixteenth Century Journal*, 19, 3 (1988), 435–50.

was really one step too far? Was flight real? Did people truly participate in the Sabbath or only think they did? Could devils really make penises disappear? These were the questions with which demonologists played again and again. When Protestant demonologists asserted that the Devil was the master of illusion and so all his effects might be in the mind rather than literally true,[57] they seemed to solve the issue of what could be believed at a stroke. But they also immensely increased the scope of illusion, for anything could *seem* to be true. Even Catholic demonologists were willing to grant that many of the Devil's effects were illusory; but it was often the funniest of these tales that had to be explained, and once told, they stuck in the mind. Who could forget the luckless flyers Peter Binsfeld describes, who 'fall from the trees and break or crush their bones'?[58]

Beyond their conscious, intentional message, these texts appeal to the senses, the unconscious and the irrational. Humour, after all, works because it appeals to the repressed, and to what cannot be easily corralled into logical argument. In the crude pranks of the burlesque Devil, we can almost hear the belly laughter of the audience. This did not stop them from watching him enter the next scene as a terrifying demon once more. Like Shakespeare's players in *Hamlet*, the German baroque imagination had no difficulty in simultaneously accommodating 'tragedy, comedy, history, pastoral, pastoral-comical, historical-pastoral, tragical-historical, tragical-comical-historical-pastoral'. But rather than merely laugh at this bizarre jumble of competing aesthetic modes, its very chaos may disclose something vital to understanding the early modern mind. The literature of demonology opened up a whole imaginative world that drew on classical reference as well as the Bible to create something vivid and new. Belief in witchcraft was never just a matter of subscribing to a set of propositions about witches and demons or even to a consistent binary world-view of a universe caught between good and evil. Like all belief, it consisted in a morass of images, half articulated convictions and contradictory positions, elements of which could occasionally come together in searing clarity to fuel suspicion that a particular individual was a witch.

---

[57] Stuart Clark, 'Protestant Demonology: Sin, Superstition, and Society (c. 1520–c.1630)', in *Early Modern European Witchcraft: Centres and Peripheries*, ed. Bengt Ankarloo and G. Henningsen (Oxford, 1990).

[58] Peter Binsfeld, *Tractat Von Bekantnuß der Zauberer und Hexen* (Trier, 1590), 60: he thinks this proves flight is real, but concedes that some call flight dreams. Del Rio also mentions those who have the bad luck to get arrested without any clothes on, or simply fall from the sky; Del Rio, *Investigations*, 97 (qu. 16).

Transactions of the RHS 16 (2006), pp. 143–62 © 2006 Royal Historical Society
doi:10.1017/S0080440106000454   Printed in the United Kingdom

AFRICA AND THE BIRTH OF THE MODERN WORLD*

By Megan Vaughan

READ 4 MARCH 2005

ABSTRACT. The Commission for Africa, which reported in March 2005, drew attention to the enduring problem of poverty in Africa, but also reinforced the common perception that Africa has a troubled relationship with the 'modern world'. This essay reviews the literature on Africa's long-term political and economic development, paying particular attention to the continent's insertion into the global system in the period described by C. A. Bayly as the 'birth of the modern world'. It concludes that, though many of the continent's current problems arise out of recent policy failures, we should not ignore longer-term, structural elements of environmental, demographic and economic history, including the consequences (direct and indirect) of the slave trade.

By some accounts Africa seems to have a troubled relationship with the modern world. The Commission on Africa will report in the spring. In 2001 preparing the way for the Commission's work the British prime minister stated that 'Africa's poverty is a scar on the conscience of the world.' Recently Commissioner Geldof has gone further – 'Africa's agony', he argues, 'has been compounded by the chill winds of the globalised world, which has effectively excluded it further.' Urging his fellow commissioners to move from 'charity to justice', Geldof warns: 'If this turns out to be another anodyne and meaningless development tract, I'm out of here and I will weep.'[1]

Whatever you make of the Africa Commission there is little dispute over the seriousness of Africa's economic (and related social) problems. Africa is the only region of the developing world which is no better off than it was twenty-five years ago. Declining growth rates, increasing poverty, falling

---

* My thanks for all the perceptive comments and criticisms of this essay made by those present at the Royal Historical Society lecture and at a later presentation at the Centre for the History of Economics at Cambridge. It will be apparent that I have drawn heavily on the incisive work of both Gareth Austin and Frederick Cooper, as well as on that of my African history colleagues in Cambridge, John Lonsdale and John Iliffe. Chris Bayly's outstanding work inspired me to write this essay.

[1] Quoted in 'Africa Commission's Uphill Task', report by BBC correspondent Steve Schifferes, 6 Oct. 2004: http://news.bbc.co.uk/1/hi/business.3682509.stm.

life expectancy and the recurrence of conflict characterise the continent. The Commission has its work cut out.[2]

Meanwhile, demonstrating that not all news out of Africa is bad news, London hosts a festival of African cultural events (Africa 05), including, of course, musical events. If you were ever any doubt about Africa's position in global culture, try and think about world music without thinking about African music. Included in Africa 05 is a major exhibition of African contemporary art at the Hayward, entitled 'Africa Remix: Contemporary Art of a Continent'.[3] While the deliberations of the Commission for Africa imply that Africa has been left behind as the rest of the world forges ahead economically, Africa Remix is almost relentless in its stress on Africa's modern, perhaps more accurately post-modern, condition – as a continent of cityscapes, of recycled rubbish, of modern warfare, of people struggling with a very contemporary kind of poverty. If you are looking for 'tribal art' it would be better not to go there, but if you want to see what contemporary African artists do with the continent's predicament, then do.[4]

I enjoyed Africa Remix, but not everyone did – including one of Britain's leading art critics – Waldemar Januszcsak. In a review in the *Sunday Times* entitled 'Art: The Poverty Gap', Januszcsak had little positive to say about this collection of art from Africa (though he is at pains to point out that he likes African music as much as the next man).[5] I was a little puzzled by the vehemence of his reactions. What, I wonder, do we outsiders expect and want from 'Africa'? While the Francophone artists come in for criticism for producing art which 'reeks of the evening class and the post-structuralist seminar', more generally Januszcsak seems disturbed by the way the exhibition engages with poverty. One of the pieces he dislikes most (and there are many) is Pascale Tayou's DVD showing an African village having a road built through it: 'This isn't road-building, it's scarring. This isn't progress, it's rape.' Januszcsak is far too sophisticated to call for a bit of primitivism of the old kind, but he gets close to it when he writes, 'The drab textures. The beige moods. Even those proper African artists who offer doses of authentic African insight

[2] The Commission reported in March 2005. The final document is published as *Our Common Interest: Report of the Commission for Africa* (London, 2005). Commentary on the Commission: Penny Jackson, 'Briefing: The Commission for Africa, Gleneagles, Brussels and Beyond', *African Affairs*, 104, 417 (2005), 657–65; Percy S. Mistry, 'Reasons for Sub-Saharan Africa's Development Deficit that the Commission for Africa Did Not Consider', *African Affairs*, 104, 417 (2005), 665–79. On Africa's ongoing economic crisis see Nicolas van de Walle, *African Economies and the Politics of Permanent Crisis* (Cambridge, 2005).

[3] The catalogue of the exhibition: *Africa Remix: Contemporary Art of a Continent*, ed. Simon Njami *et al.* (London, 2005).

[4] Of course, the idea that the entire continent's contemporary art could be dealt with in one exhibition, is itself revealing, as some reviewers pointed out.

[5] Waldemar Januszcsak, 'Art: The Poverty Trap', *Sunday Times*, 20 Feb. 2005.

suffer from this heaviness. It lies, on this evidence, at the very heart of the African experience. And it makes you weep.'

Africa seems to be producing quite a bit of weeping. One would be inclined to diagnose post-colonial melancholia if it were not for the fact that Geldof is Irish and Januszcsak of Polish extraction. But Januszcsak's comments point to two related issues – Africa's very real poverty and its cultural place in the contemporary world.

I have based the title of my essay on the recent book by my colleague Chris Bayly, *The Birth of the Modern World, 1790–1914*.[6] In this monumental work of world history, Bayly moves away from a Eurocentric version of the period and the story of European exceptionalism, stressing instead the reciprocal interactions between events in the emerging European and North American core of the industrial western economy and events elsewhere in the world. Following much social anthropological analysis of more recent processes of globalisation,[7] Bayly argues that this earlier period also witnessed the spread of global uniformities (in thought, deportment, economy, religion, political organisation) which simultaneously provoked and were informed by the elaboration of cultural and social differences.

This was an unsettling period, writes Bayly, producing conflict and turmoil. This turmoil was partly produced by the unevenness of the changes outlined here, for one of Bayly's points is that although the industrial revolution must take a central role in this story, it does not work in simple synchrony with the other developments which we associate with this period – the development of modern states, for example, and of the political ideologies which go with that. Only after 1840, argues Bayly, does the shift towards industrialisation begin to kick in at a global level, and even then not without another set of crises: rebellions in Asia, 1848 in Europe and the American Civil War. The relationships between economic change, political organisation and political ideas were complex, according to Bayly, but what can be said of this period is that

contemporary changes were so rapid and interacted with each other so profoundly, that this period could reasonably be described as the 'birth of the modern world' – a phrase encompassing the rise of the nation state, demanding centralisation of power or loyalty to an ethnic solidarity, alongside the massive expansion of global commercial and intellectual links.

Bayly is clear that 'modernity' is a state of mind as much as anything else – so that the spread of ideas and modes of living are integral to this history – not just a cultural icing to the cake.

[6] C. A. Bayly, *The Birth of the Modern World, 1790–1914: Global Connections and Comparisons* (Oxford, 2004).
[7] The literature is large and growing. Bayly draws particularly on the work of Arjun Appadurai, *Modernity at Large: Cultural Dimensions of Globalisation* (Minneapolis, 1997).

146   TRANSACTIONS OF THE ROYAL HISTORICAL SOCIETY

We Africanists have a terrible habit when it comes to works on world history. We scan the index to see whether Africa has been included in them at all – often the continent is barely mentioned. Bayly certainly cannot be accused of this. Africa may not loom as large in Bayly's account as other areas of the world, but nevertheless, throughout the book Bayly uses African examples to make a number of his points – about the development of the state outside Europe, for example, and the spread of the world religions and of liberal political theory and its interaction with local ideologies. But his African examples are often accompanied by quite major qualifications, and at times it seems that Africa (or most of it) does not sit very well with Bayly's attempt to de-centre the history of this period.

Let me begin with the easy bits, where Africa seems to fit best with Bayly's account. This is in the history of the religious and intellectual developments in the long nineteenth century. Expanding religions, argues Bayly, were like other major social formations of this period – the state and capitalism – in that they harnessed to themselves underlying changes in technology, and made full use of new opportunities for communication and travel. The world religions expanded outwards and 'downwards' in this period, tapping into and attempting to centralise pre-existing religious organisation and sentiment. Though part of this story is of a missionary or revivalist impulse from the centre(s), expanding outwards, it is also just as much a story of how Africans and others reinterpreted and re-fashioned the world religions to fit their needs and their imaginations. Christianity was 'converted' by Africans and Asians, writes Bayly.

In this field perhaps more than in any other, historians of Africa have long made the case for the role of African people in making or re-making the modern world. At the start of Bayly's period at the turn of the eighteenth and nineteenth centuries we have the extraordinary movement for the consolidation and expansion of Islam in what is now Nigeria – the Fulani jihads, or 'war of conversion', reflecting a wider movement of Islamic revival spreading from the Middle East and North Africa, but rooting itself in the specific circumstances of northern Nigeria where Fulani lineages displaced existing Hausa aristocracies and created the centralised Sokoto Caliphate. Long before the arrival of Christianity, Islam offered some Africans at least an alternative cosmopolitan connection to that of the 'West', and this connection remains an important (arguably growing) force in many parts of Africa.[8] After 1800 Christianity spread again in West Africa (there

---

[8] David Robinson, *Muslim Societies in African History* (Cambridge, 2004); *The History of Islam in Africa*, ed. Nehemia Levitzion and Randall L. Pouwels (Athens, OH, 2000).

were earlier incarnations), and African converts took the message into the interior.[9]

It was here, perhaps more than anywhere else, that the globalising and modernising developments of the early nineteenth century emphasised by Bayly are most evident. Here a group of African and African-American intellectuals in the mid-nineteenth century produced a kind of African 'renaissance' to rival the Islamic version which had been generated by their brothers to the north. Amongst them were African-born Africanus Horton (medical doctor and political thinker), Samuel Ajayi Crowther (Anglican bishop), Edward Blyden (born in West Indies, educated in Liberia), Pierre Boilat (born in Senegal, educated in France), all contributors in their various ways to that ongoing process of exchange across the Atlantic, which Paul Gilroy refers to as the *Black Atlantic*.[10] These were intellectuals who perfectly exemplify Bayly's claims for this period. They worked in a complex diasporic transnational frame (born of the forced displacement of slavery of course), they engaged with all the issues of the day – with science (including racial science), with the question of the political future of Africa, with questions of language policy, the place of women. Their contributions are well known, so I will not rehearse them all here, save to point to some of the ambiguities of this period and of its legacy – ambiguities highlighted by Paul Gilroy, Kwame Anthony Appiah and others.

These figures are incomprehensible without direct reference to the slave trade and its abolition. Saving Africa was their mission. This was understandable since all of them (African, African-American and West Indian) had, either indirectly or very directly, experienced the horrors of the slave trade and of slavery. The Christian redemptive message with which they were imbued told them that though the evils of the slave trade were perpetrated by the slavers, responsibility also rested with Africans themselves, and that it was therefore within 'Africa' (that entity which they helped to create discursively) that the sources of this evil were to be found.[11] These were not one-dimensional thinkers. They were as complex as the politics they attempted to grapple with – conservative in some ways, radical in others. Africanus Horton, for example, was deeply critical of

---

[9] On the earlier history of Christianity in the kingdom of the Kongo, see the work of John Thornton: John Thornton, *The Kingdom of the Kongo* (Madison, 1983); John Thornton, *The Kongolese Saint Anthony: Dona Beatriz Kimpa Vita and the Antonian Movement, 1684–1706* (Cambridge, 1998).

[10] Paul Gilroy, *The Black Atlantic: Modernity and Double Consciousness* (Cambridge, MA, 1992); Kwame Anthony Appiah, *In My Father's House: Africa in the Philosophy of Culture* (Oxford, 1992); Robert W. July, *The Origins of Modern African Thought* (London, 1962); Christopher Fyfe, *Africanus Horton: West African Scientist and Patriot* (Oxford, 1972); *African and the West: Intellectual Responses to European Culture*, ed. Philip D. Curtin and James W. Fernandez (Madison, 1972).

[11] On the construction of 'Africa' see V. Y. Mudimbe, *The Idea of Africa* (London, 1994).

British policy in West Africa and proposed a form of self-rule, and he employed his scientific education to challenge the pretences of scientific racism head-on.[12] He, like his colleagues, believed fervently, not only in Christianity, but in the virtues of education. With enough education the African could be the equal of the white man. They all reiterated this belief. But of course the premise here was one of inequality. Their writings are graphic in their depiction of the ghastly state of the unredeemed African, a state partly produced by the debasement attendant on the slave trade – but also inherent in the pagan culture of 'this long benighted continent' where people were, in Crowther's words, 'harassed from within and without by unjust war and kidnapping, as well as by superstitious belief in the power and influence of false gods, and of the craftiness of priests'.[13] The Muslim Hausa and Fulani of northern Nigeria fare no better in Crowther's book:

> Notwithstanding the pride of the people on account of their flowing dresses . . . they go about in them in a most filthy and disgusting state; they are never washed from the time they are made and put on to the time they are worn threadbare, and they are the receptacles for all kinds of vermin . . . Even their ablutions are an abomination . . . a description of them would insult the pure heart of the Christian.

Crowther's writings are designed to shock, peppered with descriptions scattered with meals of rotting meat, disease, mud and excrement. What he is describing in fact is poverty, and the poverty was real enough. But as a Victorian moralist he knew that the poverty came from within, that it was inseparable from depravity. Poverty was an insult to Crowther's African pride, and it offended him.

At the other end of the continent, missionary competition fuelled a growth in Christian conversions in Southern Africa. By the 1870s, Xhosa Christian converts from Lovedale Institution in the Eastern Cape were volunteering enthusiastically to follow in the footsteps of David Livingstone and convert their heathen brothers and sisters in the interior to the north, in present-day Malawi.[14] At Lovedale where these men had been educated, the promotion of Christianity was inseparable from a thorough-going Scottish education, which included a heavy dose of the classics. For the missionaries at Lovedale a genuine attachment to ideals of universalism and equality before God was synonymous with a belief in the need for a cultural and social transformation rooted in a version of the European historical experience. These Scotsmen were not ones to compromise readily, a fact which had contradictory consequences. On

[12] *Africanus Horton: The Dawn of Nationalism in Modern Africa: Extracts from the Political, Scientific and Medical Writings of J. A. B. Horton*, ed. Davidson Nicol (London, 1969); James Africanus Beale Horton, *West African Countries and Peoples* (Edinburgh,1969; first published 1868).

[13] Samuel Crowther, *Journal of an Expedition up the Niger and Tshadda Rivers* (London, 1855).

[14] T. Jack Thompson, *Touching the Heart: Xhosa Missionaries to Malawi, 1876–1888* (Pretoria, 2000).

the one hand they fought (an ultimately losing) battle against attempts to downgrade African education; on the other hand they had relatively little time for any engagement with African cultural and social traditions. This put their Xhosa emissaries in a difficult situation when charged with the duty of translating Christianity and attracting converts from among the Ngoni people of Malawi. One of them, William Koyi, was highly respected by his missionary superiors, but he also faced severe criticism when it seemed to some that his 'presents' to Ngoni chiefs were on the over-generous side. The problem which Koyi (and so many other African Christians) wrestled with in this period was that the redemptive message of Christianity also implied that Africa and Africans needed saving from themselves.

Back in South Africa Koyi's Xhosa colleague, Isaac Wauchope, was negotiating the same delicate boundaries. A committed Christian and avid member of the temperance movement, Wauchope was also a political agitator at a time when African rights (a new concept of course) were being progressively eroded and denied. He pursued his battles through his use of the pen and his literary society – the Imbumba Yama Nyama – literally meaning 'compressed meat', a reference in Xhosa to the importance of 'indissoluble unity'.[15] Wauchope, like some of his West African counterparts, had come to the conclusion that some kind of pan-tribal 'nation' was what was needed if Africans in South Africa were to avoid being trampled over, and that the battle would now have to be fought on intellectual grounds – using modern methods but referring constantly to Xhosa imagery. 'Fight with the Pen' was the title of one of Wauchope's poems, written in the Xhosa language: 'Your cattle are plundered, compatriot – Lay down the musket, Take up the pen, Seize paper and ink. That's your shield.' Unfortunately Wauchope's pen, and others like it, would prove an inadequate defence against the forces of settler colonialism in this part of Africa.

The Black Atlantic intellectuals and their Southern and Eastern African equivalents were in a tiny minority of course, but they had a lasting significance which survived the conservative and racist backlash of the late nineteenth century. They were involved in a complex negotiation of what it meant to be black and modern in the era of slavery and Abolition, they were central to the imagining of something called 'Africa' and they had big ideas about what to do with the continent. Theirs was a Victorian middle-class morality, married uneasily (in the case of some of them at least) to an attempt to re-value aspects of African culture. Amongst many other things, they seem to have had an unfailing belief in the godliness of clothing – unsurprisingly since slavery was so often marked by nakedness.

[15] *Ibid.*, 170.

And European textile manufacturers, as it happens, had their eyes on Africa as a market.

Perhaps reflecting on the contradictions of this period, Yinka Shonibare (a British Nigerian artist who was this year short-listed for the Turner Prize and whose work features in the Africa Remix exhibition at the Hayward) creates life-size headless figures clothed in the elaborate Victorian style of dress worn by the African intellectuals I have been discussing. But the raw material for their long coats and bustiers is the 'Dutch wax' printed cotton, which first found a major market in Africa in the nineteenth century and which is still popular today.[16] Shonibare's art 'remixes' the new bodily practices of the elite with the mass-produced cotton which for the most part was simply wrapped round women's waists or used to tie their babies to their backs. The story of Dutch wax print is in part an example of the kind of globalisation of desires and of trade which Bayly sees as so characteristic of this period. John Picton tells the story of how in the nineteenth century Dutch agency brought together Indonesian designs, West African tastes and textile industries in northern Europe, aided by a Glasgow dealer Ebenezer Brown Flemming, whose idea it was to market imitation batik in West Africa, manufactured in the Netherlands and England.[17] The original link came through a colour, Turkey Red. Flemming was a dealer in this dye and deep red had always been in demand in West Africa: a felted red cloth, traded by the Portuguese in the late fourteenth century, was apparently an essential element of courtly dress in Ewe/Benin, and Picton tells us that Ewe and Asante weavers were in the habit of unravelling imported red cotton cloth to re-weave the yarn. The story of Dutch wax print is then a continuation of a longer history. In the eighteenth century, for instance, West African chiefs made their desires and tastes known to European traders in Indian textiles and were extremely peeved when presented with the wrong stuff. In the 1830s, in the heart of Central Africa, hundreds of miles from any coast, King Kazembe was telling a Portuguese emissary that he did not like the kind of (Indian) cloth he had brought with him, and in any case he wanted it in rolls, not cut into pieces.[18] In the late nineteenth century, then, European manufacturers were quick to respond to West Africa consumer demand, not only for certain colours, but for some quite specific designs: blackboards, the alphabet, numbers, emblems of chiefly authority and designs based on the visualisation of local proverbs.

---

[16] *Yinka Shonibare, Double Dutch* (Rotterdam, 2002).

[17] John Picton, 'Laughing at Ourselves', in *Yinka Shonibare, Double Dutch*, 45–63; Ruth Nielsen, 'The History and Development of Wax-Printed Textiles Intended for West Africa and Zaire', in *The Fabrics of Culture: The Anthropology of Clothing and Adornment*, ed. Justine Cordwell and Ronald Schwartz (The Hague, 1979).

[18] A. C. P. Gamitto, *King Kazembe and the Marave, Cheva, Bisa, Bemba, Lunda and Other Peoples . . .* (Lisbon, 1960).

This was an eclectic mix then, patterns which in Picton's words 'mark the Africanization of these cloths, their transformation from an exotic textile (in West African terms) to a fabric of immediate relevance to the developing local modernity of the area'.[19]

But this history is also, in part at least, one of the undermining of African petty commodity production; and in the longer run Africa's enduring poverty meant that it did not live up to nineteenth-century marketing expectations. African consumers do indeed continue to make their preferences known to the manufacturers of Dutch wax, and the results are not too dissimilar from those of the nineteenth century: emblems of modernity (the mobile phone for example) vie for space on the body with traditional proverbs and reminders of chiefly authority. In some parts of Africa, however, these cloths face the tough competition of second-hand clothing imported from the United States and elsewhere, T-shirts bearing slogans signs and symbols over which African consumers have no control and whose cultural referents (*despite* globalisation) are sometimes distinctly exotic.[20] Does it matter? I do not know.

If, as Bayly argues, modernity was a 'state of mind' and a set of bodily practices, it was also inescapably about states and about economic processes.

In his attempt to de-centre the history of the 'birth of the modern world', Bayly also de-centres, up to a point, the narrative of the role of the nation state in this process. In outlining the major features of the development of the modern European state (stable legal institutions guaranteeing property rights, the development of a national sentiment, military centralisation), Bayly also argues that these developments were (at least until the mid-nineteenth century) *not so* unique, not so different from what was going on in Africa and Asia. Here too 'more focused identities, patriotic homelands owing allegiance to wider values... formed, dissolved and reformed'.

Bayly is rightly cautious in his application of this argument to Africa. The history of pre-colonial Africa is littered with failed states as well as with more enduring and successful attempts at state building. Furthermore, most historians of Africa would want to take a step back from any Whiggish narrative to ask the prior question: what is a state for, and why, in the context of the conditions prevailing in much of the continent, assume that conditions of life under a state might be better

[19] For the parallel history of the demand for textiles in nineteenth-century East Africa see Jeremy Prestholdt, 'On the Global Repercussions of East African Consumerism', *American Historical Review*, 109 (2004), 755–83.
[20] Karen Hansen, *Salaula: The World of Second-Hand Clothing and Zambia* (Chicago, 2000).

than in stateless, decentralised polities?[21] I will return to this question later, but for now let me summarise what I think is the consensus about the limits of state formation in pre-colonial Africa and the related question of economic development.

If state formation is a tricky business everywhere (as Bayly points out) there is nevertheless reason to believe that it was always particularly difficult in most parts of pre-colonial sub-Saharan Africa. The argument is in essence a simple one. Africa is a large and varied continent, but over some very large parts of it population densities were historically low, due to a combination of environmental and disease factors.[22] With some notable exceptions (which do, in fact, prove the rule – parts of northern Nigeria, and the Great Lakes Region for example) populations were thinly spread, practising extensive agriculture over large areas and shifting settlements when soils were exhausted. The dominant social and political systems of pre-colonial Africa had evolved to meet these circumstances. As is oft reiterated, with some exceptions, labour rather than land was the scarce resource. As a consequence social, cultural and religious systems placed enormous stress on fertility. Extensive kinship systems bound people together, and political organisation (which in most places was an extension of kinship) emphasised that generosity was the price one had to pay for the exercise of any authority. Powerful chiefs aimed to gather people around them and secure their allegiance. In return they were expected to protect their subjects from enemies, ensure their fertility and the fertility of the soil and feed them in times of famine. War was no less a feature of African societies than of any other, as John Iliffe's book on honour in African history reminds us,[23] but much warfare in pre-colonial Africa was directed at absorbing the competition rather than annihilating it: enemy captives constituted useful servile labour and captive women were valued for their reproductive capacities.

There is a long-running debate about the nature of domestic slavery in Africa which addresses such questions as: how servile was servile, what was the difference between being a slave and a junior member of a lineage, what relative values were accorded to productive and reproductive labour, and so on.[24] What is clear is that institutions of slavery and of pawnship offered ambitious rulers ways round the rules of kinship

---

[21] These questions are addressed explicitly by, amongst others, John Lonsdale: John Lonsdale, 'Globalization, Ethnicity and Democracy: A View from "the Hopeless Continent"', in *Globalization in World History*, ed. A. G. Hopkins (2002), 194–220.

[22] The demographic argument is made most explicitly in John Iliffe's work: John Iliffe, *Africans: The History of a Continent* (Cambridge, 1995).

[23] John Iliffe, *Honour in African History* (Cambridge, 2005).

[24] Claude Meillassoux, *The Anthropology of Slavery: The Womb of Iron and Gold*, trans. Alide Desnois (Chicago, 1991); *Slavery in Africa: Historical and Anthropological Perspectives*, ed. Suzanne Miers and Igor Kopytoff (Madison, 1977); *Africans in Bondage: Studies in Slavery and the Slave*

and inheritance which otherwise constrained their ability to extend their authority. Ambitious rulers there were, here as elsewhere, and they made efforts to devise new methods of binding others to them unconditionally – sometimes through slavery, sometimes through the exercise of fear and ritual sanction, sometimes through the creation of structures of political authority which cut across lines of inheritance, sometimes (where this was possible) through the distribution of scarce mineral resources and trade goods.

Where conditions were favourable, Africa had its states – as a generation of post-Independence historians were at pains to point out. One of the most impressive was the kingdom of the Asante, in present-day Ghana, the history of which is made accessible to us through the extraordinary work of Ivor Wilks, Tom McCaskie and others.[25] Significant as a political achievement, Asante is also a reminder of the conditions which made political centralisation possible – in this case the conjuncture of rich agricultural resources, and the occurrence of a valuable mineral, gold. Asante's rulers were far-sighted. Amongst other administrative innovations, they devised a system of death duties which enabled them to keep control of the gold. They also created a system of political institutions which integrated kings and chiefs, rather than placing them in structured opposition, as happened in many African polities, with predictable destabilising results. Elsewhere Africa's traditional rulers struggled continually with what has been called the politics of the frontier.[26] Poor soils and the distribution of water supplies rendered centralisation of population difficult (risking food security and epidemic disease), and so one's subjects were more often than not at a distance. Extending authority over neighbouring peoples brought its own problems of control where communication remained difficult and populations were mobile. Attempts to centralise military power and to tax subject populations were countered by what Albert Hirschman called the 'exit option', which in this context basically means the option of moving away both physically and socially.[27]

Trade, ed. Paul Lovejoy (Madison, 1986); *Pawnship in Africa: Debt Bondage in Historical Perspective*, ed. Toyin Falola and Paul Lovejoy (Boulder, 1994).

[25] Ivor Wilks, *Ashanti in the Nineteenth Century: Structure and Evolution of a Political Order* (Cambridge, 1977); Ivor Wilks, *Forests of Gold: Essays on the Akan and the Kingdom of Asante* (Athens, OH, 1996); T. C. McCaskie, *State and Society in Pre-Colonial Asante* (Cambridge, 2003); *The History of the Ashanti Kings and the Whole Country Itself and Other Writings*, by Ofumfuo, ed. A. Adu Boahen *et al.*, Nana Agyeman Prempah 1 (Oxford, 2002).

[26] Igor Kopytoff, *The African Frontier: The Reproduction of Traditional African Societies* (Bloomington, 1987).

[27] On the long durée of political systems in Africa see the work of Jan Vansina, *How Societies Are Born: Governance in West Central Africa before 1600* (Charlottesville, VA, 2005); *idem, Paths in the Rainforest: Toward a History of Political Tradition in Equatorial Africa* (Madison, 1990).

Over the long durée we can say then that African political systems were characterised by the ongoing push and pull between centralisation and fission. Does it matter that such a large proportion of Africa's pre-colonial population lived in decentralised polities? There is a strong argument that it did not: given the prevailing conditions, centralisation may have had little to offer (until the arrival of Europeans with other ideas that is).[28] More significant than political decentralisation was the related phenomenon of sparse population and the 'exit option'.

Here I draw especially on the work of both Gareth Austin and Frederick Cooper.[29] African pre-colonial rulers, argues Cooper, were never very good at intensively exploiting their subjects. Africa was a hard place to exploit, 'a discovery made by its own would-be rulers and later by a variety of would-be conquerors' – it was not that oppression and appropriation were unknown to Africa – far from it – but that the exit option was relatively open, not just for geographic reasons but also for social ones. Extensive kinship ties, diverse networks of affiliation, the adaptability of social systems to migration and the reconstitution of politics all made it relatively easy for people to evade would-be exploiters. The consequences of 'this capacity to fend off or escape routinised economic exploitation were not all happy ones' writes Cooper, and we will see why.[30]

Austin provides a judicious assessment of the consequences of all of this for Africa's history of economic and political development. Given the general abundance of land and the relative scarcity of labour, what were the growth strategies available to Africans?[31] Raising labour productivity in agriculture through the application of fixed capital was difficult, partly because soils in Africa are generally thin, making ploughing and intensive permanent agricultural production difficult. The exceptions again confirm the rule, for instance in the case of the application of the plough in parts of Ethiopia. It follows that in most parts of Africa it was difficult if not impossible to raise revenue from land. Though there were significant exceptions (in iron-working and textile industries for example), craft specialisation and petty commodity production were

[28] Lonsdale, 'Globalization'.
[29] Gareth Austin, 'Markets with, without, and in spite of States: West Africa in the Pre-colonial Nineteenth Century', Department of Economic History, London School of Economics, Working Paper No. 03/04, Mar. 2004; Gareth Austin, 'The Labour-Intensive Path to Industrialization: An Africanist Perspective', paper presented at the African Studies Association of the UK biennial meeting, Birmingham, 2002; Gareth Austin, 'Resources and Strategies South of the Sahara: Long-term Dynamics of African Economic Development', paper presented at the African Studies Association, Washington DC, Nov. 2005; Frederick Cooper, 'Africa's Pasts and Africa's Historians', *Canadian Journal of African Studies*, 34 (2000), 298–336; Frederick Cooper, *Africa Since 1940* (Cambridge, 2004).
[30] Cooper, 'Africa's Pasts', 321.
[31] Austin, 'Labour-Intensive Path'.

limited by the same factors – the sparseness of population, poor transport and communications.

This did not mean that there was no trade. Trading systems there were, including the ancient trans-Saharan trade, and the Indian Ocean trade which extended inland to sources of gold in present-day Zimbabwe. When, in 1352, Ibn Battuta came across cowry shells in Mali, they had already been in use for centuries by traders.[32] Aside from these long-distance systems, dense networks of exchange had also emerged in regions where complementary ecological zones met (the forest and the savannah, for example), along with some specialisation in petty-commodity production, in the textile industry, for example.

It follows from this general theory of labour scarcity in Africa that the major brake on the development of internal markets was the difficulty of securing a supply of labour to meet the demand for goods. Because prospective employers found it difficult to persuade largely self-sufficient peasants to yield their labour, ambitious accumulators usually resorted to coercion.[33] Where labour markets existed, then, they took the form of a trade in rights in people – usually captives from other groups reduced to slaves or pawns. It was a rational response. Rather than struggle to appropriate a surplus from their own peasant subjects (and face all the attendant social hurdles which that involved), Africa's big men externalised the extraction process and captured slaves from other groups. This way they also avoided (up to a point, but only up to a point) the eternal questions of legitimacy which arose from attempting to harness the labour of those who considered themselves 'kin'; this way African societies retained their deeply held valuation of people rather than things, whilst simultaneously transforming other peoples' people *into* things. But it was a precarious balancing act.[34]

It was, of course, the nature of Africa's encounter with the 'modern world' which transformed this internal African dynamic into one with lasting global implications. This encounter came with the slave trade. There was a 'tragic paradox' in the fact that a labour scarce continent became the source of labour for the New World. It might not make sense at the collective level to sell people, but it made perfect sense for individual African rulers. As Frederick Cooper argues, the export slave trade had a very particular appeal to ruthless rulers. It offered them the possibility of

[32] Jan. S. Hogendorn and Marion Johnson, *The Shell Money of the Slave Trade* (Cambridge, 1986). On currency in Africa see also *Money Matters: Instability, Values and Social Payments in the Modern History of West African Communities*, ed. J. I. Guyer (Portsmouth, NH, 1995).

[33] Austin, 'Labour-Intensive Path', for a summary of this argument.

[34] On 'wealth in people and things' see the collection of essays in the *Journal of African History*, 36 (1995), also Charles Piot, 'Of Slaves and the Gift: Kabre Sale of Kin during the Era of the Slave Trade', *Journal of African History*, 37 (1996), 31–49.

making large profits without the problem of extracting and disciplining labour.

It is not just that millions of Africans were lost to the slave trade, and all the human tragedy involved in that, but, Cooper argues, the external trade in people entrenched a model of accumulation which has persisted. Neither colonial rulers nor their post-colonial successors found it easy to pursue strategies of sustainable exploitation internally to African economies, but easy money was always to be made at the interface with the outside world, as in the period of the slave trade. Independent African rulers, writes Cooper, have presided over 'gatekeeper states' able to control the interface with the outside world better than production and commerce within.[35]

Cooper's argument seems generally convincing to me. It is broad enough to accommodate the view that much of Africa's current poverty is the result of the policy failures of the last twenty years or so, but it places this in a longer-term perspective of the relationship between Africa's ruling elites and the world economy. But of course any rendering of history at such a level of generalisation is bound to leave us with some questions, and this is where some of the most interesting and challenging work in African history and anthropology is taking place. Jane Guyer is at the forefront of this work.[36] She has argued that though the idea of wealth in people is a powerful one, it is largely unspecified. She goes on to demonstrate the multiple dimensions of the value accorded to persons in Africa, which she describes as a regime of quality as well as quantity. These multiple dimensions cannot be understood in materialist or demographic terms alone. Neither, she argues, can we assume that a pattern of accumulation built on capture was completely separate from the apparently more circuitous one originating in trading and production, because they crossed over at various points.[37] Finally, Guyer is not persuaded that we have completely answered the puzzle of why so many people were sold into slavery if it is the case that acquiring people lay at the heart of African political self-realisation.

And though most people sold into slavery in Africa were the captives of other more powerful groups (this is where centralised polities *did* have some advantages), this was not always the case. How, asks Charles Piot, can we explain the fact that some people sold their kin in return for

[35] Frederick Cooper, *Africa since 1940* (Cambridge, 2004).

[36] Jane I. Guyer, 'Wealth in People and Self-Realization in Equatorial Africa', *Man*, 28, 2 (1993), 243-65; Jane I. Guyer and S. M. Eno Belinga, 'Wealth in People as Wealth in Knowledge: Accumulation and Composition in Equatorial Africa', *Journal of African History*, 36 (1995), 91-129; Jane I. Guyer, *Marginal Gains: Monetary Transactions in Atlantic Africa* (Chicago, 2004).

[37] This is part of a larger critique of the notion of 'separate spheres' in Africa's economic history, and is elaborated in Guyer's latest book, *Marginal Gains*.

cowry shells?[38] Samuel Johnson, the nineteenth-century historian of the Yoruba, asked the same question.[39] In the case of the Kabre of Togo studied by Piot, an especially close and affectionate relationship was said to exist between a child and his or her mother's brother. Yet in the era of the slave trade it was your maternal uncle who was more likely than anyone else to sell you into slavery: beware close affective relationships would seem to be the lesson of this story. Piot explains this apparent puzzle in terms of the complex internal logic of the Kabre prestational economy, and the intersection between the local Kabre 'gift' economy and the larger political economy of slavery. As Guyer puts it, 'in lived practice, investment "portfolios" with a wealth-in-people model' were far from static. What emerges from this literature is the complex nature of the engagement of African economic and social systems with the world economy, and the moral dilemmas created by and negotiated through the sale of people.

Africa's more ruthless rulers may have attempted to avoid the moral issues involved in transforming people into things through their sale of captive strangers who were already somehow 'other', but like Guyer I am not persuaded that they avoided the question completely. After all, these were polities which prior to the slave trade had often raided for captives in order to assimilate neighbouring groups, and, in any case, as Piot reminds us, not all of those sold into slavery were strangers, some of them were kin. No wonder that men like Samuel Crowther were so horrified by what they saw in parts of nineteenth-century West Africa. It was not only their Christian sensibilities which were offended, but their traditional African sensibilities too. Meanwhile, unable to imagine the modern monster which was the sugar plantation, African rulers, including those who were themselves heavily involved in the trade, puzzled over the voracious appetite of the Europeans for slaves. In many societies consumption on this scale was a symptom of a cannibalistic kind of witchcraft. Rosalind Shaw argues that the memory of the slave trade is still very evident in Sierra Leone today in the forms taken by witchcraft accusations, and the same could be argued for other parts of Africa heavily affected by the trade.[40] Selling people needed some social justification, so captives were often accused of being witches involved in the invisible consumption of others. By this means the sellers of slaves accused their victims of precisely that in which they were themselves implicated – the

[38] Charles Piot,' Of Slaves and the Gift'.
[39] Samuel Johnson, *A History of the Yorubas from the Earliest Times to the Beginning of the British Protectorate* (London, 1921).
[40] Rosalind Shaw, 'The Production of Witchcraft/Witchcraft as Production: Memory, Modernity and the Slave Trade in Sierra Leone', *American Ethnologist*, 24, 4 (1997), 856–76; Rosalind Shaw, *Memories of the Slave Trade: Ritual and the Historical Imagination in Sierra Leone* (Chicago, 2002).

illegitimate (in local terms) transformation of persons into things. Shaw puts it like this: 'By authorising one of the principal ways in which persons were transformed into slaves, those who controlled witch-finding divinations accused those convicted as witches of an invisible "eating" of others analogous to that in which they were themselves engaged.' Yet at the same time their own participation in an 'eating' trade was inevitably also the object of social commentary. It is not easy to get away with 'eating' others.

As a whole body of work on the 'modernity of witchcraft' shows, wealth in Africa is often assumed to have been acquired through invisible means. Shaw, amongst others, suggests that such understandings of the workings of the modern world can be traced back to the era of the slave trade.

In a recent piece in the *Guardian* the Nigerian novelist, Chimamanda Ngozi Adichie (whose novel, *Purple Hibiscus*, was shortlisted for the Orange Prize) complained that virtually no one would read her novel in Nigeria, and more generally that the Nigerian public hardly reads novels at all.[41] She acknowledges the argument that Nigerians are just too poor to read – literature being a pursuit of the middle class 'and our middle class is being economically eroded'. But she goes on to point out that many Nigerians *do* read, but what they read are religious manuals and self-help books assuring their readers that there are answers to the apparent mystery of why some get fat and rich while the majority grow poor. It is a literature that assures Nigerians that wealth is a spiritual virtue or, as Adichie puts it, a 'scarcity-driven brand of religion where pastors in sleek churches assure you that what God wants you to have is that new Mercedes Benz'. Such brands of religion are precisely targeted, one could argue, because, as in the period of the slave trade, so much of contemporary Nigeria's wealth creation is externalised and therefore subject to suspicion.

If the slave trade had lasting effects on how some Africans thought about wealth creation, it was crucially important too for the ways in which it framed the encounter between Europeans and African peoples in the nineteenth century. We know that in earlier centuries such encounters (limited as they were mainly to coastal societies) involved complex interactions of the kind described by Bayly and others in many parts of the non-European world.[42] But slavery, Abolition and the development of racial thinking in the nineteenth century had profound effects on the construction of 'Africa' and on the way in which Africans would be located in the emerging global order. Not all of this was new – it had some deep roots – but if Africans struggled to solve their own moral dilemmas over slavery through their own cultural referents, Europeans (both pro and

[41] Chimamanda Ngozi Adichie, 'Blinded by God's Business', *Guardian*, 19 Feb. 2005, 7.
[42] Thornton, *The Kongolese Saint Anthony*; Peter Mark, *'Portuguese' Style and Luso-African Identity* (Bloomington, 2002).

anti-slavery) were faced with similar challenges. Debates over Abolition when combined with new scientific theories had the paradoxical effect of hardening racial attitudes. The forces of liberalism as they spread through the world, as Bayly acknowledges, bred complex reactions and produced unforeseen consequences.

We can see the seeds of this in one example from mid-eighteenth-century France, even before the advent of liberalism and before lines of race had been hardened by scientific racism. Francisque, an Indian-born slave, was taken by his master to France, and promptly evaded his control. His master attempted to claim him back, but Francisque was represented by a legal team which argued that as an Indian, Francisque was not covered by the French laws devised for slaves. These laws, they said, assumed slaves to be blacks, from Africa, and Francisque is not an African. They backed up their argument with an elaborate contrast between the supposed barbarity of the African and the civility of Francisque's Indian natal home, drawing on Buffon's climatological theories which isolated the African as peculiarly suited to slavery. And when push came to shove they resorted to physiological difference directly: here is Francisque, look at him,

> it suffices to see him to know that he has never spent a day on the burning sands of Guinea or Senegal. It is true that his nose is a bit large, his lips a little fat. But disregarding his colour, he looks more European than many Europeans who need only black skin to appear African.[43]

The lawyers won their case – Francisque was freed on the basis that though his legal status was that of slave, his Indian cultural origins and lack of African physical features meant that he was not a 'black', and by slaves, we really mean 'blacks'.

In the nineteenth century, then, Europeans approached Africa with a number of preconceptions, some with long genealogies, others the product of recent history. Africa was located at or near the bottom of the civilisational and material heap. While Asia had been the source of manufactured goods which had fuelled cultures of consumption in Europe (and which now, of course, would be subject to the competition attendant on industrialisation), Africa had been the source of nothing much but coerced labour. While for some the slave trade spoke to the greed of Europeans and the dark side of modernity, it was also true that Africans had been selling one another – more evidence, if it were needed, of the depravity of the 'dark continent'. If Africa had anything to offer at all it was likely to be hidden in the landscape, not in the fabric of the society: untapped sources of minerals – gold for example. For while some

---

[43] Megan Vaughan, *Creating the Creole Island: Slavery in Eighteenth Century Mauritius* (Durham, NC, 2005), 157, quoting Sue Peabody, *'There Are No Slaves in France'* (New York and Oxford, 1996), 65–6.

went to Africa with Christianity and Commerce in mind, others went with a more smash-and-grab approach to the economics of colonisation, backed up by the doctrine of free trade.

In order to understand the position of Africa in the 'modern world' we need a conception of history, like Bayly's, which crosses spaces, tracks global processes, regards African and European structures as mutually interacting and mutually constitutive and which recognises that globalisation was a multi-centred phenomenon. Beneath and in the interstices of apparent European hegemony, after all, a vibrant Islamic culture continued and continues to make its mark on the history, politics and economics of large swathes of the continent, and the current flow of African missionaries to Britain and other godless places reminds us of just how far the Christian centre of gravity has shifted in the modern world. But as Bayly is at pains to point out, global processes and uniformities had as their corollary the creation of local particularities. Perhaps the main problem with Bayly's thesis when applied to Africa is that it obscures the degree to which Africa was *not* fully integrated into the processes he describes as being global.

This is a hazardous argument for an historian of Africa to make. After all, for decades we have been emphasising that Africa *is* part of the world, that it was and is subject to the same forces as other parts of the world, that Africans are capitalists too, that politics in Africa are like politics elsewhere, that witchcraft is a thoroughly modern business and so on. Replacing a theory of European exceptionalism with one of African peculiarity is certainly not what I am suggesting here, but the seemingly intractable problem of poverty on the continent, to which the Commission on Africa, if nothing else, has drawn the world's attention, must also direct the historian's attention to the longer-term history of Africa's incorporation into the modern world and its global economy.

Let me return to Frederick Cooper's argument. Africa was a hard place to exploit internally due to the 'exit option' and so the history of wealth creation in Africa is one, by and large, of externalisation of the process, most evidently in the period of the slave trade. Africa, through the slave trade, and later as a producer of primary products, was intimately linked to the evolution of capitalism in Europe, but Cooper questions the degree to which institutions of 'entrepreneurship turned into self-reproducing social structures that assure, or, as Marx saw it, compel workers and capitalists alike to optimise their economic activities and innovate'. Cooper argues that the colonial rulers who came on the scene towards the end of the nineteenth century were no more successful than their predecessors in turning Africa into a 'predictable space for rational economic exploitation'. Colonial states were relatively weak. They might try to control access to land and to socially engineer the supply of labour, but their capacity to do so was limited. Much colonial development centred on extraction from isolated areas of mineral production. Elsewhere, Cooper argues, colonial rulers had to be satisfied with gaining when they could from largely autonomous African agricultural initiatives. Communication channels were narrow, geared to extraction and running from interior to coast. Independent Africa's rulers then inherited this pattern of looking outwards rather than inwards to make a profit. Africa's rulers, argues Cooper, were able to control the interface with the outside world better than production and commerce from within. Their lasting creation has been the 'gatekeeper state'. Political struggles concentrate on access to and control over the 'gate' to the outside world, since this is where large profits can be made, legally and illegally. Distrustful of competition and of any autonomous initiatives, Africa's ruling elites also became authoritarian in an attempt to control societies which in some ways remained stubbornly mobile, hard to pin down and 'undocile'.

This is not the same as saying that the forces of capitalism left 'traditional' Africa intact – this would be absurd – it is rather to argue that the impact of capitalism has been particularly uneven in Africa, behaving with an unpredictability which reinforces (not unreasonable) beliefs that its workings are closely connected to unseen forces.[44] Neither the market nor the state works in completely known ways, though both violence and neglect have often characterised the operation of the latter. In parts of Africa blessed (or some might say cursed) with oil resources the contrast between the wealth which can be created through the hard labour of the peasantry and that which can be grasped by having some position on the gate between international oil companies and the black stuff itself is *so* great that it is hard for most ordinary people to conceive of these two activities as related at all. In Nigeria in the 1980s, Karin Barber tells us, people well understood that 'Petro nairas' were produced, not through virtuous labour, but through bribery and through nefarious means connected to the occult.[45] The role of international financial institutions continues the theme of externalisation and cannibalistic consumption. Rural as well as urban Africans are well aware that key decisions affecting their livelihoods, their survival even, are made in distant capitals by people whose thinking is not entirely transparent, even if their vocabulary is one in which the word transparency comes up a lot. No wonder that literate Nigerians spend their money on self-help pamphlets purporting to demystify money-making, no wonder that

---

[44] On the radical unpredictability of African economies and its effects on local initiatives see Sara Berry, *No Condition Is Permanent: The Social Dynamics of Agrarian Change in Sub-Saharan Africa* (Madison, 1993); Guyer, *Monetary Gains*.

[45] Karin Barber, 'Popular Reactions to the Petro-Naira', *Journal of Modern African Studies*, 20, 3 (1982), 431–50.

stories of bloodsucking and cannibalism have more currency than ever in Africa, no wonder that the International Monetary Fund is accused of sucking blood through a pipeline which extends from villages in Southern Malawi to downtown Washington DC to pay for food aid.[46]

Recent histories of empire have, like Bayly's account of the birth of the modern world, stressed its multi-faceted and locally complex nature. This has been a welcome development and one in which historians of Africa have willingly participated, emphasising African agency, African appropriations of the modern techniques of literacy, the central role of African intermediaries in empire and so on. In *Captives* Linda Colley rightly argued that the experience of empire could not be viewed as co-extensive with that of Atlantic slavery, because generally the impact of empire was more uneven, sometimes shallow and far more slow; because intruders were frequently limited in number and dependent often on a measure of indigenous tolerance.[47] But for Africa, I would argue, it is precisely this combination of patchy violent intervention producing coerced labour (for the slave trade, for Leopold's rubber state, for the mines of Southern Africa) *and* skeletal administration, shallow hegemony and economic neglect which has produced such a difficult inheritance for contemporary Africans, millions of whom now voluntarily seek a life on other continents.

Africa's problems of poverty are not unique, and some of these problems have been exacerbated in the last twenty years by the interventions of international agencies. But the longer history of Africa's awkward integration into the 'modern world' has also left us with a challenging legacy.

---

[46] Megan Vaughan, 'Diary', *London Review of Books*, 25, 6 (25 Mar. 2003).
[47] Linda Colley, *Captives: Britain, Empire and the World, 1600–1850* (London, 2002).

Transactions of the RHS 16 (2006), pp. 163–80 © 2006 Royal Historical Society
doi:10.1017/S0080440106000417   Printed in the United Kingdom

THE BREAK-UP OF BRITAIN? SCOTLAND AND THE END OF EMPIRE

The Prothero Lecture

By T. M. Devine

READ 6 JULY 2005

ABSTRACT. The essay is concerned with the retreat from the British empire and specifically with the Scottish aspects of that process. It is now acknowledged that the Scottish role in the imperial project was central. Hence there is a special interest in tracing the response to the end of empire north of the border. Several historians and political scientists have argued that imperial decline was likely to destroy one of the key foundations of the Anglo-Scottish Union. This essay challenges these assumptions by demonstrating that imperial decline failed to produce much political concern in Scotland. The possible reasons for this are considered.

I

Most of the great territorial empires in world history have broken up slowly over several generations of decline and decay. This was not so in the case of Britain. As late as 1945 its empire was still virtually intact with British rule extending across the oceans of the globe and populations of around 700 million people. A mere two decades later, this figure had fallen to 5 million of which 3 million were concentrated in Hong Kong. In June 1997, even that last major outpost of empire was handed back to the Chinese when the Black Watch played *Auld Lang Syne* as the Union Jack was lowered over the territory for the very last time.

The end of empire was not only rapid, it was also remarkably peaceful. True, there were outbreaks of nationalist hostility in Cyprus, Aden and Kenya during the imperial retreat. But in Britain itself all was calm. Indeed, as several scholars have noted, the British seem to have accepted the collapse of their empire with an equanimity bordering on indifference. Here contrasts are often drawn with the experience of France and Portugal. Both had much smaller empires than the British in Africa, Asia and Indo-China. Yet in these two countries decolonisation was followed by social trauma and political convulsion at home.[1]

---

[1] John Darwin, *The End of the British Empire. The Historical Debate* (Oxford, 1991), 1–4, 34–5; *idem, Britain and Decolonisation* (1988), 324, 328; *The Oxford History of the British Empire. The Twentieth Century*, ed. Judith M. Brown and W. R. Lewis (Oxford, 1999), 330, 706.

In one important sense the relative silence in Britain, outside the right wing of the Conservative Party, is intriguing. As the break-up of empire loomed, some commentators predicted that imperial decline must place considerable strain on the Anglo-Scottish Union. As early as 1937, Andrew Dewar Gibb, Professor of Constitutional Law in the University of Glasgow and a prominent nationalist with deep imperial sympathies, noted in his *Scottish Empire* that 'The existence of the Empire has been the most important factor in securing the relationship of Scotland and England in the last three centuries.'[2] He implied that without empire this ancient political connection might not stand the test of time. Similarly in his last work, Sir Reginald Coupland, a distinguished imperial historian of the old school, considered the potential rise of Scottish and Welsh nationalism in the aftermath of decolonisation and gloomily concluded that Ireland might not be the last of the nations of the British Isles to leave the United Kingdom.[3]

This theme was taken up even more vigorously in the 1960s and 1970s as the Scottish National Party (SNP) began to achieve its first spectacular successes in elections. Commentators as varied as H. J. Hanham, Jan Morris and Tom Nairn outlined a possible relationship between the end of empire and dissolution of the Union. Hanham's *Scottish Nationalism*, published in 1969, two years after Winnie Ewing's sensational by-election SNP victory at Hamilton, observed:

> Now that the Empire is dead many Scots feel cramped and restricted at home. They chafe at the provincialism of much of Scottish life and at the slowness of Scottish economic growth, which is related to that provincialism. To give themselves an opening to a wider world the Scots need some sort of outlet, and the choice appears at the moment to be between emigration and re-creating the Scottish nation at home.[4]

For Jan Morris, an author who had written extensively about the British empire, there was no longer much scope for a shared pride between the nations of the United Kingdom with the acceleration of decolonisation. All that remained in the Union, she remarked memorably, was 'this grubby wreck of old glories' in which few could take any satisfaction. Hence, the time was ripe for a new constitutional beginning.[5] It was then left to the Marxist writer, Tom Nairn, in 1977 to provide a full-scale analysis of those issues. For him, the break-up of Britain was not only inevitable but necessary as a constructive response to the crisis in the Union triggered by the end of empire.[6]

[2] Andrew Dewar Gibb, *Scottish Empire* (1937), 311.
[3] Sir Reginald Coupland, *Welsh and Scottish Nationalism* (1954), xv, 12, 13.
[4] H. J. Hanham, *Scottish Nationalism* (1969), 212.
[5] *Daily Telegraph*, 24 Feb. 1979, cited in Keith Robbins, '"This Grubby Wreck of Old Glories": The United Kingdom and the End of the British Empire', *Journal of Contemporary History*, 15 (1980), 84.
[6] Tom Nairn, *The Break-Up of Britain* (1977), 118–20.

These observers and others had, on the face of it, a plausible case. The British empire was seen traditionally as a vital economic cement of Union as, for the Scots from the later eighteenth century onwards, the empire provided a remarkable set of opportunities in trade, the professions, military service and administration for the Scottish upper and middle classes while the entire production structure of Scottish industry from the age of cotton to the era of heavy industry was built around imperial markets.[7] Since the empire supplied a powerful material rationale for Union, it therefore seemed attractive to argue that with its disappearance the economic anchor which had for so long bound Scotland to England could easily also be cut adrift. This point was apparently given added force by the analysis of Tom Nairn, George Davie and others of the long-run history of nationalism in Scotland. For them the nineteenth and early twentieth centuries were an epoch of profound crisis for Scottish nationhood. In Europe during these decades the Scots were out of step as, throughout the continent, small historic nations asserted their rights to self-determination and independence. In Scotland, however, nationalism in this form was conspicuous by its absence. Their argument is that the Scottish professional and mercantile elites were seduced by the glittering prizes of empire, selling in the process their distinctive identity and ancient autonomy for a share of the imperial spoils. With decolonisation, on the other hand, nationalist aspirations could once again come to the fore.[8] As John Mackenzie has put it in his commentary on this argument:

> With the end of Empire the Scots could at last escape from their self-interested complicity and reunite nation with state after the dramatic rupture of that particular Union. With the loss of the colonies, the imperial cataracts can be removed from the eyes of the imperial collaborators and a new democratic dispensation can be discerned emerging from which the national opthamologist can free the Scots as much as the subordinate peoples of the white settler territories, India and the dependant empire.[9]

Thus far, however, more than fifty years after the independence of India, the dire predictions of the disintegration of the Union have proven to be false. Indeed, arguably it is more secure now than it has been at any time since the late 1960s and 1970s when Scottish nationalism seemed to have achieved an unstoppable momentum. In 2005 the SNP is becalmed with less than 20 per cent of the popular vote in Scotland and the pro-Union parties are in the ascendant in the Scottish parliament.[10]

---

[7] T. M. Devine, *Scotland's Empire 1600–1815* (2003); *idem, Scotland's Empire and the Shaping of the Americas* (Washington, 2003); Michael Fry, *The Scottish Empire* (Edinburgh, 2001).

[8] Nairn, *Break-Up*, 162; R. J. Finlay, 'Controlling the Past: Scottish Historiography and Scottish Identity in the 19th and 20th centuries', *Scottish Affairs*, 9 (1994), 127–43.

[9] John M. Mackenzie, 'A Scottish Empire? The Scottish Diaspora and Interactive Identities', in *The Heather and the Fern. Scottish Migration and New Zealand Settlement*, ed. T. Brooking and J. Coleman (Otago, 2003), 19.

[10] Lindsay Paterson *et al.*, *New Scotland, New Politics?* (Edinburgh, 2001), 83–100.

George Robertson, a former secretary of state for Scotland and director-general of NATO, famously observed that devolution would kill Scottish political nationalism stone dead. Whether this is a correct diagnosis or not, it is still tolerably clear that the advent of a Scottish parliament has not precipitated a headlong rush to full independence, despite the fears of many Unionists.

In truth, of course, the Union was itself transformed by the devolution of important powers to Edinburgh in 1999. But any direct or convincing link between the end of empire and the new constitutional settlement has yet to be demonstrated. Political scientists and modern Scottish historians have tended to look elsewhere for the root causes of devolution and have found them in the disenchantment felt in Scotland in the 1960s and 1970s when both Tory and Labour, the two 'Unionist' parties, were incapable of delivering long-term economic and social benefit as UK governments struggled against recurrent currency crises and the menace of rising inflation.[11] However, these pressures were not yet enough to trigger general hostility in Scotland to the terms of the constitutional relationship with England, as the failed referendum on a Scottish Assembly in 1979 made clear. Only in the 1990s did such a consensus emerge. Then it was fashioned not by any nostalgia for lost imperial glory but by the profound economic crises of the 1980s, the 'democratic deficit' caused by the cleavage between Scottish and English voting patterns and perhaps, above all, by growing opposition to the social policies of a succession of Conservative governments. Mrs Thatcher has an infinitely greater claim to be the midwife of Scottish devolution than the factor of imperial decline.[12]

Indeed, historically, Scottish Home Rule and empire were not incompatible. The first search for some form of devolution for Scotland took place in the late nineteenth century at the high noon of the British empire and was seen by its protagonists as a means to ensuring that the governance of empire might be improved. This was not just a theoretical discussion. A series of Home Rule Acts were promulgated between the 1880s and 1914. In 1913 the policy had secured widespread agreement and was merely awaiting parliamentary time and the solution of the Irish question. The outbreak of the First World War, however, put paid to this aspiration.[13]

There is also the problem of chronology in associating the rise of Scottish political nationalism with imperial decline in the 1940s and 1950s. The Scots mainly identified with the colonies of white settlement, Canada,

---

[11] I. G. C. Hutchison, *Scottish Politics in the Twentieth Century* (Basingstoke, 2001), 121–2; Keith Webb, *The Growth of Nationalism in Scotland* (Glasgow, 1977), 85–90.

[12] T. M. Devine, *The Scottish Nation 1700–2000* (1999), 604–5.

[13] Fry, *Empire*, 380, 388, 496; Webb, *Nationalism*, 87.

South Africa, Australia and New Zealand. These were the countries which had experienced mass Scottish immigration since the eighteenth century. Ties of kindred, friendship and identity with them were close. But these dominions had enjoyed autonomy since the Statute of Westminster in 1931 while at the same time retaining a symbolic and sentimental form of attachment to the mother country through the British Commonwealth of Nations. The process of decolonisation in Asia and Africa after 1945, which was chronologically closer to the rise of the SNP, evoked little protest or opposition in Scotland. On the contrary, the Church of Scotland vigorously supported the cause of black nationalism in Africa and, through its annual General Assembly, criticised the government for not conceding independence more quickly.[14] The position of the Church on this issue was deeply significant. To a much greater extent than today it was a national church with a membership which historically reached an all-time high in the late 1950s. Traditionally, in this stateless nation, the Church of Scotland was regarded as a kind of surrogate parliament which spoke for the country on matters of contemporary political and social importance as well as religious issues through its General Assembly. The proceedings of this body were then widely reported and discussed in the Scottish press.[15]

II

We are therefore left with a conundrum. Historians claim that Scotland was heavily involved with the imperial project, yet the passing of empire seems to have had little perceptible consequence on the nation. Certainly the anticipated causal relationship between the end of empire and the dissolution of the Union has proven thus far to be fallacious. One possible way of resolving the puzzle is to question the very premise that the British empire was of central significance to the British people. This view has a long pedigree. Some time ago, for instance, the novelist, H. G. Wells, famously remarked that nineteen Englishmen out of twenty knew as much about the British empire as they did about the Italian Renaissance.[16] Historians as different as Max Beloff and A. J. P. Taylor also insisted that imperialism was on the whole an irrelevant factor in the lives of most Britons.[17] From a similar perspective James Morris argued

---

[14] T. Royle, *Winds of Change. The End of Empire in Africa* (1996), 231; R. Ferguson, *George MacLeod* (1990), 299.

[15] Callum Brown, *The Social History of Religion in Scotland since 1730* (1987), 209–47.

[16] Bill Nasson, *Brittania's Empire. Making a British World* (Stroud, 2004), 208.

[17] John M. Mackenzie, *Propaganda and Empire* (Manchester, 1984), 1.

that few people in the United Kingdom found the empire of any great significance or interest.[18]

More recently, however, the most powerful and detailed exploration of this thesis has come from the pen of Bernard Porter in *The Absent-Minded Imperialists: Empire, Society and Culture in Britain* (2004). Despite its subtitle, Porter's focus is almost entirely Anglocentric. In 108 pages of end-notes and 30 pages of 'select' bibliography, there is only one article with a Scottish emphasis. Essentially, therefore, it is for English historians to judge the overall validity of his argument. But Porter's general thesis hardly convinces in a specific Scottish context. Far from being a marginal factor in the nation's domestic history, empire was crucial to the Scottish experience during the eighteenth and nineteenth centuries. Indeed, one author has recently claimed that so fundamental to the moulding of the modern nation was the British empire that it should rank alongside the Reformation, the Union of 1707 and the Enlightenment as one of the truly seminal developments in Scottish history.[19] So intense was Scottish engagement with empire that it had an impact on almost every nook and cranny of Scottish life over these two centuries: economy, identity, politics, intellectual activity, popular culture, consumerism, religion, demographic trends and much else.[20]

In the eighteenth century the colonial tobacco and sugar trades were two of the key drivers of Scottish industrialisation while during the Victorian and Edwardian eras the Scottish heavy industrial economy was strongly biased towards export markets and the principal outlets for ships, locomotives and engineering products were the British colonies.[21] Dundee, one of Scotland's four principal cities, became 'Juteopolis', its booming textile industry founded on the importation of raw jute from India. Gordon Stewart, later an historian who went on to write an important study of jute, recalled the imperial connections of his native city:

> I grew up in Dundee and I thought that the Scottish city was the centre of the world jute trade. This impression was dinned into me by my geography lessons at school and by a host of childhood encounters with jute. When I felt depressed by the drabness of life amidst the row of identical, rain-stained buildings on the housing scheme where I lived, I would pedal my bike down to the docks and watch hundreds of bales of jute being unloaded from the holds of great cargo steamers which had sailed half-way round the world from Chittagong and Calcutta. On the way home from school I would sit on city buses crowded with women workers coming off their shifts with wisps of jute sticking

---

[18] James Morris, 'The Popularisation of Imperial History', *Journal of Imperial and Commonwealth History*, 1 (1973), 113–18.

[19] Fry, *Empire*, 498.

[20] John M. Mackenzie, 'Essay and Reflection: On Scotland and Empire', *International History Review*, 15 (1993), 714–39.

[21] Devine, *Empire*, 69–93, 221–49; M. S. Moss and J. R. Hume, *Workshop of the British Empire. Engineering and Shipbuilding in the West of Scotland* (1977).

to their hair and clothes and their hands roughened red by the handling of jute in the factories . . . Because of the names on the sterns of the cargo ships and the faces of the crewmen, I understood there was an Indian dimension to jute. I also learned of this connection by listening to family stories about relatives and friends of my parents who had spent time in India.[22]

In Glasgow, the economic connections were equally deep. It arrogated to itself the description 'Second City of the Empire' (a term first used as early as 1824) while the broader west of Scotland region was celebrated as 'The Workshop of the British Empire'. Scottish society more generally had strong ties to empire. As one author has put it, the Scots professional and middle classes claimed 'not merely a reasonable but a quite indecent share of the [imperial] spoils'.[23] Throughout the eighteenth and for much of the nineteenth centuries, Scottish educators, physicians, soldiers, administrators, missionaries, engineers, scientists and merchants relentlessly penetrated every corner of the empire and beyond so that when the statistical record for virtually any area of professional employment is examined, Scots are seen to be over-represented.[24]

This elite emigration was but one element in a greater mass diaspora from Scotland. Between 1825 and 1938 over 2.3 million Scots left their homeland for overseas destinations. This placed the country with Ireland and Norway in the top three of European countries with the highest levels of net emigration throughout that period. The emigrants had three main destinations – USA (after 1783), British North America (which became the Dominion of Canada in 1867) and Australia. After c. 1840 the USA was the choice of most who left but Canada predominated in the early twentieth century. Also in the 1850s Australia, for a period, was taking more Scots than each of the two North American countries considered individually.[25] These huge levels of emigration generated a vast network of family and individual connections with the colonies and dominions which were consolidated by return migration (in one estimate averaging more than 40 per cent of the total exodus in the 1890s), chain migration, letter correspondence and widespread coverage of the emigrant experience in Scottish popular press and periodical literature.[26]

The British empire also had a potent influence on Scottish national consciousness and identity. Several recent analyses have emphasised that

[22] Gordon Stewart, Jute and Empire (Manchester, 1998), ix.
[23] D. Allan, Scotland in the Eighteenth Century (Harlow, 2002), 185.
[24] Devine, Empire, xxv–xxvii.
[25] M. Gray, 'The Course of Scottish Emigration, 1750–1914: Enduring Influences and Changing Circumstances', in Scottish Emigration and Scottish Society, ed. T. M. Devine (Edinburgh, 1992), 16–36.
[26] M. Harper, Emigration from Scotland between the Wars (Manchester, 1998), 6–13; idem, Adventurers and Exiles (London, 2003), 237–81; idem, 'Introduction', in Emigrant Homecomings: The Return Movement of Emigrants, 1600–2000, ed. M. Harper (Manchester, 2005), 1–15.

for the Scots elite in the years before 1914 nationalism was not in conflict with the Union but rather was integrated closely with it. The empire was the means by which the Scots asserted their equal partnership with England after 1707. By the Victorian era it was commonplace to assert that substantial imperial expansion only occurred after the Union and hence was a joint endeavour in which the Scots had played a full part.[27] This was no empty boast. Scottish publicists, through such works as John Hill Burton's *The Scots Abroad* (2 vols., 1864) and W. J. Rattray's monumental four-volume *magnum opus*, *The Scot in British North America* (1880), were easily able to demonstrate the mark that Scottish education (especially at college and university level), presbyterianism, medicine, trading networks and philosophical enquiry had had on the colonies.[28] Pride in the Scottish achievement was taken even further by those who saw the Scottish people as a race of natural empire-builders. Thus the nationalist Andrew Dewar Gibb argued in 1930:

> the position of Scotland as a Mother nation of the Empire is at all costs to be preserved to her. England and Scotland occupy a unique position as the begetters and defenders of the Empire. They alone of all the Aryan peoples in it have never been otherwise than sovereign and independent. Ireland and Wales, mere satrapies of England, can claim no comparable place. Scotsmen today are occupying places both eminent and humble throughout the Empire, and Scottish interests are bound up with every colony in it.[29]

Nonetheless, it might be objected that the argument thus far ignores the important factor of differences in the attitudes of social class to empire. Bernard Porter in *The Absent-Minded Imperialists* focuses especially on this aspect. He sees the upper and middles classes as most committed to the imperial project while the working classes were 'either apathetic towards the empire or superficial in their attitude to it'. Porter also claims a deep ignorance about the empire on the part of the majority of the British people.[30]

Again, this interpretation hardly fits the Scottish case. While it is impossible, of course, in the current state of knowledge to determine in precise terms what the ordinary Scot thought about empire it is nevertheless unlikely that the words 'apathy' and 'ignorance' are appropriate terms to use of public opinion. Exposure to imperial themes started early in Scotland. In 1907 the Scottish Education Department in its memorandum on the teaching of history in schools directed that

[27] R. J. Finlay, 'The Rise and Fall of Popular Imperialism in Scotland, 1850–1950', *Scottish Geographical Magazine*, 113 (1997), 13–21; John M. Mackenzie, 'Empire and National Identities. The Case of Scotland', *Transactions of the Royal Historical Society*, sixth series, 8 (1998), 215–32.
[28] David S. Forsyth, 'Empire and Union: Imperialism and National Identity in Nineteenth Century Scotland', *Scottish Geographical Magazine*, 113 (1997), 6–12.
[29] A. D. Gibb, *Scotland in Eclipse* (1930), 187.
[30] Bernard Porter, *The Absent-Minded Imperialists: Empire, Society and Culture in Britain* (Oxford, 2004), 115–33.

the curriculum should develop from the study of Scotland to British and international themes but always throughout stressing the nation's role in the empire. Text books embodying this approach were soon available in schools and the most popular was *Cormack's Caledonia Readers* which placed emphasis on empire. As Robert Anderson has shown, the British empire had a key part to play in late nineteenth-century history teaching because it provided the kind of blend of British and Scottish history which reflected Scotland's position in the Union state.[31]

But this was not all. The 1900s also saw the celebration of Empire Day in schools when flags were exchanged between Scottish schools and those elsewhere in the empire. The stories of such imperial heroes as General Gordon, Sir Colin Campbell (of Indian Mutiny fame), the missionary Mary Slessor and, above all, David Livingstone would have been very well known to Scottish schoolchildren.[32] Biographies of Livingstone, the 'Protestant Saint' and the most famous and venerated Scotsman of the nineteenth century, were widely read and also awarded as prizes in schools and Sunday Schools, a practice which continued unabated through to the 1960s.[33] Of course it was not simply children who were taught to respond to these imperial heroes. They were also celebrated by the trade union movement, working men's clubs and Labour politicians, such as Keir Hardie, as models of Scottish virtue and exemplars for the nation. Knowledge of and loyalty to empire was also communicated by such organisations as the Junior Empire League with around 20,000 members and the Boys' Brigade. This last was formed in Glasgow in 1883 and not only promoted Christian values but also inculcated fidelity to the imperial ideal within its membership. The 'BBs' became enormously popular among ordinary young Scots boys well into the twentieth century.[34]

Among the mass of the population, however, perhaps the main symbols of empire were the Scottish regiments. Recognised as the spearheads of imperial expansion, and widely celebrated in music, story, painting and statue as the tartan-clad icons of the Scottish nation, they enjoyed, as Stuart Allan and Allan Carswell have put it, 'unchallenged prominence in Scottish society as symbols of national self-image'.[35] Ironically, despite the fame of the Highland soldier, the kilted battalions were mainly recruited during the Victorian age from the working class of the Scottish cities. Their exploits were widely reported not simply in the popular press but

[31] R. D. Anderson, *Education and the Scottish People 1750–1918* (Oxford, 1995), 212–13, 218–19.

[32] *Ibid.*, 218–19.

[33] Andrew C. Ross, 'Christian Missions and the Mid-Nineteenth-Century Change in Attitudes. Race: The African Experience', in *The Imperial Horizons of the British Protestant Missions, 1880–1914*, ed. Andrew Porter (2003), 102–3.

[34] Mackenzie, 'Identities', 226.

[35] Stuart Allan and Allan Carswell, *The Thin Red Line. War, Empire and Visions of Scotland* (Edinburgh, 2004), 40.

in such famous paintings as *The Thin Red Line*. The regiments made a remarkable impact on Scottish consciousness. Seen as the heirs of a martial national tradition which went back for centuries, they also acted as important catalysts for the wide diffusion of the military ethic throughout the country.[36] One major spin-off was the Volunteer movement which developed into a permanent reserve force for the army and attracted many thousands of young Scotsmen. The Volunteers were a focus for local pride but they also strongly identified with the British empire. Both the Volunteers and the Boys' Brigade adopted army ranks and nomenclature, undertook military drill and were regularly inspected by army officers. The important influence of both organisations goes a long way to explaining the exceptional scale of voluntary recruitment into the army in Scotland when war broke out in 1914.[37] More generally, the fame and significance of the Scottish military tradition lives on even to the present day as illustrated by the extraordinary and continuing success of the Edinburgh Military Tattoo and political controversies during the 2005 General Election over the proposed reorganisation of the historic Scottish regiments.

III

There therefore seems on the face of it to be a huge gap between the imperial enthusiasms of the nineteenth century and the apparent equanimity with which Scotland accepted decolonisation in the middle decades of the twentieth century. It will be argued here that the crucial period for understanding this transformation in attitude to empire occurred between the 1920s and 1950s, despite the fact that imperial sentiment did not entirely fade away during these decades.

There is, after all, plenty of evidence of continuity in the years after 1918. The massive war losses suffered by Scotland, officially counted at 74,000 but unofficially reckoned to be over 110,000, were commemorated in the Scottish National War Memorial, completed in Edinburgh Castle in 1927. It was not simply a remarkable tribute in stone to the nation's fallen but also to the sons and grandsons of Scotland from the empire. The Roll of Honour included all those who had served in Scottish regiments and in those of the dominions overseas, eloquent affirmation of the continuing importance of the imperial bond.[38] The link between empire and the

[36] Devine, *Empire*, 290–319; Heather Streets, 'Identity in the Highland Regiments in the Nineteenth Century; Soldier, Region, Nation', in *Fighting for Identity. The Scottish Military Experience c. 1550–1900*, ed. S. Murdoch and A. Mackillop (Leiden, 2002).

[37] H. J. Hanham, 'Religion and Nationality in the Mid-Victorian Army', in *War and Society*, ed. M. R. D. Foot (1973), 173.

[38] E. W. McFarland, 'Introduction: "A Coronach in Stone"', in *Scotland and the Great War*, ed. Catriona M. M. Macdonald and E. W. McFarland (East Lothian, 1999), 1–2.

nation Church also seemed intact. The cult of David Livingstone reached its apotheosis in the 1920s when many small donations by ordinary Scots financed the creation of the Livingstone Memorial Centre in Blantyre, Lanarkshire, in the cotton mill complex where the legendary explorer and missionary had worked as a boy. The Centre remained a place of pilgrimage for schools and Sunday Schools until the 1950s.[39] The public face of imperial Scotland seemed also to have changed little. A great imperial exhibition was held in Glasgow in 1938, the fourth in a series which since the 1890s had attracted literally millions of visitors.[40] As late as 1951 a colonial week was held in the same city. Empire was also still very much on the political agenda. In the inter-war years factional arguments raged in the Scottish nationalist movement over the nature of the relationship which a self-governing Scotland would have with the empire. Even the Labour Party temporarily diluted earlier hostility and some of its leading intellectuals in Scotland, including John Wheatley, argued that through the empire could come not only economic regeneration but also the hope of protecting a socialist Britain from the menace of international capitalism.[41]

In some ways, however, all this was a mirage, a false image of continuity after the trauma of the Great War. Andrew Dewar Gibb in 1937 recognised the change. With the granting of dominion status to the colonies of white settlement, he observed 'the hegemony of Britain in the Empire is steadily becoming more formal and more ornamental'.[42] Popular imperialism also waned. Scholars now regard the Glasgow Empire Exhibition of 1938 not so much as a catalyst for regenerating imperial enthusiasms as an event of mere nostalgic significance.[43] Iain Hutchison has also noted that in the 1945 election both Scottish Tory and Labour candidates referred even less frequently in their manifestos to imperial themes than their English counterparts.[44] This was a symbolic and ominous prelude to the results of that election, when the Unionists, *par excellence* the party of empire, were roundly defeated by Labour which had a quite different set of political and social priorities for the future governance of Scotland.

The traditional career route of middle-class Scots into imperial administration was crumbling. In this respect the Indian Civil Service

[39] John M. Mackenzie, 'David Livingstone: The Construction of the Myth', in *Sermons and Battle Hymns: Protestant Popular Culture in Modern Scotland*, ed. G. Walker and T. Gallagher (Edinburgh, 1990), 24–42.

[40] P. Kinchin and J. Kinchin, *Glasgow's Great Exhibitions* (Bicester, 1988).

[41] R. J. Finlay, '"For or Against?": Scottish Nationalists and the British Empire, 1919–39', *Scottish Historical Review*, 71 (1992), 184–206; Finlay, 'Imperialism', 20.

[42] Gibb, *Eclipse*, 187.

[43] B. Crampsey, *The Empire Exhibition of 1938: The Last Durbar* (Edinburgh, 1988).

[44] Hutchison, *Politics*, 121–2.

(ICS) had long enjoyed pre-eminence in the rank order of colonial administrations. By 1939, Scots accounted for 13 per cent of the Europeans on the ICS books.[45] This was still marginally greater than the Scottish proportion of UK population. Nonetheless, this was a significantly lower ratio than in the eighteenth and for much of the nineteenth centuries. Indeed, Anthony Kirk-Greene suggests that demoralisation was rampant in the ICS after 1918 because of a perceived decline in its career prospects as Indian self-government became a likely prospect. Though recruitment to the service did not dry up, the ICS was confronted with what has been described a critical shortage of satisfactory recruits from Britain which became especially acute from the 1920s.[46]

Scottish elite families were still exporting their male progeny but were no longer constrained to the same extent by opportunities within the formal empire. The great Scottish business syndicates of Jardine, Matheson and Co., the Hongkong and Shangai Bank, Burmah Oil Company, Guthries and Company and several others had become global rather than simply imperial corporations. The USA, Latin America, China and Japan all provided rich pickings for ambitious and educated Scots. They no longer, if they ever had, felt themselves restricted by imperial frontiers.[47] Above all, career goals were still more easily satisfied in London than in faraway places. Historians have been more interested in the exotic and have therefore tended to concentrate on the Scottish transoceanic experience. In truth, the London financial and business world had always been crucial.[48] The modern 'Scottish Raj' in the UK cabinet and the high-profile Scottish presence in the British media is simply the latest variant in a trend which goes back for many generations.

IV

No single cause conspired to erode Scotland's emotional attachment to empire. But the profound crisis which overwhelmed the nation in the period between the world wars in the twentieth century was a major factor. To understand this fully, however, it is necessary to describe the context of the long-term relationship between the Scottish economy and empire in the Victorian and Edwardian era. Such a perspective strongly suggests that the disastrous inter-war experience was the culmination of structural weaknesses which reached much further back in time.

---

[45] A. Kirk-Greene, *Britain's Imperial Administrators 1858–1966* (Basingstoke, 2000), 17.
[46] *Ibid.*, 88.
[47] R. A. Cage, *The Scots Abroad. Labour, Capital, Enterprise, 1750–1914* (1985).
[48] Devid Stenhouse, *On the Make. How the Scots took over London* (Edinburgh, 2004).

Certainly the close connections with imperial markets helped to boost productive capacity enormously in Scotland. One very significant consequence was a marked increase in Scottish population due to the economy's creation of more employment opportunities for the new generation. Thus, in 1701, Scotland had a total population of around 1.1 million. By 1831 the figure stood at 2.3 million and in 1911 had reached 4.7 million. Further confirmation of the dynamic nature of the economic system was the massive increase in immigration in the Victorian era, most notably from Ireland, but also including significant numbers of Italians, Jews and Lithuanians. This level of immigration over such a short period was something quite new in Scottish history and testimony to the economy's capacity to generate more employment opportunities.

Again, trading with the empire made some Scots very rich indeed. A handful of families amassed colossal fortunes. Sir Charles Tenant of the chemical empire, William Baird, the ironmaster, Sir James and Peter Coats of the threadmaking dynasty and William Weir, colliery owner and iron manufacturer, were among the forty individuals in Britain reckoned to be worth £2 million or more in the nineteenth century. Recent research has shown that the super-rich were also as well represented in Scotland as in any other part of the United Kingdom.[49] In addition to these fabulously wealthy but exceptional tycoons there were the solid ranks of the prosperous middle classes who ranged in occupational status from highly paid professionals such as lawyers to small businessmen and senior clerks. In his analysis of national income, published in 1867, the Victorian economist, R. Dudley Baxter, reckoned that 267,300 people were in this group in Scotland, had an annual income of between £100 and £1,000 and represented nearly one fifth of the total number of what he termed 'productive persons' in the country. The impact of the spending of this middle class could be seen in the elegant suburbs which blossomed around the major cities in the nineteenth century: Broughty Ferry near Dundee, the graceful terraces of the West End of Glasgow and the substantial villas of Newington and Corstorphine in Edinburgh.[50]

The increases in the outflow of capital from Scotland after 1870 were also in part a reflection of the increases in savings among the Scottish middle classes. Most of this came through Scottish solicitors and chartered accountants raising funds on behalf of overseas clients from professional and business families at home. It was said that Edinburgh in

---

[49] W. D. Rubenstein, 'The Victorian Middle Classes: Wealth, Occupation and Geography', *Economic History Review*, second series, 30 (1977), 609–11, 614.

[50] Stena Nenadic, 'The Victorian Middle Classes', in *Glasgow*, II : *1830 to 1912*, ed. W. H. Fraser and I. Maver (Manchester, 1996), 271–2.

the 1880s was 'honeycombed' with agents of these companies who were the main channel for this substantial mobilisation of middle-class capital.[51] Certainly, Scottish middle incomes were on average fewer and lower than London and the metropolitan areas of the south but in the early twentieth century on a par with the major English industrial centres in Lancashire and Yorkshire. These regions, however, hardly compared with Scottish levels of overseas investment, one of the most telling manifestations of the new wealth. These grew from an estimated £60 million in 1870 to £500 million by 1914. Not all of this went to the imperial territories – land, mining and railway developments in the USA were also major beneficiaries – but much did. In the 1880s it was reckoned that three-quarters of the British companies established for overseas investment were of Scottish origin. Nearly half of all Australian borrowing in the late nineteenth century came from Scotland. Tea planting in Ceylon, jute production in India and railways in the Canadian West also benefited. One estimate for 1914 suggested that the value of overseas investment was equivalent to £110 for every Scot compared to the average of £90 for the United Kingdom as a whole.[52] Here was unambiguous confirmation that Scotland's imperial economy had indeed generated huge increases in capital. The social elites and many in the business and professional classes had done rather well out of empire.

The picture is, however, somewhat gloomier for the rest of the population. Scotland was a grossly unequal society in the heyday of its imperial success. R. D. Baxter's calculations for 1867 suggest that around 70 per cent of 'productive persons' in Scotland, or almost a million people in total, belonged to his two bottom categories of 'lower skilled' and 'unskilled' which consisted of male workers who earned on average below £50 per annum.[53] For many at this level short-term unemployment was always a threat. Shipbuilding and the other capital goods industries were subject to intense and savage fluctuations in 1884–7, 1894, 1903–5 and 1908. In that last year, unemployment among Clydeside skilled engineers rose to nearly 20 per cent and among shipyard workers to almost a quarter. In the four major cities there were large pools of seasonal and casual labour, reckoned in the early 1900s at around 25 per cent of the work force, who were engaged in jobs such as portering, catering and street-selling where earnings were both paltry and unpredictable. For most of the period between 1830 and 1914 Scottish industrial wage rates

[51] Quoted in A. S. J. Bastier, *The Imperial Banks* (1929).
[52] C. H. Lee, 'Economic Progress: Wealth and Poverty', in *The Transformation of Scotland; The Economy since 1700*, ed. T. M. Devine, C. H. Lee and G. C. Peden (Edinburgh, 2005), 138–41.
[53] T. C. Smout, *A Century of the Scottish People 1830–1950* (1986), 109, 111.

were lower than the English average. The Board of Trade estimated in 1912 that real wages (after taking into account living costs) were fully 10 per cent less in Scottish towns than in their counterparts in England. Living costs on the other hand were higher.[54] For Glasgow, recent work by Richard Rodger has shown that the city's inhabitants paid on average over 5 per cent more for their food and rent (which accounted for four-fifths of the weekly working-class budget) than the population of Manchester, Leeds, Salford and Nottingham – and this against a background of low wages and volatile levels of employment on Clydeside.[55]

That Victorian industry was not a source of general prosperity is confirmed by the examples of Scottish migration and housing in this period. Precisely at the time when manufacturing was achieving remarkable success in overseas markets the Scots, as noted above, were leaving their native land in large numbers for the USA, Canada and Australasia. Over 2 million people emigrated from Scotland between 1815 and 1939, a rate of outward movement that, per capita, was around one and a half times that for England and Wales. This figure did not include another 600,000 who moved south of the border. In the 1850s, for instance, the loss of young men from Scotland through emigration was considerably greater than that experienced in the years of human carnage during the First World War. Scotland was therefore almost alone among European countries in having experienced both large-scale industrialisation and a great outward movement of population. Most other societies prone to high levels of emigration were poor rural economies. It seemed that many Scots were voting with their feet in the search for better prospects than were easily available to them at home.[56]

The condition of working-class housing confirmed that mass poverty was a marked feature of Scotland's age of empire and provoked endless investigation and comment by the early twentieth century. From these surveys it is abundantly clear that there was little real progress made between 1870 and 1914. Clive Lee has recently concluded that, 'by the eve of the First World War Scotland stood on the brink of a housing catastrophe'.[57] In 1911 nearly 50 per cent of the Scottish population lived in one- or two-roomed dwellings compared with just over 7 per cent in England. Rents were significantly higher north of the Border, 10 per cent greater than in Northumberland and Durham and almost 25 per cent higher than the other English midland and northern counties. Over

[54] T. M. Devine, 'Industrialisation', in *Transformation*, ed. Devine, Lee and Peden, 65–6; *idem*, 'Scotland', in *The Cambridge Economic History of Modern Britain*, 1 : *Industrialisation, 1700–1860*, ed. Roderick Floud and Paul Johnson (Cambridge, 2004), 388–416.
[55] R. Rodger, 'The Labour Force', in *Glasgow*, ed. Fraser and Maver, 163–85.
[56] T. M. Devine, 'The Paradox of Scottish Emigration', in *Emigration*, ed. Devine, 1–15.
[57] C. H. Lee, *Scotland and the United Kingdom* (Manchester, 1995), 46.

two million Scots in 1914, nearly half the population, lived more than two persons to a room, the contemporary definition of 'overcrowding'. The housing problem reflected the reality of low and fluctuating incomes. For families on limited earnings it made economic sense to take small tenement flats at a rental sufficiently affordable to avoid arrears or eviction. The problem was not so much availability of reasonable housing as the ability of very many to pay for it. In 1914, for instance, in Glasgow alone there were over 20,000 unoccupied houses or about a tenth of the city's total stock. The housing crisis was the most striking manifestation of the depth of Glasgow's poverty problem in the very decade when it proclaimed itself 'Second City of the Empire'.[58]

The conclusion must be that despite high levels of emigration Scotland suffered from a chronic over-supply of labour in the heyday of empire.[59] Low pay, underemployment, casual work and broken time were all consistent with that pattern. Some Scots had grown wealthy but the majority, despite modest gains in the later nineteenth century, remained mired in poverty and endured a hard daily struggle to make ends meet. The imperial economy was also building up potential problems for the future. The dependency on low wages and semi-skilled or unskilled labour placed the nation at a strategic disadvantage in the twentieth century when home demand propelled the new consumer economy with its focus on household good, motor vehicles, cycles, furniture and electrical products. Scotland missed out on most of this 'second Industrial Revolution'. Even before 1914, the economic structure seemed precarious. The heavy industries were all inter-connected, geared to overseas markets, especially in the empire, and at risk from such mighty competitors as the USA and Germany. The threat was especially real because the Scots excelled at the making of simple capital goods such as iron, steel, locomotives, bridges and the like which could easily be rapidly imitated by emerging competitors. Imperial markets had therefore left a flawed legacy by 1914 with serious consequences for Scotland when international trade collapsed during several years between the wars.

The manifestations of crisis were everywhere. Unemployment soared to unprecedented levels in the early 1930s. In the industrial heartland of the western lowlands, 'The Workshop of the British Empire', over a quarter of the entire labour force, nearly 200,000 individuals were out of work in 1932. New industries failed to develop and poor housing and

<hr />

[58] *Census of Population, Scotland* (1911), II , 566–7; S. Damer, 'State, Class and Housing', in *Housing, Social Policy and the State*, ed. J. Melling (1980), 90.
[59] The following two paragraphs are based on Devine, *Scottish Nation*, 201–66, 268–72, and C. H. Lee, 'Unbalanced Growth: Prosperity and Deprivation', in *Transformation*, ed. Devine, Lee and Peden, 209–24.

slum conditions remained as bad as ever with overcrowding six times greater in 1935 than south of the Border. Fears were expressed in the business community of long-term economic decline and the erosion of indigenous Scottish control as several failing firms were bought up by financial interests from England. The unprecedented scale of emigration in the 1930s intensified these anxieties. So great was the exodus that the Scottish population actually fell by nearly 40,000 in that decade, the only period since records began in which absolute decline between censuses occurred.

Now, rather than being seen as evidence of the virility of an imperial race, emigration was viewed as a scourge and confirmation of a terminal national crisis. The novelist and poet, Edwin Muir, saw it as a 'silent clearance' in which 'the surroundings of industrialisation remain, but industry itself is vanishing like a dream'. His apocalyptic vision was of a country 'being emptied of its population, its spirit, its wealth, industry, art, intellect, and innate character'. As his fellow intellectual, George Malcolm Thomson, put it: 'The first fact about the Scot is that he is a man eclipsed. The Scots are a dying race.'[60]

The most arresting illustration of the economic irrelevance of empire was the experience between the wars of the Dundee jute industry. Already, by the 1890s, Bengal had overtaken its Scottish parent to become the world's dominant centre for the jute sacks and hessian cloth which carried the world's foodstuffs and raw materials. Not surprisingly, in the depressed market conditions in the 1930s, Dundee jute interests pleaded on numerous occasions for tariffs to be imposed on the cheap imports from Calcutta. But their pleas were in vain. Now it was Dundee which looked more like the colony, and Bengal the metropole: 'jute presents an unusual example of a powerful industry emerging in a colonial setting which almost destroyed the rival industry back in Britain while the empire was still flourishing'.[61]

All this shattered faith in Scotland as the powerhouse of empire. Long before decolonisation took place, imperial markets were no longer seen to be of much benefit. Though the economy recovered during the Second World War and the immediate post-war period, the fully enfranchised masses now had other social priorities which could be delivered through the ballot box. It was therefore hardly surprising that the majority of the Scottish people reacted to the end of empire with indifference, despite Scotland's historic role before 1900 in imperial expansion. After 1945, state intervention in industry, political commitment to full employment and, above all, the Welfare State, slowly delivered security and material

---

[60] Edwin Muir, *Scottish Journey* (Edinburgh, 1935), 110; G. M. Thomson, *Caledonia or the Future of the Scots* (Edinburgh, 1932), 18–19.
[61] Stewart, *Jute*, 2–4.

improvement to the mass of Scots. These were the issues which now had widespread popular appeal, especially in the light of Scotland's social history over the previous century. The age of empire may have passed, but, ironically, the Union was now even more important than before. As one of the poorer parts of the United Kingdom, Scotland was likely to gain more than other regions from the introduction of an interventionist social and economic policy which was being implemented in the very decade that decolonisation accelerated through the independence of India.[62] State support from cradle to grave became the new anchor of the Union state.

---

[62] C. H. Lee, 'Unbalanced Growth: Prosperity and Deprivation', in *Transformation*, ed. Devine, Lee and Peden, 231.

ROYAL HISTORICAL SOCIETY
REPORT OF COUNCIL
SESSION 2005-2006

Officers and Council

- At the Anniversary Meeting on 25 November 2005 Dr J.P. Parry succeeded Professor J. Hoppit as Honorary Treasurer; the remaining Officers of the Society were re-elected.
- The Vice-Presidents retiring under By-law XVII were Professor H.T. Dickinson and Dr C.J. Kitching. Professor R.J.A.R. Rathbone, PhD, and Professor P.M. Thane, MA, PhD, were elected to replace them.
- The Members of Council retiring under By-law XX were Dr S.R. Ditchfield, Professor M. Finn and Professor F. O'Gorman. In accordance with By-law XXI, amended, Professor P.G. Burgess, MA, PhD, Professor S.R.I. Foot, MA, PhD and Professor G.A. Stone, MA, PhD were elected in their place.
- Professor R.A. Burns joined the *Studies in History* Editorial Board, replacing Professor M. Taylor.
- The Society's staffing arrangements have again changed over the year. In April 2006 Jane Boland was succeeded temporarily as Executive Secretary by Joy McCarthy. Sue Carr has been appointed to the post with effect from 25 August 2006. Melanie Batt continued as the Society's Administrative Assistant.
- haysmacintyre were appointed auditors for the year 2005-2006 under By-law XXXIX.
- Cripps Portfolio continued to manage the Society's investment funds under the new name Heartwood Wealth Management.

Activities of the Society during the Year

The Annual Report, for the first time, contains individual reports of the activities of the seven Committees which support the work of Council - Research Policy, Teaching Policy, General Purposes, Publications, Finance, Membership and Research Support – and the remarks which now follow is a preface to these more detailed reports.

Throughout the year the Society has maintained its prominent role in defending and advancing the interests of the discipline and the profession.

The President and Honorary Secretary had a useful meeting with Professor Philip Esler, Chief Executive of the AHRC, on 21 June 2006. We expressed our disquiet at the proposal to replace the peer-reviewed RAE with metrics based on 'a basket' of up to 40 different variables, and were pleased to learn that a 'light-touch' RAE was still a possible alternative. We discussed the AHRC's current review of postgraduate funding and reiterated the Society's concern that extra support be made available for postgraduates tackling particularly challenging areas of study, such as Chinese History. The sustainability of major resources such as the Society's on-line Bibliography of British and Irish History was also debated. Outstanding issues are now being pursued through further contacts and correspondence with HEFCE and sympathetic MPs.

The President and Professor Bates, one of our Vice-Presidents, have continued to attend occasional ministerial meetings on the role of history in the school curriculum and its relationship with proposed teaching on 'citizenship'. Regular meetings of the Society, the Institute of Historical Research, History UK (HE) and the Historical Association have continued this year to pool ideas and co-ordinate responses to developments within the discipline. Conferences at the Institute of Historical Research, usually in conjunction with the Society, play an important part in building bridges with schools, the educational establishment, politicians and the wider public.

Over the past year the Society has responded to consultative documents on a wide range of issues, including the European Science Foundation's listing of journals, the British Library's Content Strategy, the AHRC's questionnaire to Learned Societies, the QAA's Subject Benchmark Statement for History and the British Academy's Survey on its Research Grants. It has also made nominations for the AHRC Peer Review College and History Panel.

As usual, the Society made two very successful visits outside London, the first to Dublin on 21–22 October, as reported in the Spring 2006 Newsletter, and the second to the University of Hull on 31 March 2006. A Society visit to mainland Europe is being planned for later in the decade.

The maintenance and enhancement of the Society's current website has caused considerable technical difficulties, to the frustration of Council as well as the Fellowship, and the decision has been taken to replace it with a more attractive, informative and user-friendly version. A working party is making excellent progress and the new website should be unveiled early in the New Year.

Council and the Officers record their debt of thanks in another challenging transitional year to the former Executive Secretary, Jane Boland, to Joy McCarthy during the interregnum, and to the Administrative Assistant, Melanie Batt, for their expert and dedicated work on these and other activities. We welcome Sue Carr as the new Executive Secretary and look forward to working with her.

Meetings of the Society

5 papers were given in London this year and 2 papers were read at locations outside London. Welcome invitations were extended to the Society to visit the History Departments at the Dublin universities and the University of Hull. (Future visits are planned to include the University of Hertfordshire on 20 October 2006, the University of Wales Bangor on 27 April 2007 and the University of Essex on 19 October 2007).

At the ordinary meetings of the Society the following papers were read:

o 'The Break-Up of Britain? Scotland and the end of the Empire'
   Professor Tom Devine (6 July 2005: Prothero Lecture)
o 'What were the Penal Laws for?'
   Dr Ian McBride (21 October 2005 at the Royal Irish Academy, Dublin)
o 'From Scientific Conversation to Shop Talk'
   Professor Jim Secord (27 January 2006)
o 'Representing Africa: ambassadors and Princes from Christian Africa to Renaissance Italy and Portugal, 1402–1608'
   Professor Kate Lowe (10 March 2006)
o 'King Henry I and Northern England'
   Professor Judith Green (31 March 2006 at the University of Hull)
o 'The Origins of the English Hospital'
   Dr Sethina Watson (19 May 2006: Alexander Prize Essay)

• At the Anniversary meeting on 25 November 2005, the President, Professor Martin Daunton, delivered his first address on 'Britain and Globalization since 1850: Creating a Global Order, 1850–1914'.

Conferences

i) a joint conference was held with The Centre for English Local History, University of Leicester, to mark the 50th Anniversary of W. G. Hoskins' *Making of the English Landscape*, at the University of Leicester on 7–10 July 2005;
ii) a one day seminar to commemorate the Society's former President, Professor Gerald Aylmer, on 'Historical Research: the role of the National Museum Collections' was held at the Imperial War Museum on 6 October 2005. A report appeared in the Autumn 2005 Newsletter;
iii) a seminar on 'History in the School Curriculum' was held at the Royal Irish Academy, Dublin, on 22 October 2005;

iv) a one day conference with the History of Parliament Trust to mark the 400th anniversary of the Gunpowder Plot, was held at Westminster Hall on 4 November 2005. A report appeared in the Spring 2006 Newsletter;

v) a conference on 'New Directions in British Historiography of China' was held at the Institute of Historical Research on 26 November 2005. A report appeared in the Spring 2006 Newsletter;

vi) a joint conference with the Institute of Historical Research and the Historical Association on 'History and the Public' was held at the IHR on 13–14 February 2006.

The conference focused on how those with professional responsibility for the interpretation of the past communicate with the huge – and seemingly insatiable – public enthusiasm for matters historical. The central conclusion was that the subject of History and the Public is both extremely important and extremely complex. On the one hand, the public's enthusiasm and expertise needs to be listened to. On the other hand, on occasion the public needs quite simply to be better informed. It was noted that some of the most powerful current initiatives have come from sectors which might not be deemed to fall within the traditional definition of historical. The Council for British Archaeology, for example, has a policy of 'Archaeology for All'; the Archive Awareness Campaign has brought together archivists, family historians and genealogists. There are going to be follow-up conferences in Swansea and Liverpool; there should without doubt be more. In due course further issues will be raised around the even broader theme 'Why History Matters'. And as long as Government continues to drive forward agendas within the frameworks of social inclusion, 'Every Child Matters', citizenship and Britishness, there must be extensive debate not just around 'Why?', but also around 'How?' and 'To Whom?'.

vii) a joint conference with the YMCA, 'Christian Movements', was held in Birmingham on 17–19 February 2006;

viii) a conference, 'Cultures of Political Counsel?', was held on 7–9 April 2006, at the University of Liverpool.

The Colin Matthew Memorial Lecture for the Public Understanding of History - previously known as the Gresham Lecture - was given on Wednesday 2 November 2005 by Dr Michael Wood on 'Travels in Time: History and Identity in Today's World'. These lectures continue to be given in memory of the late Professor Colin Matthew, a former Literary Director and Vice-President of the Society. The lecture in 2006 will be on Wednesday 1 November when Dame Joan Bakewell, CBE, one of the most respected presenters and commentators on British radio and

185

television over a period of some thirty years, will speak on 'The Curse of the Poke Bonnet: Television's Version of History'.

Future conferences are to include:

i) a joint conference with the German Historical Institute London on 'How violent were the Middle Ages?', to be held in July 2006 at Cumberland Lodge, Windsor;
ii) a joint conference with the National Maritime Museum, on the Seven Years War, on 14–15 July 2006 at Greenwich;
iii) a joint conference with the Bibliographical Society on 'Historians and Bibliographers in Conversation', on 4 November 2006 at the IHR;
iv) a conference to mark the Tercentenary of the Union with Scotland is scheduled to be held in 2007;
v) Professor Miri Rubin would be hosting a conference on 'The Global Middle Ages' in 2007.

Prizes

The Society's annual prizes were awarded as follows:

- The Alexander Prize was awarded in 2006 to Sethina Watson, BA, MSt, DPhil, for her essay 'The Origins of the English Hospital'.
- The David Berry Prize for 2005, for an essay on Scottish history, was awarded to Dr Alec Ryrie for his essay, 'Congregations, Conventicles and the nature of early Scottish Protestantism'.

The judge's citation read:

'This is a vigorous and purposeful examination of the relationship of religion and politics that subverts later protestant teleologies and offers many insights into contemporary mentalities.'

- The Whitfield Book Prize for a first book on British history attracted 35 entries. The generally high quality of the entries was again commended by the assessors.

The Prize for 2005 was awarded to:

Matt Houlbrooke, *Queer London: Perils and Pleasures in the Sexual Metropolis, 1918–1957* [University of Chicago Press]

The judges' citation read:

'We thought this a subtle and exciting work of social history, using a range of sources to excellent effect and building a clear and original argument, whilst vividly evoking the experiences of homosexual men in early and mid-twentieth century London. In general it is well-written, readable, and well located within appropriate theory. The book is well-designed and the illustrations used to excellent effect.'

The judges nominated two proxime accessits:

i. Amy Froide, *Never Married. Singlewomen in Early Modern England* [Oxford University Press]

'A highly original and very interesting study of a very large section of the population which has been curiously marginalized in the historiography. She creates a convincing picture of the role of unmarried women in the economy and the community, especially of urban areas, and of their relationships with kin. She is especially effective in analysing the emergence of the negative stereotype of the 'old maid' over her period. It is a fine, original piece of work.'

ii. Maya Jasanoff, *Edge of Empire: Conquest and Collecting in the East, 1750–1850* [Fourth Estate]

'We thought this was an ambitious and original take on the growth of the British Empire. Her conception of the Empire as 'collected', just as individual collectors, whom she describes, collected artefacts in the colonies, provides a different and helpful perspective on the Empire from more purposive and conspiratorial interpretations. This approach also enables her to explore the variety of relationships between colonizers in different parts of the Empire and at different times and processes of cultural exchange between them. Also valuable and original was her emphasis on the parallels between, and interconnectedness of, the growth of the French and the British Empires. It is readable and fascinating.'

• Thanks to the continuing generous donation from The Gladstone Memorial Trust, the Gladstone History Book Prize for a first book on a subject outside British history was again awarded. The number of entries this year was 30.

The Prize for 2005 was awarded to:

Robert Foley, *German Strategy and the Path to Verdun: Erich von Falkenhayn and the Development of Attrition, 1870–1916* [Cambridge University Press]

The judges wrote:

'It seems most appropriate that, on the occasion of the 90th anniversary of the Battle of the Somme, the 2005 Gladstone History Prize has been awarded to Dr Robert Foley of the University of Liverpool for his book. It was the Battle of the Somme which contributed enormously to the German failure at Verdun and thwarted von Falkenhayn's intention to bleed the French Army white through a strategy of attrition (*Ermattungsstrategie*). This strategy of attrition was to some extent at odds with the more favoured and traditional German alternative of seeking a rapid and conclusive decision on the battlefield through a strategy of annihilation (*Vernichtungsstrategie*). In a highly readable and articulate presentation Dr Foley has revealed in admirable and meticulous detail all the tensions and rivalries which existed in the German High Command around these two alternative strategies. Through his rigorous and wide ranging research in a number of military and foreign ministry archives in Germany and elsewhere, complemented by considerable secondary reading and full awareness of the historiographical context, Dr Foley has produced a book of admirable scholarship deserving of the award of the Gladstone History Prize.'

- In order to recognise the high quality of work now being produced at undergraduate level in the form of third-year dissertations, the Society continued, in association with *History Today* magazine, to award an annual prize for the best undergraduate dissertation. Departments are asked to nominate annually their best dissertation and a joint committee of the Society and *History Today* select in the autumn the national prizewinner from among these nominations. The prize also recognizes the Society's close relations with *History Today* and the important role the magazine has played in disseminating scholarly research to a wider audience. 39 submissions were made.

First prize was awarded to Anna Mason [Wadham College, Oxford] for her essay 'The English Reformation and the Visual Arts Reconsidered';
Highly Commended was Matthew Greenhall [University of Durham] for his essay 'From Cattle to Claret: Scottish economic influence in northeast England 1660–1750'.

Articles by the two prize-winners presenting their research will appear shortly in *History Today* editions in 2006. It was not possible for the entrants and their institutional contacts to visit The National Archives at Kew, as in previous years. It is planned to revive the visit in January 2007.

- Frampton and Beazley Prizes for A-level performances were awarded following nominations from the examining bodies:

Frampton Prizes:

AQA:
Andrew J Dooley, Birmingham
Edexcel Foundation incorporating the London Examination Board:
No award
OCR:
Austen Saunders, Leicester
Welsh Joint Education Committee:
Alice Lawson, Dover and Charlotte Hunter, Deeside

Beazley Prizes:

Northern Ireland Council for the Curriculum Examinations and Assessment:
Thomas Lowe, Belfast
Scottish Examination Board:
Catherine Jung, Dundee Lydia Jones, North Berwick and Jamie J. Hay, Clackmannanshire

- The Director of the Institute of Historical Research announced the winner and runners-up of the Pollard Prize, at the Annual Reception on 5 July 2006. The prize is awarded annually to the best postgraduate student paper presented in a seminar at the IHR.

The Pollard Prize winner for 2006 was Rupa Viswanath (Columbia), 'Spiritual slavery, material malaise: "Untouchables" and religious neutrality in colonial South India' (nominated by Imperial History Seminar);

Second place: Katherine Halliday (New College, Oxford), 'New light on the 1549 risings' (nominated by Tudor-Stuart Seminar);

Third place: Jacqueline Rose (Clare College, Cambridge), 'Kings shall be thy nursing fathers: Royal Ecclesiastical Supremacy and the Restoration Church' (nominated by Religious History of Britain Seminar).

RESEARCH POLICY COMMITTEE, 2005–6

On behalf of the Society, each year the Committee helps to organise the G.E. Aylmer Seminar in honour of one of our past presidents. As reported in the Newsletter, the Aylmer Seminar for 2005 was held at the Imperial War Museum on 6 October 2005, in association with the National Museum Directors' Conference. The subject was *Historical Research: the role of the National Museum Collections*. Regrettably few academic historians attended. It was agreed that The National Archives would be invited to host the next seminar, to take place in early 2007, on the subject of publishing and technological change.

The Committee continues to follow the unfolding of the Bologna Process and to inform the Society of important developments. Dr Liesbeth van Houts has taken responsibility for this and the Committee is exploring ways in which academics and learned societies can contribute to, say, proposed changes to doctoral programmes.

The Committee monitors the activities of AHRC through the Society's representatives on its panels and committees, including: the current review of doctoral training; the European Science Foundation project of producing Europe-wide rankings of journals in the arts and humanities; its consultation over its role in relation to museums and archives; its evaluation of its research funding in Modern History; and its apparent confusion over its responsibility for funding research in later twentieth century history.

The Committee carefully follows RAE arrangements, actual and proposed, present and future, including the vexed issue of metrics. Developments in research support in Wales, Scotland and Northern Ireland are also closely watched.

In September 2005 Dr Stephen Taylor gave a presentation to the Committee on 'The Future of the Monograph', which has generated a lively and on-going debate in the Newsletter. In September 2006 Bill Stockting of the National Archives addressed the Committee on the Archives UK: Connecting Archives Project.

TEACHING POLICY COMMITTEE, 2005–6

The Royal Historical Society is a learned society and its central purpose is that of promoting scholarship by publication and lectures and of supporting research and the interests of the history profession as a whole. This last must include an interest in teaching at all levels since school pupils and undergraduate as well as postgraduate students form both the future of the profession and an important part of our audience. The numbers of those studying history and the quality and range of history taught to them is clearly of concern to us. Moreover government consultation on education now frequently includes consultation with professional and learned societies. It is important therefore that the Society is fully informed about teaching matters and aware of problems so that it can take full advantage of its greater opportunities to influence decisions in its consultations with government, its agencies and research councils. The Teaching Policy Committee monitors and discusses matters of importance in teaching, and works closely with the Historical Association, History UK (HE) and the Institute of Historical Research to avoid duplication of effort and to co-ordinate responses where appropriate.

This year a major concern has been the proposed changes to the content and assessment of A levels. The Society has hosted two meetings on this topic, on 26 October 2005 (shortly before the criteria on history were to be drafted) and on 13 January 2006 (when the draft criteria were available). The meetings included representatives of all three examining boards, of the Qualifications and Curriculum Authority, the HA, History (UK) and IHR, and were particularly valuable in the breadth of discussions there. Some of the points raised included ways in which minority subjects or periods (such as medieval or eighteenth-century history) might be protected, the status of historical narrative, ways of using and assessing primary source materials in the school syllabus, and the value of the personal research project. The second meeting provided the opportunity to discuss the draft criteria for the new A level syllabuses and the History Officer at QCA took note of a number of important problems in the wording of the draft. These meetings showed that the Society has a valuable role to play in facilitating discussions between key players in educational changes and that it can also contribute to these debates, raising the concerns of the historical profession. One outcome of the discussions has been the cooperation between the Society and the IHR in the organisation of the conference on 'History in British Education:

Issues of Progression and Assessment' to be held at the IHR in October 2006.

The Committee has also flagged a further area of major concern. This is the possible decline of specialist history teaching in some schools. The Committee meeting on 5 July 2006 received an invited paper on this problem by Ros Ashby, Head of the PGCE Team at the Institute of Education, London. Pressures affecting specialist teaching in schools include the limited opportunities for continuing professional development for teachers, the closing of PGCE courses for historians at some Universities, the pressure on time given over to history and some evidence of history being included in humanities departments in schools. These pressures, together with some reported instances of history no longer being taught by specialist historians at secondary level, could affect the future provision of exciting and top-quality history teaching in schools. This in turn could lead to a decline in the numbers of pupils fired to continue the study of history at GCSE and A level. This could have a knock-on effect at university level, which would have profound dangers for the future of the profession. The committee will continue to investigate and monitor these changes in conjunction with the HA. The co-operation between the Society, the IHR, HA and History (UK) in organising the conference to be held at the IHR on 'Why History Matters' in February 2007 is important in this context.

GENERAL PURPOSES COMMITTEE, 2005–6

The General Purposes Committee has numerous responsibilities, in particular making arrangements for the card of session, and for conferences, monitoring the representation of the Society on various outside bodies, and arranging for the assessment of the various prizes awarded by the Society. During the year the Committee invites and then considers proposals for speakers for paper readings, and for the Colin Matthew Lecture and the Prothero Lecture. The Committee works hard to try to ensure a balance of papers throughout the year, on different periods, and geographical and subject areas.

The Committee is also responsible for the appointment of assessors for the various prizes that the Society awards, and, where appropriate, for the reassessment of the terms and conditions under which these awards are made. In 2005–6 the Committee approved a major change to one prize and the establishment of two others.

The Alexander Prize has been reconfigured and from 2006 will be awarded for the best published scholarly journal article or essay by a doctoral student or early career historian. In addition to the recognition of his or her published work the winner will be invited to submit a further paper for consideration for publication in the Society's *Transactions*.

Two new prizes have been established, and will be awarded for the first time in 2006–7. The first is The Royal Historical Society/*History Scotland* prize, to be given to the best undergraduate dissertation on Scottish History. It complements the highly successful prize awarded jointly with *History Today*, which is now open to undergraduate dissertations on any subject other than Scottish history. In both cases, the winners (and perhaps the runners up) may, at the discretion of the editors, have their essay published in *History Today* or *History Scotland*.

The second is The Rees Davies Graduate Prize. This is an essay prize specifically for those graduates awarded grants by the Society to attend conferences under its research support scheme. These sponsored graduates will be encouraged to enter a revised version of their paper for an annual essay competition (length: 5–10,000 words). The prize will be publication of the essay in the following year's edition of the Society's *Transactions*, three years' free membership of the Royal Historical Society, and a cash prize of £100. The aim of the prize is to create a strong link between the Society's research support activities and its publication activities – in the process raising awareness among a rising generation that the Society is more than simply another possible source of small grants. All graduates sponsored during the 2005–6 academic year will be invited to submit revised versions of their papers for consideration with a view to the first prize being awarded in early 2007, followed by publication in *Transactions 2007*.

Publications

PUBLICATIONS COMMITTEE, 2005–6

All the Society's publications have continued to prosper during 2005–6 and there are several developments to report. An important landmark was reached with the publication of the fiftieth volume in the Studies in History. In these times when the future of the monograph is under more intense discussion than ever before, it is both important and salutary that this series continues to attract proposals of the very highest quality and that Boydell & Brewer continue to publish the volumes to such a high standard. The series has been one of the flagships of the Society's policy to encourage early career development and it has been sustained over the years by a lot of selfless work by the Literary Directors and by members of the Studies in History Editorial Board. The Society has also invested funds to hasten publication of volumes in advance of the RAE deadline.

It is hard to underestimate the value of the Bibliography on British and Irish History Online to scholars and increasingly to students and the wider public. The Society's team added approximately 14000 records to the database in 2005–6; the sister project Irish History Online (IHO) added another 6000. IHO has now incorporated all the material covered in *Writings in Irish History 1970–2001*. The total number of records in the database now stands at 407,000. Linkages to *Oxford DNB* have been enhanced, and the establishment of Z-39–50 connectivity means that the bibliography is compatible with bibliographic and footnoting software like Endnote. Council records its gratitude to Ian Archer, Peter Salt and Simon Baker, for their expert management of the project.

It is pleasure to announce that funding for a further three years from January 2007 has been secured from the AHRC's Resource Enhancement Scheme. The application process was not been an entirely smooth one and the Society owes a great debt to the Literary Directors and to Dr. Jane Winters of the IHR for overcoming difficulties. The challenge of obtaining secure long-term funding for the Bibliography is one which the Society must meet and overcome in the coming years. It seems extraordinary that the national and international importance of one of the prime resources for the study of British and Irish History is not recognised by funding bodies and does not have the guaranteed long-term funding as a national resource. The Society is investigating the prospects for the longer term sustainability of the resource.

Digitisation of the Society's Publications proceeds apace. The Society is delighted by the positive response from holders of copyright to allow the digitisation by the Million Books Project of the vast majority of the Camden Series volumes to go ahead. All volumes of the *Transactions* are shortly to be digitised and included in J-Stor.

Transactions, Sixth Series, Volume 15 was published during the session, and *Transactions*, Sixth Series, Volume 16 went to press, to be published in November 2006.

In the Camden, Fifth Series, *Newsletters from the Caroline Court, 1631–1638: Catholicism and the Politics of the Personal Rule*, ed. Michael C. Questier (vol. 26) and *The Clarke Papers, Volumes V and VI*, ed. Frances Henderson (vol. 27) were published during the year. *Debating the Hundred Years War: Pur ce que plusieurs (La Loy Salicque) and a declaracion of the trew and dewe title of Henrie VIII*, ed Craig Taylor (vol. 28) and *British Envoys to Germany, 1816–1861 Volume III: 1848–1850* ed. M. Mosslang, S. Freitag and Peter Wende (vol. 29) went to press for publication in 2006–7.

The *Studies in History* Editorial Board continued to meet throughout the year. The second series continued to produce exciting volumes. The following volumes were published, or went to press, during the session

o *French Revolutionaries and English Republicans: The Cordelier Club in the early 1790s* Rachel Hammersley
o *Making Trieste Italian, 1918–1954* Maura Hametz
o *Henry III of England and the Staufen Empire, 1216–1272* Bjorn Weiler

- The Culture of Commerce in England, 1660–1720 Natasha Glaisyer
- Lollardy and Orthodox Religion in Pre-Reformation England: Reconstructing Piety Robert Lutton
- Creating Capitalism: joint stock enterprise in British politics and culture, 1800–1870 James Taylor
- Gladstone and Dante: Victorian Statesman, Medieval Poet Anne Isba
- Gender, Crime and Judicial Discretion, 1780–1830 Deirdre Palk
- Women in Thirteenth-Century Lincolnshire Louise J. Wilkinson
- Women and Violent Crime in Enlightenment Scotland Anne-Marie Kilday
- Scottish Public Opinion and the Union of 1707 Karin Bowie
- Gender and Space in Early Modern England Amanda Flather

As in previous subscription years, volumes in Studies in History series were offered to the membership at a favourably discounted price. Many Fellows, Associates and Members accepted the offer for volumes published during the year, and the advance orders for further copies of the volumes to be published in the year 2006–2007 were encouraging.

The Society acknowledges its gratitude for the continuing subventions from the Economic History Society and the Past and Present Society to the Studies in History series.

Finance

The Finance Committee approves the Society's accounts each financial year and its estimates for the following year. This year, as before, the accounts were very professionally and efficiently audited by haysmacintyre. They are presented elsewhere in Transactions, with slight changes in format to reflect new charity accounting requirements (SORP 2005). This provides, among other things, an analysis of the estimated cost of the Society's various categories of charitable activity.

In general, expenditure and income in 2005–6 did not deviate significantly from the expectations set out in the estimates last summer. On the income side, the profit-share scheme with Cambridge University Press has now settled down to produce a substantial profit each year, helped by reductions in production costs at CUP. The Finance Committee reviews the scheme each year. It also examines the cost of the Society's other major activities. During the year, for example, it has kept under review the subsidy to the Studies in History series, the support given to the Bibliography project, the Society's Research Support policy, and the costs of the Society's lectures and conferences. It also receives a detailed analysis of monthly expenditure.

The Committee's estimates for 2005–6 balanced rather precariously. Moreover, that balance depends on the decision – ratified again by Council this year - that the Society is permitted each year to draw down up to 4% of the value of its investment portfolio (which is run on a total return basis). The Committee monitors the performance of the portfolio regularly and invited the investment manager to its September meeting. The managers, Cripps, changed their name to Heartwood in the course of the year. 2005–6 was a satisfactory year for the portfolio, bearing in mind that it is run conservatively with a strong income bias. It yields 3.8%; total return for 2005–6 was just over 11%, just above the benchmark that we use (10.4%). This growth was helped by a shift away from bonds; the proportion in the portfolio has fallen from 36% to 23% in the last two years. Though the market value of the main fund has risen by 21% to £2.2 million in the last two years, this is merely a correction; the Society's investments are back at the levels of 2001 but still below those of 1998. The Committee also reviews management charges and transaction levels and continues to be satisfied with Heartwood's approach and conduct.

The Committee reviewed membership fees and kept them unchanged for the time being. It also maintained the budget for Research Support to postgraduate students at £20,000 per year.

It also considered the question of fund-raising, specifically in order to increase the amount of support that it can give to research students and other young scholars. To this end Professor Margot Finn agreed to be co-opted onto the Committee, and to sit on a sub-committee to consider fund-raising strategy further, in conjunction with the Hon. Treasurer and Hon. Secretary. Two new bursaries are to be awarded in 2006–7, one in memory of a recent generous donor, Miss V.C.M. London, and one in honour of Fellow Martin Lynn, which has been kindly provided by his widow.

- The Society welcomed a further bequest of £6,000 from the estate of deceased Fellow Miss Vera C. M. London of Shropshire. This was in addition to the legacy of £39,000 already received.
  FINANCE COMMITTEE, 2005–6

- Council records with gratitude the further benefactions made to the Society by:
  o Mr. L.C. Alexander
  o The Reverend David Berry
  o Professor Andrew Browning
  o Professor C.D. Chandaman
  o Professor G. Donaldson
  o Professor Sir Geoffrey Elton
  o Mr. E.J. Erith
  o Mr. P.J.C. Firth
  o Mrs. W.M. Frampton

- o Miss B.F. Harvey
- o Mr. A.E.J. Hollaender
- o Professor C.J. Holdsworth
- o Miss V.C.M. London
- o Dr Martin Lynn
- o Professor P.J. Marshall
- o Mr. E.L.C. Mullins
- o Sir George Prothero
- o Dr. L. Rausing
- o Professor T.F. Reddaway
- o Miss E.M. Robinson
- o Miss J.C. Sinar
- o Professor A.S. Whitfield

Membership

MEMBERSHIP COMMITTEE, 2005–6

The Society is always keen to expand its fellowship and membership in order to ensure that it is as representative as possible of the scholarly historical community in Britain and Ireland, as well as engaging with historians who live and work abroad. The Membership Committee reviews all of the applications the Society receives for fellowship and membership and makes recommendations to Council. We are a committee of three, at present Paul Seaward, Geoffrey Hosking and David Palliser. Over the year 2005–6, 85 applications for fellowship and 16 applications for membership were received, and 80 fellows and 16 members were elected.

Applications are reviewed carefully against the published eligibility criteria: for fellows, the publication of one or more than one book of historical scholarship based on original research; or the publication of a body of scholarly work (for example, learned articles, essays, catalogues, calendars); or a major contribution to historical scholarship in a form other than publication, for instance, the organisation of exhibitions, collections, or conferences, or the editing of local history serials. Membership is more broadly defined, with the aim of attracting a wider group of people who may not necessarily regard themselves as academic historians but are contributing in many and important ways to the study of history: applications will be considered from individuals who are engaged in advanced historical scholarship and research, or teaching history in higher or further education, or who have rendered many years of service to history at national or local level. Applicants may, for example, be in the later stages of, or have completed, their doctoral dissertations; equally they may be active local historians or archivists. They may, but need not, have one or more scholarly publications to their name. Occasionally we propose to applicants, where we do not feel that their application quite matches our criteria, that they become members of the society instead. We are currently reviewing our criteria to ensure that they are as clear and up-to-date as possible.

We are delighted to receive new applications for either fellowship or membership, and hope that fellows will encourage others to apply, for both categories. Full details are available on the Society's website. Please remind any applicant to fill in the necessary forms carefully – we receive a number of applications which are not properly completed, and therefore take longer to process – and that they will need a reference from an existing fellow of the Society.

- The following were announced in the Queen's Honours' Lists during the year:

  Professor Sir Roderick Floud – Fellow - received a Knight of the British Empire

  Professor Averil Millicent Cameron, C.B.E. – Fellow - D.B.E. for services to classical scholarship

  Miss Brenda Margaret Bolton – Associate - M.B.E. for services to ecclesiastical history

  Professor J.L. Nelson – Honorary Vice-President – D.B.E. for services to History

  Professor F.C.R. Robinson – Fellow – C.B.E. for services to Higher Education and to the History of Islam

- Council was advised and recorded with regret the deaths of 6 Fellows, 10 Retired Fellows, 1 Honorary Vice-President, 3 Corresponding Fellows, 2 Associates and 3 Members.

  These included
  Professor M. S. Anderson – Retired Fellow
  Professor C. A. Bolt – Retired Fellow
  Dr D. J. Boorstin – Corresponding Fellow
  Mrs H. E. Combes – Member and Office Administrative Assistant 1999–2001
  Dr C. G. Durston – Fellow & Co-convenor of History UK (HE) [formerly HUDG]
  Professor U. F. J. Eyck – Retired Fellow
  Mr G. Fleming – Fellow
  The Rev. Professor W. H. C. Frend – Retired Fellow

Mr I.. J. Gorton – Retired Fellow
The Rev V. H. H. Green – Fellow
Mr M. W. Greenslade – Member
Professor P. Grierson – Honorary Vice-President
Mrs L. E. Jerram-Burrows – Associate
Dr P. J. Jones – Retired Fellow
Professor G. I. Langmuir – Corresponding Fellow
Captain M. Lee – Member
Professor G. Mingay – Associate
Dr J. A. Rawley – Retired Fellow
Professor J. D. Ritchie – Fellow
Mr B. E. Robson – Fellow
Professor Sir Peter Russell – Retired Fellow
Mr A. N. Ryan – Retired Fellow
Professor B. H. Slicher Van Bath – Corresponding Fellow
Dr J. W. R. Taylor – Retired Fellow
Dr G. A. Worsley – Fellow and Alexander Prize Winner 1992

- The membership of the Society on 30 June 2006 numbered 2936, comprising 1974 Fellows, 569 Retired Fellows, 16 Life Fellows, 15 Honorary Vice-Presidents, 92 Corresponding Fellows, 68 Associates and 202 Members.
- The Society exchanged publications with 15 Societies, British and Foreign.

Representatives of the Society

- The representation of the Society upon other various bodies was as follows:
  o Professor David Ganz on the Anthony Panizzi Foundation;
  o Dr. Julia Crick on the Joint Committee of the Society and the British Academy established to prepare an edition of Anglo-Saxon charters;
  o Professor N.P. Brooks on a committee to promote the publication of photographic records of the more significant collections of British Coins;
  o Professor G.H. Martin on the Council of the British Records Association;
  o Mr. P.M.H. Bell on the Editorial Advisory Board of the *Annual Register*;
  o Professor C.J. Holdsworth on the Court of the University of Exeter;
  o Professor M.C. Cross on the Council of the British Association for Local History; and on the British Sub-Commission of the Commission International d'Histoire Ecclesiastique Comparée;

- Professor L.J. Jordanova on the Advisory Council of the reviewing committee on the Export of Works of Art;
- Professor W. Davies on the Court of the University of Birmingham;
- Professor R.D. McKitterick on a committee to regulate British co-operation in the preparation of a new repertory of medieval sources to replace Potthast's *Bibliotheca Historica Medii Aevi*;
- Professor W.R. Childs member of the Court of the University of Sheffield;
- Dr. J. Winters on the History Data Service Advisory Committee;
- Professor R.A. Burns on the user panel of the RSLP Revelation project 'Unlocking research sources for 19th and 20th century church history and Christian theology';
- Dr. M. Smith on the Court of Governors of the University of Wales, Swansea;
- Dr. R. Mackenney on the University of Stirling Conference;
- Professor N. Thompson member of the Court of the University of Wales;
- Dr. C.J. Kitching on the National Council on Archives.
- Council received reports from its representatives.

Grants

RESEARCH SUPPORT COMMITTEE, 2005–6

The Committee has, as usual, met six times in the course of the year to carry out the entirely agreeable task of allocating funds to research students needing financial help to carry out specific elements of their research in Britain and overseas, and help others to present papers to sessions of relevant, significant conferences. Under another funding head, the Committee also tries to assist organisers seeking to cushion, by partial subsidy, the costs of student attendance at their conferences. All of this work reflects the Society's enthusiastic commitment to the encouragement of young scholars and their historical research. The Society's funds are however limited and research expenses are increasingly costly; accordingly in the course of the year the Committee must carefully read and then discuss the applications of many more candidates than it can ultimately benefit. Budgetary limits also mean that we must decide how much of a funding request we can meet as we are only rarely able to provide students with the total sum for which they have asked. In addition to this regular work, the Committee has this year had the task of deciding upon the criteria for two newly and generously endowed awards which have been established in the memories of two highly regarded and much missed Fellows, Miss Vera London of Church Stretton and Dr Martin Lynn of the Queen's University, Belfast.

The development of the scholarly careers of young historians and the wider dissemination of their research achievements, one of the major concerns of the Royal Historical Society, lay behind the launch in 2005 of a new speakers' programme for which the Committee is responsible. Under this scheme, the Royal Historical Society's Postgraduate Speakers Series, history departments are encouraged to become acquainted with the work of young historians. Past recipients of research awards or conference grants have been, with their consent, listed and their names, along with a description of their research, are circulated to the convenors of history research seminars in the United Kingdom. Convenors may then invite speakers from that list in the knowledge that the Society will pay for the visiting scholars' expenses. The success of the initiative in its one year trial in 2005–6 has led to its continuation for 2006–8.

Sadly not all of the Committee's business this year has, however, been devoted to giving money to deserving students of history; it has also necessarily had to spend time on the better management of generosity. From the beginning of 2006 the Committee has discussed its increasing concern with the apparent unwillingness of some of its beneficiaries to honour the few, undemanding conditions of our awards; for example it regards any failure to provide the Society with a report outlining the ways in which Society grants have been spent as unprofessional as well as unacceptable. In addition to this the Committee and the Honorary Treasurer have unhappily also had to spend time discussing the implications of a case of a student who intentionally misspent a large grant and who has subsequently failed to reimburse the Society. While there is no way in which rare cases such as this can be entirely prevented, the Committee is very well aware that the money at the Society's disposal is limited and is, after all, drawn from the subscriptions of Fellows and Members, and from the generosity of donors. Council has now approved a new set of procedures proposed by the Committee which we hope will meet some of our concerns by enhancing accountability without significantly complicating the process of application.

- The Royal Historical Society Centenary Fellowship was not awarded for the academic year 2005–2006.
- The Society's P.J. Marshall Fellowship was awarded in the academic year 2005–2006 jointly to Katherine Rebecca Chambers [St John's College, Cambridge] studying 'The Laity in the writings of Paris masters in the late twelfth and early thirteenth centuries' and Avi Lifschitz [Lincoln College, Oxford] studying 'Debating Language: Academic Discourse and Public Controversy at the Berlin Academy under Frederick the Great'. Professor Marshall had confirmed his plans

to support a Fellowship every year for the next few years for which the Society wishes to express its grateful acceptance of his generosity.
• Grants during the year were made to the following:

Travel to Conferences [Training Bursaries]

o Shin AHN, PhD, University of Edinburgh
The 19th World Congress of the International Association for the History of Religions: 'Religion – Conflict and Peace', held in Tokyo, Japan, on 23–31 March 2005.
o Jackson Webster ARMSTRONG, PhD, Trinity Hall, University of Cambridge
Fifteenth Century Conference: The Peoples of the British Isles, held at the University of Wales Swansea, 8–10 September 2005.
o Manuel BARCIA PAZ, University of Essex
World History Association Annual Meeting held at the University of Ifrane, Morocco, 27–29 June 2005.
o Jonathan Gilder BATESON, DPhil, University of Oxford
Annual Meeting of the American Association for the History of Medicine, held in Birmingham, Alabama, USA, 7–10 April 2005.
o Kimberly BERNARD, PhD at the University of Wales, Swansea
'Crosstown Traffic', held at the University of Warwick, 4–7 July 2004.
o Robert Gregory BODDICE, PhD at the University of York
Northeast Conference on British Studies held at McGill University, Montreal, 1–2 October 2004.
o Thomas Edward CADOGAN, PhD at SOAS, University of London
The 47th Annual Meeting of the African Studies Association, held in New Orleans, USA, 11–15 November 2004.
o Vanessa Ann CHAMBERS, PhD, Institute of Historical Research, London
The Society History Society 30th Annual Conference, held at Trinity College, Dublin, on 7–9 January 2005.
o Nancy COLLINS, PhD at University College London
Seventh Annual International Conference of the Urban History Association held in Athens-Piraeus, Greece, 27–30 October 2004.
o Catherine FERRIS, PhD, University College London
Social History Society Annual Conference, held at Trinity College, Dublin, on 7–9 January 2005.
o Lauren French FOGLE, PhD, Royal Holloway, University of London
22nd Annual Conference of the Illinois Medieval Society, held at the University of Southern Illinois, USA, on 22–25 February 2005.
o Miguel GARCIA-SANCHO, PhD, Imperial College, London
Conference, 'Gathering Things, Collecting Data, Producing Know–ledge', held at Ischia, Italy, 28 June–5 July 2005.

o [Thomas] Michael GOEBEL, PhD, University College London
  Conference, Xo Jornadas Interescuelas/Departamentos de Historia,
  held at Rosario, Argentina, 20–23 September 2005.
o Kristian GUSTAFSON, PhD, Downing College, Cambridge
  Royal Military College of Canada Annual Military History Sym-
  posium, held at Kingston, Ontario, on 16–18 March 2005.
o Nicola Claire GUY, PhD, University of Durham
  Second Southeast European Studies Association Conference, held at
  Ohio State University, USA, on 28–30 April 2005.
o Jane HAMLETT, PhD at Royal Holloway, University of London
  'North American Conference on British Studies', held in Philadelphia,
  USA, 29–31 October 2004.
o David Ian HARRISON, PhD, University of Liverpool
  Conference, 'We Band of Brothers', held at the University of Sheffield,
  17–19 November 2004.
o Emma JONES, PhD, Royal Holloway, University of London
  Conference, 'Health and History: International Perspectives', 9th
  Biennial conference of the Australian Society of History of Medicine,
  held at Auckland, New Zealand, on 16–19 February 2005.
o Heidrun KUGELER, DPhil, Faculty of Modern History, University
  of Oxford
  Fourth International Interdisciplinary Conference on Germany-
  speaking Europe, held at Duke University, Durham, NC, USA, 7–10
  April 2005.
o Simone LAQUA, PhD at the University of Oxford
  Sixteenth-Century Studies Conference 2004, held in Toronto, Canada,
  28–31 October 2004.
o Amanda MARTINSON, PhD at the University of St Andrews
  Conference on 'The World of Henry II', held at the University of East
  Anglia, 13–17 September 2004.
o Stamatina MASTORAKOU, DPhil, University of Oxford
  Seventh Biennial History of Astronomy Workshop, held at the
  University of Notre Dame, USA, 7–10 July 2005.
o Matthew MILNER, PhD at the University of Warwick
  2004 Sixteenth Century Studies Conference held in Toronto, 28–31
  October 2004.
o Izabel Anna ORLOWSKA, PhD at SOAS, University of London
  Conference, 'The Power of Expression: Identity, Language and
  Memory in Africa and the Diaspora', held in New Orleans, USA,
  11–14 November 2004.
o Eyal POLEG, PhD, Queen Mary, University of London
  Conference, 'Bookish Traditions: Authority and the Book in
  Scripturalist Religions', held at the Central European University,
  Budapest, 4–15 July 2005.

o Manjeet Kaur RAMGOTRA, PhD at the London School of Economics
American Political Science Association 100th Annual Meeting, 'Global Inequalities', held in Chicago on 2–5 September 2004.
o Meredith L.D. RIEDEL, DPhil at Exeter College, Oxford
19th Annual Texas Medieval Conference held at the University of Dallas, Texas, on 16–18 September 2004.
o James Thomas ROBERTS, PhD, Institute of Medieval Studies, University of Leeds
International Society of Anglo-Saxonists, Biennial Conference 2005 'England and the Continent', held at the International Society of Anglo-Saxonists, Bavarian American Centre, Munich, on 1–6 August 2005.
o Nicole ROBERTSON, PhD, University of Nottingham
Social History Society Annual Conference, held at Trinity College, Dublin, on 7–9 January 2005.
o Jason ROCHE, PhD at the University of St Andrews
'Society for the Study of the Crusades and the Latin East; Istanbul Conference', held in Istanbul, Turkey, 25–29 August 2004.
o Carlos SANTIAGO CABALLERO, PhD, London School of Economics and Political Science
European Society for Environmental History Third International Conference, 'History and Sustainability', held in Florence, Italy, on 16–19 February 2005.
o Ayako SAKURAI, PhD, Department of History and Philosophy of Science, University of Cambridge
Annual meeting of the Japanese Socio-Economic History Society, held at Hitotsubashi University, Tokyo, 30 April–1 May 2005.
o Gareth SHAW, PhD at the University of Hull
'Conference of Quaker Historians and Archivists', held at the George Fox University. Portland, Oregon, USA, 25–27 May 2004.
o Erik SPINDLER, DPhil, Faculty of Modern History, University of Oxford
40th International Congress of Medieval Studies, held at the campus of Western Michigan University, Kalamazoo, Michigan, USA, 5–8 May 2005.
o John STRACHAN, PhD, University of Manchester
51st Annual Meeting of the Society for French Historical Studies, held at Stanford University, USA, on 17–19 March 2005.
o Anke TIMMERMANN, PhD, Robinson College, Cambridge
Conference, 'Material Cultures and the Creation of Knowledge', held at the University of Edinburgh, 22–24 July 2005.

o Jelmer Antoon VOS, PhD at SOAS, University of London
The 47th Annual Meeting of the African Studies Association, held in
New Orleans, USA, 11–14 November 2004.
o Konstantinos ZAFEIRIS, PhD at the University of St Andrews
Sixth Conference of the Society for the Study of the Crusades and the
Latin East: '1204: A Turning Point in Relations Between Eastern and
Western Christendom' held in Istanbul, Turkey, 26–29 August 2004.

[38]

Research Expenses Within the United Kingdom:

o David John CLAMPIN, PhD at the University of Wales Aberystwyth
Visits to The National Archives, Kew.
o Julie DAY, PhD, University of Leeds
Visit to various archives in England, November 2004–July 2005.
o Daniel ENGLUND, PhD at the University of Durham
Visits to libraries and archives in London and Gloucester, June–July
2004.
o Nicola GUY, MA at the University of Durham
Visits to the School of Slavonic and East European Studies Library, the
Maughlin Library, King's College London and The National Archives,
8–12 June 2004 and visit to Somerset Record Office, December 2004,
and The National Archives, January 2005.
o Ashfuque HOSSAIN, PhD, University of Nottingham
Visit to Glasgow University Archive Services.
o Zehra MAMDANI, MPhil, Hughes Hall, University of Cambridge
Visit to The National Archives, Kew.
o Swapnesh MASRANI, PhD at the University of St Andrews
Visits to archives in Dundee, Edinburgh, Forfar and Tayport, August –
September 2004.
o Christine V SEAL, PhD, University of Leicester
Visit to various archives in England from February – December 2005.
o Elizabeth Kate VIGURS, PhD, University of Leeds
Visit to archives in the London area, January – March 2005.
o Mark WALLACE, PhD at the University of St Andrews
Visits to The National Archives and the Library and Museum of
Freemasonry, 10–13 August 2004.

[10]

Research Expenses Outside the United Kingdom:

o Katharine Sarah AYLETT, PhD, University of Leeds
Visit to the National Library of Russia, St. Petersburg.

○ Noah Londer CHARNEY, PhD, St. John's College, Cambridge
Visit to various archives in Italy, 5 February–5 March 2005.

○ Delphine DOUCET, PhD at Royal Holloway, University of London
Visits to archives in Germany, 10 August – 2 September 2004.

○ Michael GOEBEL, PhD at University College London
Visits to archives and libraries in Buenos Aires, Argentina, 21 September–20 December 2004.

○ Vassiliki KARALI, PhD, University of Edinburgh
Visit to various archives in Maryland, U.S.A.

○ Mohammed KARIM, PhD at De Montfort University
Visits to the Republic of Uzbekistan State Archives, September–October 2004.

○ EE Hong (Agnes) KHOO, PhD at the University of Manchester
Visits to archives in South Korea, 1–21 September 2004.

○ Mikhail KIZILOV, DPhil, Merton College, Oxford
Various archives in Austria, April 2005.

○ Philippa Constance LANE, PhD, University of Essex
Visit to various archives in South Africa.

○ Georgios LIAKOPOULOS, MPhil/PhD, The Hellenic Institute/History Department, Royal Holloway, University of London
Visit to The Ottoman Archives, Istanbul, Turkey, 1 July–1 August 2005.

○ Katherine LIM, DPhil at the University of Oxford
Visits to Archives in Venice, August 2004 – September 2005.

○ Jaime MORENO TEJADA, PhD, King's College London
Visits to various archives in Ecuador, 20 June–20 December 2005.

○ James MARSHALL, MLitt at the University of Newcastle
Visits to Museums and Fieldwork in Greece, October–November 2004.

○ Jennifer McNUTT, PhD, University of St. Andrews
Visit to archives in Geneva, August 2005.

○ Paolo NATALI, PhD, University of Cambridge
Visit to various archives in the U.S.A.

○ Gabriela Edreva PETKOVA-CAMPBELL, PhD at University of Newcastle upon Tyne
Visit to the History Department, School of East European Studies of Sodertorns Hogskola, Sweden.

○ Mihail Raychev RAEV, PhD at Trinity College, Cambridge
Visit to archives in Russia, Ukraine and Belarus.

○ Ignacio RIVAS, PhD, University College London
Visit to various archives in Spain, June – September 2005.

○ David Rodriguez SARIAS, PhD at Sheffield University
Visit to various archives in the U.S.A.

○ Charlotte SCHRIWER, PhD at the University of St Andrews
Visits to Archives and Libraries in Cyprus, Jordan and Syria, 1 July–1 September 2004.

o Paul Daniel SHIRLEY, PhD, University College London
Visit to various archives in the Bahamas and the US, May   July 2005.
o Seumas SPARK, PhD at the University of Edinburgh
Visits to War Cemeteries in Egypt, Germany, the Netherlands and
Italy, summer 2004.
o John STRACHAN, PhD, University of Manchester
Visit to archives in France, 15–23 February 2005.

[23]

Conference Organisation [Workshop]

o Malcolm BARBER, Conference, 'The Medieval Chronicle IV', held
at the University of Reading on 15–19 July 2005.
o Lawrence BLACK
Conference, 'Taking Stock: The Co-operative Movement in British
History', held at the People's History Museum, 13–14 May 2005.
o Patrick J. BONER
British Society for the History of Science Postgraduate Conference
held at the Department of History & Philosophy of Science, University
of Cambridge, 5–7 January 2005.
o Caroline BOWDEN
Conference, 'Consecrated Women: Towards a History of Women
Religious of Britain and Ireland', held at the University of Cambridge,
on 16–17 September 2005.
o Janet BURTON and Karen STÖBER
Conference, 'Monasteries and Society in the Later Middle Ages', held
at Gregynog Hall, Newtown, Mid Wales, 4–7 April 2005.
o Penelope J. CORFIELD
Conference, 'The Political and Cultural Left in Britain in the 1790s',
held at the Institute of Historical Research, London, 29 June 2005.
o Ildiko CSENGEI
The British Society for Eighteenth-Century Studies, 34th Annual
Conference, held at St. Hugh's College, Oxford, 6–8 January 2005.
o Flora DENNIS
Conference, 'Domestic Encounters: 1400 to the Present', held at the
Royal College of Art, London, on 14 March 2005.
o C.C. DYER
Conference, 'W.G. Hoskins and the Making of the British Landscape',
held at the University of Leicester, 7–10 July 2005.
o Dagmar ENGELKEN and Abayomi KRISTILOLU
'Critical Perspectives on Empire and Imperialism: Past and Present,
Interdisciplinary Postgraduate Conference', held at the University of
Essex, 24–25 September 2004.

o David FRENCH
Conference, 'Anglo-American Relations from the Pilgrim Fathers to the Present', held at University College London on 17–10 February 2005.

o K.S.B. KEATS-ROHAN
Conference, 'Prosopography: Approaches and Applications', held at Jesus College, Oxford, 15–18 July 2005.

o Andy KING
'War and Peace; New Perspectives on Anglo-Scottish Relations, c. 1286–1406', held at the University of Durham, 1–2 September 2004.

o Beat KUMIN
Third Warwick Symposium on Parish Research, held at the University of Warwick, on 14 May 2005.

o Michael LEWIS
Conference, 'Beyond Imperial Centre and Global Periphery: Reconnecting the Global and the Local Location', held at the Centre for Research in the Arts, Humanities and Social Sciences (CRASSH), Cambridge, on 11–12 March 2005.

o Simon MACLEAN
Conference, 'Interpreting the Past in Medieval Germany', held at the University of St. Andrews, on 19–22 July 2005.

o Rachel MAIRS
'Current Research in Egyptology IV', held at the University of Cambridge, 7–9 January 2004.

o Amy McKINNEY
Conference 'Religious Thought and Practice in Ireland, 1700–1980', held at Queen's University, Belfast, on 19 March 2005.

o Nicola MILLER
Conference 'When was Latin America modern?', held at UCL and the Institute for the Study of the Americas, London, on 16–18 February 2005.

o Luc RACAUT
European Reformation Research Group annual conference 2005, held at the University of Newcastle upon Tyne, on 1–3 September 2005.

o Patricia SKINNER
'Texts, Histories, Historiographies: the Medieval Worlds of Timothy Reuter', held at the University of Southampton, 24–26 July 2004.

o Naomi TADMOR
Conference, 'Kinship in Britain and Beyond, 500–2000', held at the University of Cambridge and Downing College, 25–26 July 2005.

o Duncan TANNER
Conference, 'New directions in modern British political history, c. 1867–2001: from the body politic to the politics of the body', held

at the Centre for Contemporary British History, Institute of Historical Research, London, 7–9 April 2005.
o Craig TAYLOR
Conference, 'France and England in the Later Middle Ages', held at the Centre for Medieval Studies, University of York 2–5 April 2005.
o Joan TUMBLETY
'Spaces and places': the 19th annual conference of the Society for the Study of French History, held at Avenue Campus, University of Southampton, 4–5 July 2005.
o Alexandra WALSHAM
Conference, 'Syon Abbey and its Books, c. 1400–1700', held at the University of Exeter, Crossmead Conference Centre, 7–8 October 2005.
o Katherine D. WATSON
Conference '"Assaulting the Past": Placing Violence in Historical Context', held at St. Anne's College, Oxford, on 7–9 July 2005.
o Bjorn WEILER
Conference, 'Thirteenth-Century England 11: Plantagenet Britain, 1180–1330', held at the University of Wales Conference Centre, Gregynog, on 9–12 September 2005.
o Charlotte WILDMAN
Conference, 'Modern Britain: New Perspectives', held at the University of Manchester, 3 November 2004.
o Deborah YOUNGS
The Fifteenth Century Conference, 'The peoples of the British Isles', held at the University of Wales Swansea, on 8–10 September 2005.

[30]

Bursaries for Holders of ORS Awards

o Katherine CHAMBERS, St John's College, Cambridge.
o Natalya CHERNYSHOVA, King's College London.
o Cameron Mitchell SUTT, St. Catharine's College, Cambridge.

[3]
[Total = 104]

29 September 2006

THE ROYAL HISTORICAL SOCIETY
FINANCIAL STATEMENTS
FOR THE YEAR ENDED 30 JUNE 2006

haysmacintyre
Chartered Accountants
Registered Auditors
London

THE ROYAL HISTORICAL SOCIETY REFERENCE AND ADMINISTRATIVE INFORMATION

Members of Council:

THE ROYAL HISTORICAL SOCIETY
REPORT OF THE COUNCIL OF TRUSTEES
FOR THE YEAR ENDED 30 JUNE 2006

The members of Council present their report and audited accounts for the year ended 30 June 2006.

STRUCTURE, GOVERNANCE AND MANAGEMENT

The Society was founded on 23 November 1868 and received its Royal Charter in 1889. It is governed by the document 'The By-Laws of the Royal Historical Society', which was last amended in November 2002. The elected Officers of the Society are the President, six Vice-Presidents, the Treasurer, the Secretary, the Librarian and not more than two Literary Directors. These officers, together with twelve Councillors constitute the governing body of the Society, and therefore its Trustees. The Society also has two executive officers: an Executive Secretary and an Administrative Assistant.

Appointment of Trustees

The names of the Trustees are shown above. The President shall be *ex-officio* a member of all Committees appointed by the Council; and the Treasurer, the Secretary, the Librarian and the Literary Directors shall, unless the Council otherwise determine, also be *ex-officio* members of all such Committees.

In accordance with By-law XVII, the Vice-Presidents shall hold office normally for a term of three years. Two of them shall retire by rotation, in order of seniority in office, at each Anniversary Meeting and shall not be eligible for re-election before the Anniversary Meeting of the next year. In accordance with By-law XX, the Councillors shall hold office normally for a term of four years. Three of them shall retire by rotation, in order of seniority in office, at each Anniversary Meeting and shall not be eligible for re-election before the Anniversary Meeting of the next year.

All Fellows of the Society are able to nominate Councillors; they are elected by a ballot of Fellows. Other Trustees are elected by Council.

At the Anniversary Meeting on 25 November 2005, the Officers of the Society were re-elected, or in the case of Dr Parry (Hon. Treasurer) newly elected. The Vice-Presidents retiring under By-law XVII were Professor H. T. Dickinson and Dr C. J. Kitching. Professor R. J. A. R. Rathbone and Professor P. M. Thane were elected to replace them. The Members of Council retiring under By-law XX were Dr S. R. Ditchfield, Professor M. Finn and Professor F. O'Gorman. In accordance with By-law XXI, amended, Professor P. G. Burgess, Professor S. R. I. Foot and Professor G. A. Stone were elected in their place.

Trustee training and induction process

New Trustees are welcomed in writing before their initial meeting, and sent details of the coming year's meeting schedule. They are advised of the Committee structure and receive papers in advance of the appropriate Committee and Council meetings, including minutes of the previous meetings. Trustees are Fellows of the Society and have received regular information including the annual volume of *Transactions of the Royal Historical Society* which includes the annual report and accounts. They have therefore been kept apprised of any changes in the Society's business. Trustees may have previously served on Council, in which case their previous knowledge of procedures will assist their understanding of current issues. Details of a Review on the restructuring of the Society in 1993 are available to all Members of Council.

Standing Committees

The Society has operated through the following Committees during the year ended 30 June 2006:

MEMBERSHIP COMMITTEE   Professor W. R. Childs – Chair (to November 2005)
Dr P. C. Seaward – Chair (from November 2005)
Professor G. A Hosking
Professor D. M. Palliser

RESEARCH SUPPORT COMMITTEE   Dr P. Seaward – Chair (to November 2005)
Professor R. J. A. R. Rathbone – Chair
(from November 2005)
Dr M. Finn (to November 2005)
Professor F. O'Gorman (to November 2005)
Professor S. R. I. Foot (from November 2005)
Professor D. M. Palliser (from November 2005)
Professor G. A. Stone (from November 2005)

OBJECTIVES AND ACTIVITIES

The Society exists for the promotion and support of historical scholarship and its dissemination to historians and a wider public through a programme of publications, papers, sponsorship of lectures, conferences and research and by representations to various official bodies where the interests of historical scholarship are involved. It is Council's intention that these activities should be sustained to the fullest extent in the future.

ACHIEVEMENTS AND PERFORMANCE

Grants

The Society awards funds to assist advanced historical research. This year it distributed more than £20,000 in grants to 101 individuals. It operates several separate schemes, for each of which there is an application form. The Society's Research Support Committee considers applications at meetings held regularly throughout the year. In turn the Research Support Committee reports to Council. The Royal Historical Society Postgraduate Speakers' Series was introduced at the beginning of the year, on a trial basis. Full details and a list of awards made are provided in the Society's Annual Report.

Lectures and other meetings

During the year the Society holds meetings in London and at universities outside London at which papers are delivered. It is also associated with other organisations to support conferences on various topics and at various locations. It continues to sponsor the joint lecture for a wider public with Gresham College. Full details are provided in the Annual Report.

Publications

This year, as in previous years, it has pursued this objective by an ambitious programme of publications. A volume of *Transactions*, two volumes of edited texts in the *Camden* Series and further volumes in the *Studies in History* Series have appeared.

Library

The Society's Library continues to house its collection in the Council Room. It also continues to subscribe to a range of record series publications housed in the room immediately across the corridor from the Council room, in the UCL History Library.

Membership services

In accordance with the Society's 'By-laws', the membership is entitled to receive, after payment of subscription, a copy of the Society's *Transactions*, and to buy at a preferential rate copies of volumes published in the *Camden* series, and the *Studies in History* series. Society Newsletters continue to be circulated to the membership twice annually. The membership benefits from many other activities of the Society including the frequent representations to various official bodies where the interests of historical scholarship are involved.

Investment performance

The Society holds an investment portfolio with a market value of about £2.42 million (2005: £2.25 million). It has adopted a "total return" approach to its investment policy. This means that the funds are invested solely on the basis of seeking to secure the best total level of economic return compatible with the duty to make safe investments, but regardless of the form the return takes.

The Society has adopted this approach to ensure even-handedness between current and future beneficiaries, as the focus of many investments moves away from producing income to maximising capital values. In the current investments climate, to maintain the level of income needed to fund the charity, would require an investment portfolio which would not achieve the optimal overall return, so effectively penalising future beneficiaries.

The total return strategy does not make distinctions between income and capital returns. It lumps together all forms of return on investment – dividends, interest, and capital gains etc, to produce a "total return". Some of the total return is then used to meet the needs of present beneficiaries, while the remainder is added to the existing investment portfolios to help meet the needs of future beneficiaries.

The Society's investments are managed by Heartwood Wealth Management (formerly Cripps Portfolio), who report all transactions to the Honorary Treasurer and provide six monthly reports on the portfolios, which are considered by the Society's Finance Committee which meets three times a year. In turn the Finance Committee reports to Council.

The Society closely monitors its investments. The decision was recently taken to assess the main portfolio against the FTSE APCIMS balanced benchmark along with the smaller Whitfield and Robinson portfolios.

During the year the general fund portfolio generated a total return of 11% compared with its benchmark return of 10.4%. The Whitfield and Robinson portfolios generated returns of 13.7% and 11.5% respectively against their benchmark of 13.5%.

FINANCIAL REVIEW

Results

The Society's finances continued to recover with total funds increasing from £2,252,861 to £2,420,828, an increase of £167,967. This was largely due to an improvement in the stock market and the receipt of legacies and donations of £11,444.

Membership subscriptions fell marginally from £73,275 to £72,782 and investment income amounted to £87,202 compared to £92,310 in 2005.

Income from royalties increased from £28,919 to £36,247, income from conferences generated £259 and grants for awards decreased from £8,309 to £2,000. Total costs fell from £231,807 to £215,309 reflecting lower meeting costs.

Fixed assets

Information relating to changes in fixed assets is given in notes 5 and 6 to the accounts.

Risk assessment

The trustees are satisfied that they have considered the major risks to which the charity is exposed, that they have taken action to mitigate or manage those risks and that they have systems in place to monitor any change to those risks.

Reserves policy

The Council have reviewed the Society's need for reserves in line with the guidance issued by the Charity Commission. They believe that the Society requires approximately the current level of unrestricted general funds of £2.2m to generate sufficient total return, both income and capital, to cover the Society's expenditure in excess of the members' subscription income on an annual basis to ensure that the Society can run efficiently and meet the needs of beneficiaries.

The Society's restricted funds consist of a number of different funds where the donor has imposed restrictions on the use of the funds which are legally binding. The purposes of these funds are set out in notes 13 to 15.

FUTURE PLANS

Council agreed to reduce the number of meetings a year, from six to five; to ensure that Council finds time to explore issues of policy, external and internal to the Society; to focus on increasing the visibility of the Society where it provides financial support, for example to postgraduate students; to continue to promote conferences relating to policy issues with which the Society is engaged, but to withdraw from offering financial and administrative support for conferences which would go ahead regardless of the support of the Society.

During the year the Society appointed a Working Party to review the use and functionality of the website, bearing in mind the Society's current objectives, and recommend a costing strategy for the redesign and maintenance of the website.

The Society has revised its criteria for the Alexander Essay Prize with effect from 1 January 2006. A new annual joint prize with *History Scotland* is announced to run parallel to the joint prize with *History Today*, to be awarded for the best undergraduate dissertation, on this occasion on Scottish history. The Rees Davies Graduate Prize, named in honour of the recent President, will be awarded for the first time in 2007. The P. J. Marshall Fellowship will be awarded more frequently, owing to a most generous gift by the Society's past President and current Honorary Vice-President. Owing to the generosity of the family of the late Martin Lynn, a Scholarship in his name will be awarded in 2006-7 to assist postgraduate research on a topic in African history.

STATEMENT OF TRUSTEES' RESPONSIBILITIES

Law applicable to charities in England and Wales requires the Council to prepare accounts for each financial year which give a true and fair view of the state of affairs of the Society and of its financial activities for that year. In preparing these accounts, the Trustees are required to:

- select suitable accounting policies and apply them consistently;
- make judgements and estimates that are reasonable and prudent;
- state whether applicable accounting standards have been followed, subject to any material departures disclosed and explained in the accounts;
- prepare the accounts on the going concern basis unless it is inappropriate to presume that the Society will continue in business.

The Council is responsible for ensuring proper accounting records are kept which disclose, with reasonable accuracy at any time, the financial position of the Society and enable them to ensure that the financial statements comply with applicable law. They are also responsible for safeguarding the assets of the Society and hence for taking reasonable steps for the prevention and detection of error, fraud and other irregularities.

In determining how amounts are presented within items in the profit and loss account and balance sheet, the trustees have had regard to the substance of the reported transaction or arrangement, in accordance with generally accepted accounting policies or practice.

So far as each of the trustees is aware at the time the report is approved:

• there is no relevant audit information of which the council's auditors are unaware, and;
• the trustees have taken all steps that they ought to have taken to make themselves aware of any relevant audit information and to establish that the auditors are aware of that information.

AUDITORS

A resolution proposing the appointment of auditors will be submitted at the Anniversary Meeting.

By Order of the Board

29 September 2006   Honorary Secretary

THE ROYAL HISTORICAL SOCIETY
INDEPENDENT REPORT OF THE AUDITORS
FOR THE YEAR ENDED 30 JUNE 2006

We have audited the financial statements of The Royal Historical Society for the year ended 30 June 2006 which comprise the Statement of Financial Activities, the Balance Sheet, and the related notes. These financial statements have been prepared under the accounting policies set out therein.

This report is made solely to the charity's trustees, as a body, in accordance with the regulations made under the Charities Act 1993. Our audit work has been undertaken so that we might state to the charity's trustees those matters we are required to state to them in an auditor's report and for no other purpose. To the fullest extent permitted by law, we do not accept or assume responsibility to anyone other than the charity and the charity's trustees as a body, for our audit work, for this report, or for the opinions we have formed.

Respective responsibilities of trustees and auditors
As described in the Statement of Trustees' Responsibilities the charity's trustees are responsible for the preparation of the financial statements in accordance with applicable law and United Kingdom Accounting Standards (United Kingdom Generally Accepted Accounting Practice).

We have been appointed as auditors under section 43 of the Charities Act 1993 and report in accordance with regulations made under section 44 of that Act. Our responsibility is to audit the financial statements in accordance with relevant legal and regulatory requirements and International Standards on Auditing (UK and Ireland).

We report to you our opinion as to whether the financial statements give a true and fair view and are properly prepared in accordance with the Charities Act 1993 and whether the Trustees' Report is consistent with the financial statements. We also report to you if, in our opinion, the charity has not kept proper accounting records and if we have not received all the information and explanations we require for our audit.

We read the Trustees' Report and consider the implications for our report if we become aware of any apparent misstatements within it.

Basis of audit opinion
We conducted our audit in accordance with International Standards on Auditing (UK and Ireland) issued by the Auditing Practices Board. An audit includes examination, on a test basis, of evidence relevant to the amounts and disclosures in the financial statements. It also includes an assessment of the significant estimates and judgements made by the trustees in the preparation of the financial statements, and of whether the accounting policies are appropriate to the charity's circumstances, consistently applied and adequately disclosed.

We planned and performed our audit so as to obtain all the information and explanations which we considered necessary in order to provide us with sufficient evidence to give reasonable assurance that the financial statements are free from material misstatement, whether caused by fraud or other irregularity or error. In forming our opinion we also evaluated the overall adequacy of the presentation of information in the financial statements.

Opinion
In our opinion:

- the financial statements give a true and fair view, in accordance with United Kingdom Generally Accepted Accounting Practice, of the state of the charity's affairs as at 30 June 2006 and of its incoming resources and application of resources in the year then ended;
- the financial statements have been properly prepared in accordance with the Charities Act 1993; and
- the Trustees' Report is consistent with the financial statements.

haysmacintyre
Chartered Accountants
Registered Auditors

Fairfax House
15 Fulwood Place
London
WC1V 6AY

THE ROYAL HISTORICAL SOCIETY

STATEMENT OF FINANCIAL ACTIVITIES
FOR THE YEAR ENDED 30 JUNE 2006

	Notes	Unrestricted Funds £	Endowment Funds £	Restricted Funds £	Total Funds 2006 £	Total Funds 2005 £
INCOMING RESOURCES						
Incoming resources from generated funds						
Donations, legacies and similar incoming resources	2	11,444	–	–	11,444	43,587
Investment income	6	85,177	–	2,025	87,202	92,310
Incoming resources from charitable activities						
Grants for awards		2,000	–	–	2,000	8,390
Conferences		259	–	–	259	13,534
Subscriptions		72,782	–	–	72,782	73,275
Royalties		36,247	–	–	36,247	28,919
Other incoming resources		750	–	–	750	964
TOTAL INCOMING RESOURCES		208,659	–	2,025	210,684	260,979
RESOURCES EXPENDED						
Cost of generating funds						
Investment manager's fee		13,794	284	–	14,078	15,302
Charitable activities						
Grants for awards	3	34,393	–	15,541	49,934	38,691
Lectures and other meetings		18,467	–	–	18,467	32,881
Publications		60,564	–	–	60,564	71,672
Library		4,577	–	–	4,577	5,944
Membership services		47,056	–	–	47,056	45,809
Governance		20,633	–	–	20,633	21,508
TOTAL RESOURCES EXPENDED	4	199,484	284	15,541	215,309	231,807
NET INCOMING/(OUTGOING) RESOURCES		9,175	(284)	(13,516)	(4,625)	29,172
Transfers		65	–	(65)	–	–
Other recognised gains and losses						
Net gain on investments	6	165,065	7,527	-	172,592	223,794
NET MOVEMENT IN FUNDS		174,305	7,243	(13,581)	167,967	252,966
Balance at 1 July 2005		2,176,148	60,895	15,818	2,252,861	1,999,895
Balance at 30 June 2006		£2,350,453	£68,138	£2,237	£2,420,828	£2,252,861

THE ROYAL HISTORICAL SOCIETY

Balance Sheet as at 30 June 2006

	Notes	2006 £	2006 £	2005 £	2005 £
FIXED ASSETS					
Tangible assets	5		1,903		741
Investments	6		2,419,077		2,257,250
			2,420,980		2,257,991
CURRENT ASSETS					
Stocks	7	3,595		4,168	
Debtors	8	19,991		12,218	
Cash at bank and in hand		13,114		3,634	
		36,700		20,020	
LESS: CREDITORS					
Amounts due within one year	9	(36,852)		(25,150)	
NET CURRENT (LIABILITIES)			(152)		(5,130)
NET ASSETS			£2,420,828		£2,252,861
REPRESENTED BY:					
Endowment Funds	13				
A S Whitfield Prize Fund			46,770		42,076
The David Berry Essay Trust			21,368		18,819
Restricted Funds	14				
A S Whitfield Prize Fund – Income			1,608		1,409
BHB Fund			–		5,679
P J Marshall Fellowship			–		8,390
The David Berry Essay Trust – Income			629		340
Unrestricted Funds					
Designated – E M Robinson Bequest	15		134,437		123,123
General Fund	16		2,216,016		2,053,025
			£2,420,828		£2,252,861

Approved by the Council on 29 September 2006

President . . . .

Honorary Treasurer . . . .

The attached notes form an integral part of these financial statements.

THE ROYAL HISTORICAL SOCIETY

NOTES TO THE ACCOUNTS FOR THE YEAR ENDED 30 JUNE 2006

1. ACCOUNTING POLICIES

a) *Basis of Preparation*
The financial statements have been prepared in accordance with the revised Statement of Recommended Practice "Accounting and Reporting by Charities" (SORP 2005) and with applicable accounting standards issued by UK accountancy bodies. They are prepared on the historical cost basis of accounting as modified to include the revaluation of fixed assets including investments which are carried at market value.

As a result of the introduction of SORP 2005, the income and expenditure of the Society had been reanalysed. There is no impact on the net incoming/(outgoing) resources for the year or on the balance sheet.

b) *Depreciation*
Depreciation is calculated by reference to the cost of fixed assets using a straight line basis at rates considered appropriate having regard to the expected lives of the fixed assets. The annual rates of depreciation in use are:
Furniture and equipment   10%
Computer equipment   25%

c) *Stock*
Stock is valued at the lower of cost and net realisable value.

d) *Library and archives*
The cost of additions to the library and archives is written off in the year of purchase.

e) *Subscription income*
Subscription income is recognised in the year it became receivable with a provision against any subscription not received.

f) *Investments*
Investments are stated at market value. Any surplus/deficit arising on revaluation is included in the Statement of Financial Activities. Dividend income is accounted for when the Society becomes entitled to such monies.

g) *Publication costs*
Publication costs are transferred in stock and released to the Statement of Financial Activities as stocks are depleted.

h) *Donations and other voluntary income*
Donations and other voluntary income is recognised when the Society becomes legally entitled to such monies.

i) *Grants payable*
Grants payable are recognised in the year in which they are approved and notified to recipients.

j) *Funds*
Unrestricted: these are funds which can be used in accordance with the charitable objects at the discretion of the trustees.
Designated: these are unrestricted funds which have been set aside by the trustees for specific purposes.
Restricted: these are funds that can only be used for particular restricted purposes defined by the benefactor and within the objects of the charity.
Endowment: permanent endowment funds must be held permanently by the trustees and income arising is separately included in restricted funds for specific use as defined by the donors.

The purpose and use of endowment, restricted and designated funds are disclosed in the notes to the accounts.

k) *Allocations*
Wages, salary costs and office expenditure are allocated on the basis of the work done by the Executive Secretary and the Administrative Secretary.

l) *Pensions*
Pension costs are charged to the SOFA when payments fall due. The Society contributed 10% of gross salary to the personal pension plan of one of the employees.

2. DONATIONS AND LEGACIES	2006 £	2005 £
G. R. Elton Bequest	1,696	1,648
Donations via membership	555	260
Gladstone Memorial Trust	600	600
Sundry income	8,593	41,079
	£11,444	£43,587

3. GRANTS FOR AWARDS

	Unrestricted Funds £	Restricted Funds £	Total 2006 £	Total 2005 £
RHS Centenary Fellowship	2,500	–	2,500	9,694
Alexander Prize	252	–	252	24
Sundry Grants	200	–	200	259
Research support grants (see below)	20,342	–	20,342	21,814
A–Level prizes	520	–	520	500
A. S. Whitfield prize	–	1,111	1,111	1,065
E. M. Robinson Bequest				
– Grant to Dulwich Picture Library	2,500	–	2,500	–
Gladstone history book prize	1,111	–	1,111	432
P. J. Marshall Fellowship	–	9,624	9,624	–
British History Bibliography project grant	–	4,380	4,380	–
David Berry Prize	–	426	426	348
History Today Prize	16	–	16	–
Staff and support costs	6,952	–	6,952	4,555
	£34,393	£15,541	£49,934	£38,691

During the year Society awarded grants to a value of £20,342 (2005: £21,814) to 85 (2005: 104) individuals.

GRANTS PAYABLE

	2006 £	2005 £
Commitments at 1 July 2005	1,650	2,850
Commitments made in the year	42,982	34,136
Grants paid during the year	(42,132)	(35,336)
Commitments at 30 June 2006	£2,500	£1,650

Commitments at 30 June 2006 and 2005 are included in creditors.

4. TOTAL RESOURCES EXPENDED

	Staff costs £	Support costs £	Direct costs £	Total £
Cost of generating funds				
Investment manager's fee	–	–	14,078	14,078
Charitable activities				
Grants for awards (Note 3)	4,122	2,830	42,982	49,934
Conferences	4,235	1,415	12,817	18,467
Publications	8,470	5,661	46,433	60,564
Library	2,117	1,416	1,044	4,577
Membership services	25,297	14,153	7,606	47,056
Governance	6,353	2,831	11,449	20,633
Total resources expended	£50,594	£28,306	£136,409	£215,309

STAFF COSTS

	2006 £	2005 £
Wages and salaries	46,557	51,157
Social Security costs	3,802	4,931
Other pension costs	235	1,869
	£50,594	£57,957

SUPPORT COSTS

	2006 £	2005 £
Stationery, photocopying and postage	14,097	12,672
Computer support	1,792	538
Insurance	1,670	1,670
Telephone	659	354
Depreciation	715	554
Bad debts	7,064	1,600
Other	2,309	2,188
	£28,306	£19,576

The average number of employees in the year was 2 (2005: 2). There were no employees whose emoluments exceeded £60,000 in the year.

During the year travel expenses were reimbursed to 20 Councillors attending Council meetings at a cost of £4,449 (2005: £4,198). No Councillor received any remuneration during the year (2005 nil).

Included in governance is the following:

	2006 £	2005 £
Audit and accountancy	7,931	7,373
Other services	558	558

5. TANGIBLE FIXED ASSETS

	Computer Equipment £	Furniture And Equipment £	Total £
COST			
At 1 July 2005	31,347	1,173	32,520
Additions	1,877	–	1,877
At 30 June 2006	33,224	1,173	34,397
DEPRECIATION			
At 1 July 2005	30,606	1,173	31,779
Charge for the year	715	–	715
At 30 June 2006	31,321	1,173	32,494
NET BOOK VALUE			
At 30 June 2006	£1,903	£–	£1,903
At 30 June 2005	£741	£–	£741

All tangible fixed assets are used in the furtherance of the Society's objects.

6. INVESTMENTS

	General Fund £	Robinson Bequest £	Whitfield Prize Fund £	David Berry Essay Trust £	Total £
Market value at 1 July 2005	2,069,713	123,309	44,550	19,678	2,257,250
Additions	310,439	17,082	13,152	–	340,673
Disposals	(317,406)	(20,706)	(13,326)	–	(351,438)
Net gain on investments	154,291	10,774	4,978	2,549	172,592
Market value at 30 June 2006	£2,217,037	£130,459	£49,354	£22,227	£2,419,077
Cost at 30 June 2006	£1,832,320	£79,743	£37,588	£10,730	£1,960,381

	2006 £	2005 £
U K Equities	1,604,958	1,456,751
U K Government Stock and Bonds	561,321	586,362
Overseas equities	141,827	59,074
Uninvested Cash	110,971	155,063
	£2,419,077	£2,257,250
Dividends and interest on listed investments	86,203	91,953
Interest on cash deposits	999	357
	£87,202	£92,310

7. STOCK

	2006 £	2005 £
Transactions Sixth Series	731	1,015
Camden Fifth Series	1,957	2,195
Camden Classics Reprints	907	958
	£3,595	£4,168

8. DEBTORS

	2006 £	2005 £
Other debtors	14,603	9,621
Prepayments	5,388	2,597
	£19,991	£12,218

9. CREDITORS: Amounts due within one year

	2006 £	2005 £
Sundry creditors	2,873	2,175
Subscriptions received in advance	3,935	3,376
Accruals and deferred income	30,044	19,599
	36,852	£25,150

10. LEASE COMMITMETS

The Society has the following annual commitments under non-cancellable operating leases which expire:

	2006 £	2005 £
Within 2–5 years	£15,272	£15,272

11 LIFE MEMBERS

The Society has ongoing commitments to provide membership services to 16 Life Members at a cost of approximately £50 each per year.

12. UNCAPITALISED ASSETS

The Society owns a library the cost of which is written off to the Statement of Financial Activities at the time of purchase. This library is insured for £150,000 and is used for reference purposes by the membership of the Society.

13. ENDOWMENT FUNDS

	Balance at 1 July 05 £	Incoming resources £	Outgoing resources £	Investment gain £	Balance at 30 June 06 £
A. S. Whitfield Prize Fund	42,076	–	(284)	4,978	46,770
The David Berry Essay Trust	18,819	–	–	2,549	21,368
	£60,895	£ –	£(284)	£7,527	£68,138

A. S. Whitfield Prize Fund

The A. S. Whitfield Prize Fund is an endowment used to provide income for an annual prize for the best first monograph for British history published in the calendar year.

The David Berry Essay Trust

The David Berry Essay Trust is an endowment to provide income for annual prizes for essays on subjects dealing with Scottish history.

14. RESTRICTED FUNDS

	Balance at 1 July 05 £	Incoming resources £	Outgoing resources £	Transfers £	Balance at 30 June 06 £
A. S. Whitfield Prize Fund Income	1,409	1,310	(1,111)	–	1,608
BHB Fund	5,679	–	(4,380)	(1,299)	–
P. J. Marshall Fellowship	8,390	–	(9,624)	1,234	–
The David Berry Essay Trust Income	340	715	(426)	–	629
	£15,818	£2,025	£(15,541)	£(65)	£2,237

A. S. Whitfield Prize Fund Income

Income from the A S Whitfield Prize Fund is used to provide an annual prize for the best first monograph for British history published in the calendar year.

BHB Fund

The British History Bibliographies project funding is used to provide funding for the compilation of bibliographies in British and Irish History. The transfer is in respect of costs incurred on behalf of the Fund within the general fund in previous years.

P. J. Marshall Fellowship

The P. J. Marshall Fellowship is used to provide a sum sufficient to cover the stipend for a one-year doctoral research fellowship alongside the existing Royal Historical Society Centenary Fellowship at the Institute of Historical Research in the academic year 2005-2006. The transfer from the general fund is to cover administrative costs incurred in this and previous years.

The David Berry Essay Trust Income

Income from the David Berry Trust is to provide annual prizes for essays on subjects dealing with Scottish history.

15. DESIGNATED FUND

	Balance at 1 July 05 £	Incoming resources £	Outgoing resources £	Investment gain £	Transfers £	Balance at 30 June 06 £
E. M. Robinson Bequest	£123,123	£3,812	£(3,272)	£10,774	£–	£134,437

E. M. Robinson Bequest

Income from the E. M. Robinson bequest is to further the study of history and to date has been used to provide grants to the Dulwich Picture Gallery.

16. GENERAL FUND

	Balance at 1 July 05 £	Incoming resources £	Outgoing resources £	Investment gain £	Transfers £	Balance at 30 June 06 £
	£2,053,025	£204,847	£(196,212)	£154,291	£65	£2,216,016

17. ANALYSIS OF NET ASSETS BETWEEN FUNDS

	General Fund £	Designated Fund £	Restricted Funds £	Endowment Funds £	Total £
Fixed assets	1,903	–	–	–	1,903
Investments	2,217,037	130,459	–	71,581	2,419,077
	2,218,940	130,459	–	71,581	2,420,980
Current assets	24,961	6,478	5,261	–	36,700
Less: Creditors	(27,885)	(2,500)	(3,024)	(3,443)	(36,852)
Net current (liabilities)/assets	(2,924)	3,978	2,237	(3,443)	(152)
Net assets	£2,216,016	£134,437	£2,237	£68,138	£2,420,828